SUCCEEDING WITH CHANGE

Succeeding with Change

Implementing Action-driven Strategies

Tony Eccles

McGRAW-HILL BOOK COMPANY

London · New York · St Louis · San Francisco · Auckland
Bogotá · Caracas · Lisbon · Madrid · Mexico · Milan
Montreal · New Delhi · Panama · Paris · San Juan · São Paulo
Singapore · Sydney · Tokyo · Toronto

Published by
McGRAW-HILL Book Company Europe
Shoppenhangers Road, Maidenhead, Berkshire, SL6 2QL, England
Telephone 01628 23432
Fax 01628 770224

British Library Cataloguing in Publication Data

Eccles, Tony
  Succeeding with Change: Implementing Action-driven Strategies
  I. Title
  658.406

  ISBN 0–07–709004–7

Library of Congress Cataloging-in-Publication Data

Eccles, Tony
  Succeeding with change: implementing action-driven strategies/Tony Eccles.
    p. cm.
  Includes bibliograhical references and index.
  ISBN 0-07-709004-7
  1. Organizational change---Management. 2. Strategic planning. I. Title.
HD58.8.E27
658.4'06--dc20   94-21403 CIP

2345   BL   98765

Typeset by Computape (Pickering) Ltd, North Yorkshire
and printed and bound in Great Britain by Biddles Ltd, Guildford, Surrey.
Printed on permanent paper in compliance with the ISO Standard 9706

To my wife, Jackie,
whose intelligence, vitality and kindness
enrich our lives

Contents

Acknowledgements

I would particularly like to thank Lord Weinstock, managing director of GEC, his deputy managing director, Malcolm Bates; Brian Kent, chairman of Staveley Industries; Mike Bett, personnel director, later deputy chairman of British Telecom and before that, director of personnel at the British Broadcasting Corporation and GEC; Mike Heron, European regional director and personnel director of Unilever and latterly chairman of the Post Office; Michael Gifford, chief executive of the Rank Organisation; Neville Bain, group chief executive of Coats Viyella and previously deputy chief executive and finance director of Cadbury-Schweppes; Dominic Cadbury, chief executive and then chairman of Cadbury Schweppes; Jon Young, personnel director of Denton Hall and Jonathan Tatten, managing partner; Lord Sheppard, chairman of Grand Metropolitan and Keith Holloway, commercial director; Sir Alastair Morton, co-chairman, Eurotunnel; Geoff Gaines, formerly head of group management development of Guinness, now partner at KPMG-Peat Marwick; Judy Lowe of Strategic Consulting and Faith Gibson of Gemini Consulting—all of whom were interviewed for this book, along with the chairmen and managing directors of a number of other business enterprises who preferred to talk off the record, and all of whom were immensely helpful.

Many are the other sources of insight and enlightenment – students and colleagues at both London and Manchester Business Schools, Templeton College; peers and writers of all kinds; countless senior managers in innumerable strategy seminars; relations and friends. Particularly important academic influences have been those of Charles Handy, Henry Mintzberg, John Hunt, Chris Bartlett, Sumantra Ghoshal, Richard Pascale, Dean Berry, Paul Lawrence, Jay Lorsh, Tom Lupton, John Morris, James Brian Quinn, Gary Hamel, C. K. Prahalad, Yves Doz, Andrew Pettigrew and Gerry Johnson. Some views have come from my trying to make more sense of my own fifteen years in industry with the Ocean Group, with Unilever and in the media industry. Thanks are also due to several readers of the draft of this book. Gareth Jones, John Hunt, Adam Brand, Michael Hay and Ann Bone all provided very useful and detailed comments, as did my editors at McGraw-Hill, Kate Allen, Karin Henderson, Natalie Burfitt and Roger Horton. Caroline Hodgkinson and Sharon Wilson gave valuable secretarial support and young Robertson Eccles (then 5) assisted me with my typing.

1 Introduction

- **Core propositions**
- **Is change so difficult?**
- **Definitions**
- **The viscosity of the organization**
- **Turning inertia into momentum**

This book has arisen from a dissatisfaction and a puzzle. The dissatisfaction comes from the lack of literature on strategy implementation. There are few books specifically about strategy implementation and some of those discuss the genesis of strategy as much as they concern themselves with implementation. That is all very well, for any good strategist should be contemplating the practicalities of implementation as soon as the shape of the new strategy begins to emerge. Yet that approach diverts attention from the implementation process itself. Hence, this work has limited concern about the generation and exact content of the strategy that is to be implemented, and its interaction with the implementation process is deliberately minimized in order to sustain the emphasis on implementation.

Implementation can involve factors outside the firm. For instance, the need to strengthen a firm's distribution system may involve the acquisition of a distribution firm, and one may or may not be available at a sensible price. Financial market conditions, the possession of productive technology, competitor and customer actions, all can help or impede the implementation of a strategic change. Much of the writing about competitive strategy has been about these external market conditions and rivalry between firms; the context in

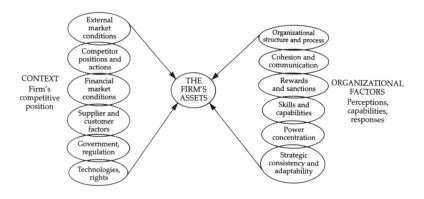

Figure 1.1   *Strategic factors*

which changes occur. This context is illustrated in Figure 1.1. External strategic factors are important, of course, but to make them effective, firms must have an internal strategy too—and a way of implementing it.

This book focuses mainly on the internal, organizational factors of strategy (which are also shown in Figure 1.1): the strategic elements within the firm which must be orchestrated in order to implement market strategies. A firm that lacks internal coherence and organized relevance to that external context has little chance of effective implementation; it might be able to buy that distribution firm, but be incapable of utilizing it to maximum advantage. The evidence from top executives is that these internal factors are vital elements in the successful execution of a strategic change.

The issue of implementation is important, for if an organization can develop a new and convincing strategy and then find difficulty in implementing it, what the people in the company are saying is: 'We can think, but we can't act.' That can happen. One large and famous global company became well known for the quality of its endlessly repeated strategic debates. A new chairman and chief executive had to be installed before it could, and did, flourish and prosper through decisive action. Fortunately, not all organizations languish like that.

This book is primarily designed to help managers. It seeks to persuade the reader about the practicality of making radical shifts in the way an organization runs; about the opportunities for implementation of strategic change; and it incorporates several core propositions—interwoven throughout the book—which it endeavours to support with logic and evidence.

CORE PROPOSITIONS

1. Implementation is not always complicated or difficult to accomplish.
2. Implementation can take place quickly.
3. Concentrated power is an aid to rapid implementation.
4. A dedicated and united top management can make things happen.
5. Without planning, an organization is handicapped in its execution of strategy.
6. The key variable of implementation (assuming that the requisite resources and capabilities are available) is that of obtaining sufficient endorsement for the proposed strategic change.
7. Strategy formulation habitually precedes implementation; these two elements are not inextricably interwoven.
8. There are easier and faster ways of changing an organization than starting by trying to change its culture.
9. Empowerment does not reduce top management's responsibility for the performance of the organization.
10. Empowerment is of little value in times of rapid, radical, frame-breaking change; it works better in more stable circumstances.
11. Implementation cannot be successfully delegated; sustained senior management involvement is vital.
12. Impediments to better strategic performance are often inside the firm.

IS CHANGE SO DIFFICULT?

The puzzle about implementation is that, while it is widely believed that making strategic changes in organizations takes years if not decades, some businesses seem able to make rapid alterations in their strategies and practices without the sky falling in on them. How can that be? Must strategic changes take a long time? What are the conditions and circumstances that lend themselves to rapid transformations that succeed?

In this book, the strategy implementation picture is painted on as broad a canvas as possible, because that seems better for our purpose than the reductionism that breaks complex systems down into hierarchically lower levels of organization in the hope that analysis of the bits will enable a more illuminating reconstruction of the whole.[1] That may work well in biology. In organization studies, too often it just leaves a heap of bits and some unconvincing attempts to embed them in a whole.

We do not have a good and convincing theory about change, which is why practical evidence of success with change is valuable. Yet there are regularities in the needs of implementation, general characteristics which assist or impede the implementation of strategy in commercial organizations. This book draws out experiences from several sources into 14 general factors that help change, and does it in a prescriptive fashion that is meant to be directly helpful to managers. Although not recommended, a manager in a real hurry could even read this introductory chapter and then start at Chapter 4, though he or she should be wary of jumping to conclusions, for executives need to know why and when, as well as what and how. Managerial circumstances have regularities and similarities, but there is always some contingent condition, some unusual combination of elements. The rules must be tailored to the firm in question in its particular state, in its context, at that time. General rules are still flexible prescriptions and every manager should be alert to the implications of the specific underlying factors.

The two main empirical sources for this book are a number of major consulting and operational assignments on strategic change, together with distillations from extended discussions with top managers (mainly chairmen or chief executives). All the top managers were very candid and several of them were kind enough to cooperate while preferring not to have their inputs publicized. The interviewees brought experiences from diverse, though generally large, corporations. These are the ones that are alleged to be sclerotic, arthritic, bureaucratic and clumsy. If they can change quite rapidly, there is hope for all organizations. The industries they inhabit range from food, textiles, accounting, telecommunications, postal services, leisure, entertainment, toiletries, engineering, construction, consultancy and life assurance, to sports management and law—thus providing a mix of manufacturing and service businesses employing in aggregate about one million people world wide. Most of their enterprises are international, some global, in their activities, though the cultural heartlands of their operations are the Anglo-Saxon regions of Europe and North America.[2]

A third empirical basis is that of 300 vignettes—typically postgraduate student projects on change in individual companies, many of them in the companies in which the students were young middle managers. The perspective, therefore, is not just top-down. The striking feature of the young managers' analyses was the great extent to which they saw the lead, the tone, the urgency and the energy of strategy implementation as needing to emanate from the top managers in their organizations and how personalized that leadership role needed to be. Top managers cannot delegate that symbolic, inspirational role. The argument will be advanced that democratizing the organization through empowerment and employee participation still leaves the top management of the firm with huge responsibilities for acting as key decision makers on behalf of the whole organization. The present fashion for claiming that top executives are merely orchestrators, mentors, guides, coaches and facilitators, finds little support here.

This is not to see middle managers and staff as being dependent. They just want to know the score, see their place in things and, from that, judge what they should do. Again and again in working with operational managers, one sees their desire to perform to the goals set by the organization's leaders, its board members, the key divisional figures and the managers of their units. The hunger for those top managers to signal their leadership is widespread and sustained. Simple observation of management processes in action shows top management's role to be vital in the shaping of organizational performance.

Empirical findings about implementation can never be completely convincing when the phenomena they seek to explain are so wide-ranging and the evidence contradictory. So the claim is not of an overturning of all other beliefs in a mad attempt to find empirical congruence, but the proffering of argument and evidence to add to the quirks and partialities of our understanding of how organizations do or do not work, for 'despite an enormous literature and prodigious research, we are still in desperate need of adequate theories of management, leadership and strategy'.[3] Consequently, this book concerns itself with reflection, proposition and discussion, which build on the implications of the evidence, not all of which can be displayed since some of the background facts must remain confidential to the organizations from which they came.

The book's reflections and propositions lead through misconceptions about change, the usefulness of management power in speeding change along, and then it turns to the vital need for strategic change to be endorsed through the growth of concerted will. The discussion of factors that help change, outlines a categorization of six contexts of management-inspired change: Takeover change, Injection change, Succession change, Renovation change, Partnership change and Catalytic change (Chapter 5). The differences and similarities between those types of change are analysed to delineate 14 factors that underpin successful change in these different contexts, arising under four categories: Purpose and initiative (Chapter 6); Concordance and trust (Chapter 7); Leadership, capabilities and structure (Chapters 8 and 9); and Building on action and success (Chapter 10). The book concludes with a discussion about some methods by which rapid and effective change can be achieved, once the organization's management has decided where it stands on each of the 14 factors.

References are only included where they seem appropriate. In the perpetual dilemma between writing a highly academic treatise dense with the jargon of scholars, versus the easy reading and lightness of widely read management texts, this book has veered steadily towards the latter as draft succeeded draft, dropping many of the more arcane references and some of the more mind-numbing quotations. It is on economist Edith Penrose's side. When faced at a conference by an earnest researcher who described a management team as 'operationalizing their paradigm reconfiguration', she asked him: 'Do you mean they are changing their view?'[4] Steering a line between density and lucidity, the bias has, it is hoped, leant towards lightness. Managers do not read as much as they intend, so why make it discouraging for them?

The attempt is made to be as straightforward and helpful as possible to managers by minimizing the number of caveats attached to propositions. Managers have to grapple with the swirling motions of organizational change. Management may be difficult; dilemmas abound. Yet much of it is not very complicated. As Napoleon Bonaparte remarked about a different form of competitive struggle: 'War is a simple art: its essence lies in its accomplishment.' So it is hoped that this work also displays what Rosemary Stewart called 'a healthy scepticism for the value of the elaboration of management theories' when she quoted Torrington *et al.*[5] who wrote 'In some ways the development of management ideas now seems to have gone too far, in making management something far more elaborate and mysterious than reality dictates.' Since so much of strategy implementation seems to be plain common sense, it is not obvious that the implementation process has to be elaborate.

Some of that implementation process works on people's feelings, beliefs and inclinations; these are not easy to calibrate or weigh. But too many of us are data-dependent, valuing excessively what we can quantify, as though that automatically confers validity. Without investing the analysis with pseudo-science ('48 per cent of chief executives said that their top teams were not as effective as they should be') the attempt has been made to concentrate on things that work, even if the reason is not always obvious. As Nigel Bogle of Bartle, Bogle and Hegarty has said: 'Unexplainable success is more important than sophisticated reasons for failure.' Instead of asking 'How does this work?', it can be as fruitful to ask 'What is this intended to do, and does it do it?'— delightful and useful though it would be to know how it did work. Rather than seek reasons for failure, this book attempts to illuminate some underlying rules for success in the implementation of rapid strategic changes.

DEFINITIONS

Before moving into the substance of the book, it is worth defining the meaning of the term 'strategic change' since the word strategy is used quite loosely in daily organizational life to describe a variety of linked elements. Whether it is:

- as a goal ('Our aim is to become world No. 1 in our industry')
- as a policy ('Our method is to invest only in large projects in the leisure industry')
- as a plan ('We intend to put lots of money into R&D and to build up the best salesforce to market new products as they come through') or, occasionally,
- as an organizational framework ('We always run each of our businesses as an autonomous profit centre')

the word 'strategy' is usually used to describe what the organization is trying to achieve and/or how it is trying to achieve it.

One striking aspect of the plethora of definitions is the increasingly grandiose language used to specify what a commercial organization is trying to do. Words like vision and mission are now commonly invoked to describe a firm's purpose and aspirations. A narrower definition of strategy will be used here; one that seeks to take account of these more recent alternatives.

The second striking thing is the large number of texts by reputable authors in which they shy away from all definitions. You can look in vain for a definition of the key words in a book's title. Disregarding the prudent judgement of authors who prefer not to offer a hostage to fortune by defining their terms—except in phrases of often paralysing complexity or obviousness—the following are this book's working definitions, with the caveat that some are, for practical purposes, almost interchangeable.

Vision

Vision might be termed a far-sighted vista of the ultimate (imagined, perceived) state; a revelation; an image in the mind. In business it is automatically assumed to be a view of the desired state. A view of a future disaster is not welcome as a vision. As with optimistic views of the after-life, a vision is supposed to reveal a benign circumstance. 'I have a vision for our company; we will go bankrupt' is not a very elevating line for a chief executive who is seeking to motivate his or her staff and reassure suppliers, customers and capital providers. Leaders and managers are not expected to remain fatalistic in the face of a challenge. They are supposed to be able to rise above that and take advantage of even a cataclysm, and visions are generally directed at strengthening the company's economic position.[6] Alternatively, vision in its more aspirational forms can be a delineation of desire, in pursuit of which the firm seeks to reach a position of reputational, achieving grace. A vision is a picture of the state in which an organization would like to be in the future.

Mission

Mission is frequently expressed, in similarly grandiose style, as being a crusade to reach a target; the vision expressed as a goal—possibly couched in rather pompous terms, so that it is an evangelical version of a goal or a task to which the organization attempts to adhere, and, moreover, one that is meant to elevate the mundane (would, for instance, the bringing of skateboards to the Ukrainians count highly on any world list of human achievements?), to uplift the organization's members and even to thrill its suppliers and customers. Mission can be a self-imposed duty or task; or a set of ethical commitments or operating principles, for example, when it is a set of guidelines to behaviour; or the way the company wishes to do business, rather than a direct business goal.

Goal

Goal has similar connotations to both vision and mission since it is an objective, a target, a desired end condition. Compared to vision and mission, goal seems positively prosaic. For our purposes, goal, vision and mission are the sensible words to describe the organization's aspirations in its market and competitive arena, since it leaves space for the word strategy to be used in more organizational terms to define the chosen way of pursuing the goal. The firm's overall expression of its main objectives is here defined as its strategic goal, vision and mission; the main ways to accomplish them are the substance of strategy implementation.[7]

Strategy

Hence, for the purposes of this book, a strategy is defined as the broad method or route chosen to try to accomplish that mission, to fulfil that vision, to achieve that goal. It is the way you intend to go in order to reach the desired state; the path that has been selected from an array of possible paths that appear to take the firm towards the goal. So the chosen strategy endeavours to answer the question: How are we going to get there from here?

This suggests that strategy implementation is the action that moves the organization along its choice of route towards its goal—the fulfilment of its mission, the achievement of its vision—and it follows that a strategic change could be triggered

    (a)   by alterations to the existing goal, or
    (b)   by alterations to the existing route

(c)   when dissatisfaction with the current performance galvanizes effort towards more challenging achievement, even if neither route nor goal is being altered.

The formulation of strategy will thus define which (combination) of these three elements is relevant. Conditions for strategy implementation are then defined as being:

- when a new vision is embraced and pursued (i.e. the goal alters materially)
- when a transformation occurs in the way the vision is pursued (i.e. a different route is used for reaching the goal)
- when a reorganization is undertaken (i.e. a revised way of organizing to traverse the route)
- when the policies/criteria of the organization alter such that those in the organization have to modify their approach, objectives and behaviour (i.e. the rules for traversing the route are modified).

The new goal might be expansion in Europe rather than in North America; an accent on software not hardware; specialist versus full service. The route could switch from takeovers to alliances; distribution not production; licensed rather than self-developed; tailored not mass produced. The altered policies/criteria could relate to the organization's stance (organic growth instead of cost cutting; long term, not short term); to criteria (sales growth, not profit margin; cash flow rather than ROA); to organization and systems (linkages, not autonomy; global product divisions, not national management units; distributed expertise rather than HQ dominance).

Strategic change campaigns come in a variety of guises, as illustrated in Figure 1.2, whether it is through the modest incremental changes of *refining* existing operations, through the more muscular activities of *rectifying* failures; *constructing* via acquisitions, divestments and alliances; *building* up capabilities and resources to gain critical strength; or, most potently, through *transforming* the company and changing the rules of the competitive game.

These five campaigns can be categorized under three

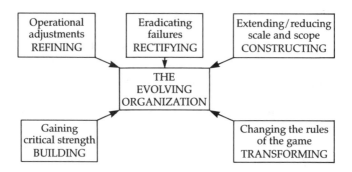

Figure 1.2   *Strategic campaigns*

headings, as in Figure 1.3. (The three categories of *breakdown*, *maintenance* and *development* were developed by John Morris at Manchester Business School in the late 1960s.) The maintenance heading, although accounting for the bulk of day-to-day activity in organizations, does not qualify as a major strategic change, but is just the mere succession of day-to-day developments that occur in all alert organizations as they refine their operations through a multitude of minor changes. Major change occurs within the breakdown and development categories.

BREAKDOWN	MAINTENANCE	DEVELOPMENT
Repairing (can be major change)	Keeping station (minor changes)	Doing new things (often major change)
Rectifying	Refining	Building Constructing Transforming

Figure 1.3   *Thrust of strategy for the organization*

Strategy Implementation

Hence strategy implementation will almost certainly entail

- revised stance/policies for the organization
- fresh criteria of performance
- modified organization structure, systems and rewards
- the addition of new skills
- enhanced or redeployed assets.

Implementation also involves purposive change, for purpose and intention are fundamental. After all, the realization of things that you did not intend or alterations that you did not seek, promote or induce, are just changes, perhaps not wayward, but certainly not implemented as the result of specific, conscious, intended choice and commitment—even if there is a consistency of behaviour in what emerges.[8] This notion of intentionality is at the heart of strategy. The view here is that strategy implementation is *the realization of intentions*. And intentions are usually those of the board and top management. A radical plan for strategic change rarely emanates from the lowest levels in an organization.

Nor do most strategies just happen to arise. While there can be little argument that some strategies do emerge as a pattern in a stream of actions, some prior thought must have been given towards an overall idea of the strategic goal.[9] Otherwise, strategy implementation is utterly simple, being just whatever the organization has happened to do. The assumption in this book is that both strategy formulation and strategy implementation in a company are, to the best of its management's abilities, purposeful, well-planned, holistic, coordinated initiatives which are sensitized to feedback about their progress and sensitive to changes in the circumstances that made them relevant. It assumes that people's behaviour is goal-directed. For our purposes an action can only be entitled to be called a strategy if it fits the organization's intentions. Otherwise it is just an event. The event may later turn out to have strategic connotations, but that is a different matter.

THE VISCOSITY OF THE ORGANIZATION

The main elements that determine the speed and ease of implementation are (a) the power and concerted will of the management, (b) the capabilities and level of knowing support of the employees and (c) the cost and amount of relevant assets and resources that the organization can put behind the proposed changes. Speedy implementation will depend on the state of the company; how poised it is to alter. The organization's combination of alertness, knowledge, confidence and resources will affect the rate at which a change can be made. Together, these elements act upon the inertia, the embedded habits and the resistance to change, and they determine the cost, feasibility and timescale of alteration. The net effect of the elements adds up to the firm's internal resistance to implementation, what can be called *the viscosity of the organization*.

Viscosity is a measure of resistance to movement. In organizational terms, a rigid bureaucracy will have high viscosity; it will require more force to overcome inertia just to get moving and, once on the move, slow progress will be made only at the cost of high levels of expended energy. The situation will be similar in an organization where trust is low and the atmosphere sullen. Change will be a struggle. Where the existing capabilities are inappropriate or inadequate for the new situation, change will be costly and, to effect significant change, the management will need to seek an ingenious, low-cost, low-threat route to the chosen goal. That may be all to the good, for a frontal assault is not necessarily smart, and with limited resources the management will need to look for maximum leverage.

A more fluid, low-viscosity organization will be character-ized by a readiness to change, a familiarity and confidence about change and its benefits, a good match between capabilities and organizational needs, the enthusiastic backing of well-informed and involved personnel, high trust in management's motives and abilities and an open manage-ment, confident and cooperative and buoyed up by the support from below. Its people are able to undertake the tasks of implementation with confidence. A firm with substantial assets will be more effective at marshalling resources behind the change programme and lubricating the frictions of change. That is why it should be much easier to implement changes in a profitable company than in one struggling for survival. The problem is that an ill-managed staff may only wake up to the need for change when they are almost bankrupt. Herein lies the rub, for 'it is difficult to come into a successful organization and get people to believe in the need for change' (Brian Kent, chairman, Staveley Industries plc). The secret of constant organizational renewal is to start that process before the existing strategy peters out; to build a new future while maintaining the present system's impetus.[10] The well-managed organization instils a change culture *before* the firm's funds are depleted by drooping performance.

Prancing through waves or wading through treacle?

The central question about internal resistance when a firm seeks to make a significant strategic change, can be posed as a question of viscosity. Is it prancing through waves or wading through treacle? As the company leaves the certain shores of stability—which may be certain only in their growing inhospitability—and moves through the shallows of minor change into the depths of major change, is it waving or drowning?

Grand Metropolitan has low viscosity as a matter of deliberate policy; British Telecom has lowered its viscosity over recent years as it has become more market-oriented and more conscious that it is competing for customers; IBM is frantically trying to liquify its more frozen features in order to flow at the same pace as the computer market, having spent several unproductive years in an icy backwater. The viscosity of the organization prior to the change is predetermined by the foresight of those who have previously been in charge of the firm. When the need for implementation arrives, it is no use regretting a lack of foresight; one can only repeat that old joke that, 'if I were you, I wouldn't start from here', and then get on with the changes irrespective of the starting position in which a company finds itself. For a company that does not currently face major organizational change, the lesson is that the development of capabilities and an embracing of a change culture are both prudent investments—insurance policies of foresight if you like—that should be made before you need them.

It is also worth remembering that intensifying and extending strengths can be as important and valid as rectifying weaknesses. Fluid, prepared organizations still need to look for ingenious, low-cost solutions, just like bureaucratic organizations. If multiplier effects can be discovered, so much the better; why expend resources unnecessarily? The difference is that the fluid organization will have more options to choose from, more freedom of manoeuvre, more backing and trust from its employees and probably more initial and relevant impetus. In short, it will be more prepared for implementation and more capable of handling it well.

It is obvious that reducing organizational viscosity should assist the process of change. Short of driving the firm into frenetic hyperactivity, for any given organizational state, a lowering of viscosity will help, as will the prior possession of organizational momentum. This is why enterprising managements seek to promote change as a normal, expected, welcome, exciting virtue which assists the achievement of organizational and personal ambitions. Yet, whatever the initial level of momentum, there comes a time in most organizations when a higher than normal order of change is needed. Since even fast-moving bodies have inertia (i.e. a resistance to a change in momentum), the process of overcoming it is important—particularly if the organization wants to alter direction. The question then is how to turn inertia into momentum?

TURNING INERTIA INTO MOMENTUM

Increases in momentum come from acting on the potential sources of useful force:

- Arousal of latent energy through the application of visionary leadership and the demonstration of the need to change
- Enhancement of latent energy through the assembly of relevant resources, skills and capabilities
- Commitment of energy to the task(s) of change through endorsement of the plans, empowerment, involvement and teamwork
- Applying energy in the right direction through focused action plans.

Effective methods of overcoming inertia problems include:

1. Reduced friction (more interunit collaboration, removal of inept rules and procedures, better communication, sharing of best practices)
2. Reduced hysteresis (*the heat dissipated from internal friction*) (better conflict resolution, less combative internal rivalries, more appropriate levels of unit and functional interdependence, greater compatibility of systems)
3. Increased leverage (use of organizational multipliers; i.e. things that have positive knock-on effects out of proportion to their cost)
4. Better aim (from management, from uniting management and workforce, from better analysis and planning)
5. Increased energy (additional resources and heightened enthusiasm together with convergent goals and with appropriate rewards in place)
6. Better energy deployment (relevant skills, employee participation, active feedback, developing the skills of all via empowerment)
7. Reduced mass (ditching deadweight, turning fat into muscle, delayering, removing overheads and operating constraints)
8. Better organizational design (organizational structures, linkages, systems, disposition of power, better fit both between organizational resources and with markets served).

The first six of these eight methods relate to cooperation

and each is concerned with the beneficial effects of better amity, mutual respect and trust, openness, commitment—all the good things in an organization that cannot be developed overnight. These six methods are strongly recommended, but some organizations are in too much of a hurry to have time to acquire their advantages.

The last two methods are more in management's control and are more likely to come from unilateral action by the top management group. This doesn't make these two methods more desirable, but likely to be effective in a stressful situation when the floundering organization has to be lightened immediately by identifying and throwing deadweight and clutter overboard. Crisis situations

> break down resistance because the cost of not taking action becomes obvious and practically demands that the CEO takes action to preserve his/her credibility . . . rapid, non-consultative decisions which may, in low stress situations, generate resentment are, in fact, preferred as a consequence of stress. In such situations, promptness and decisiveness become valued leader characteristics. . . . The increased anxiety of subordinates makes them more accepting of leader influence in crisis periods.[11]

Forced drive

This reinforces the point that a chief executive will often seek to escalate perceptions of crisis in order to strengthen his or her mandate to lead and to emphasize the requirement for strong leadership. The result is what Michael Frye has christened 'Forced Drive', in which any lack of consensus, commitment or enthusiasm is overcome by incisive action by top management.[12] Natural drive comes later when the pressures have become internalized by those lower down; when the consensus, commitment, team work and enthusiasm have been strengthened. In the meantime, if implementation is to succeed in an organization under stress, the most effective, most expeditious method is for management to use its power and judgement to drive the changes forward decisively and quickly.

An underlying assumption in this book is that companies

that seek to undertake radical strategic change are not likely to be as poised, prepared and harmoniously motivated as they would wish. The use of managerial power may be the only practical way to galvanize the organization. Even if people are poised to change, the visible commitment of management is an absolute necessity if rapid and effective change is to be accomplished. The evidence from organizations suggests that top management must continue to shove, cajole and encourage others as well as remain obviously involved in the change process. Those lower down in the organization, with their shoulders to the wheel, soon give up pushing once the top manager walks away. Any idea that a company's staff will take the necessary actions when they are devoid of leadership and example seems quixotic, and a central thrust of this book is that managers cannot abdicate their prime responsibility for ensuring that the firm's strategic intentions are realized.

REFERENCES

1. Richard Dawkins, *The Blind Watchmaker*. Penguin, 1988, p. 13.
2. Geert Hofstede, *Cultures and Organizations: Software of the Mind*. McGraw-Hill, 1991; Fons Trompenaars, *Riding the Waves of Culture*. Economist Books, 1993; Charles Hampden-Turner and Fons Trompenaars, *The Seven Cultures of Capitalism*, Piatkus, 1994.
3. J.-C. Spender, *Industry Recipes: The Nature and Sources of Managerial Judgement*. Blackwell, 1989, p. 107. See also K. Thomas and W. Tymon, Jr, Necessary properties of relevant research: Lessons from recent criticisms of the organisational sciences. *Academy of Management Review*, **7** (3), 1982, p. 345.
4. Strategic Management Society Conference, San Francisco, October 1989.
5. D. Torrington, J. Weightman and K. Johns, *Effective Management: People and Organisations*. Prentice-Hall, 1990; reviewed by Rosemary Stewart, *The Times Higher Educational Supplement*, 27 July 1990.
6. Frederick Gluck, Vision and leadership in corporate strategy. *McKinsey Quarterly*, Winter 1981, pp. 13–27.
7. Christian Scholz, Corporate culture and strategy—the problem of strategic fit. *Long Range Planning*, **20** (4), 1987, pp. 78–87.
8. Henry Mintzberg, Opening up the definition of strategy, in *The Strategy Process* (ed. James Brian Quinn, Henry Mintzberg and Robert M. James). Prentice-Hall 1988, p. 14.

9. Henry Mintzberg and James A. Waters, Of strategies, deliberate and emergent. *Strategic Management Journal*, 6, 1985, pp. 257–72.

10. Charles Handy, *The Empty Raincoat*. Hutchinson, 1994, pp. 50–2.

11. Arvind Bhambri and Larry Greiner, A conditional theory of CEO intervention and strategic change. Strategic Management Society Conference, San Francisco, October 1989, pp. 8 and 24.

12. Reported by Sarah Curtis in *Royal Society of Arts Journal*, **CXXXIX** (5414), January 1991, p. 883.

PART I

Change and its misconceptions

2 Speeding up change and using power

- Rapid change
- Cherishing the assets
- Is implementation so complicated?
- Can power be used?
- Persuasive leaders
- Delegation, drift and dissipation
- Managers' implementation tactics
- The Spartacus challenge

Successful, speedy, implementation can make a vital difference. If the managers of two competing companies have the same intended and sensible strategy and one firm can implement its intentions better, faster and with less cost than its rival, then it can win the competitive battle by virtue of those superior implementation skills. Indeed, it may so pre-empt a vital circumstance by, say, signing up the best distributors or consummating the best alliance, that rivals cannot readily catch up, particularly if its better implementation skills are used again and again to sustain its advantage.

Factors which assist or impede strategy implementation are therefore important because it is evident that such speed in implementing decisions can be a vital facet of the health of organizations, given that a company's ability to change quickly offers it that significant prospective competitive advantage—or at least the avoidance of disadvantage. There is often no choice but to change quickly; the organization may be faced with the prospect of 'Adapt or collapse'.

Change can occur quickly; for while the notion that change takes a long time remains pervasive,[1] there are heartening contra examples. For instance, Waterman[2] has written of the rapid changes in performance at the Louisville General Hospital where, in a year, attitudes and performance were transformed.

> Tired of taking the kind of flak that says that for-profit hospitals don't serve the community, Humana decided to assume the management of Louisville's General Hospital ... (which) had eliminated jobs, reduced services, and began to turn away the indigents it was supposed to serve ... the speed of the (Humana) turnaround surprised everyone, even Humana. By fiscal year 1985 the hospital realized a $3.7 million profit, despite an 11.6% increase in indigent care that cost Humana over $6 million.

Humana brought in business practices that yielded more service and lower cost. It treated people—staff and patients— with dignity, and encouraged open and honest communication with lots of feedback. 'There is no magic in the way Humana turned the place around. It was work, but they simply did the thing they do well.'[2]

This example demonstrates the benefit that comes when you have a workforce which is aware that its present practices are embarrassingly ineffective despite its own dedicated hard work, and you bring in people who have, and transmit, the confidence that they will improve matters. There was no inherent reason for a major shift in attitude, behaviour and performance to take an age. The level of achievement was materially altered and a new strategy (i.e. a better way to reach your goal) had been implemented. It had required strenuous work, but had not been impossibly difficult.

The alleged difficulties of effecting strategic change in organizations may not be one of life's great myths, but it is a belief which, in business, is mighty convenient for supine managers, recalcitrant workers and fee-loving consultants who all have an interest in having a strategic transition seen as a Herculean task on an extended timescale.

So why do we play down the evidence from company doctors and acquisition specialists who expect, and sometimes achieve, rapid implementation of change in the organizations they take over? Strategists also urge the managers of companies to act quickly and decisively, seemingly sanguine about the effects and unswayed by concerns that a diffident approach might be better received, content with an organization that has changed its habits and is now performing better, as long as insurrection is not breaking out and deflecting the organization from its objectives.

The behavioural scientist might, in contrast, focus on deep-seated cultures and sensitive organisms, feeling unhappy if the people in the organization are reporting cognitive dissonance, personal alienation and other indications of angst—which the strategist and manager are prepared to shrug off as being merely the temporary phenomena of adjustment and, perhaps, as being an inevitable cost that is to be offset by the new advantages.

Merger and acquisition (M&A) studies do not suggest that incoming owners should put on kid gloves and remain gently sensitive to the previous culture for years. Far from it; the usual recommendation is that the new owners should make their mode of running their acquisition immediately, clearly and decisively obvious, so that there is no doubt about their intent and there is little opportunity for confusion, rumour and disorder to fester. In acquisitions, the application of external power, a rapid alteration of the context in which the acquired organization is to operate, plus the evanescence of previous assumptions, all combine to create a situation in which the staff of the acquired company expect change and, by so doing, make the implementation of major change more feasible.[3] Turnaround studies also support the view that rapid change is not only feasible but, in many circumstances, desirable and, in severe cases, critical to the organization's very survival.[4]

RAPID CHANGE

It seems inconceivable, if one is in charge of an organization with substantial power at one's disposal, that strategic change should take years. Even one year may be a long time. As one experienced acquirer from Hanson has put it: 'Three

months after we arrive (in a newly acquired company)
there must be significant changes; after that, newness is a
wasting asset.'[5] For example, Hanson bought the Berec
battery company (which had unhelpfully taken its well-
known brand name out of its title), promptly changed the
name back to Ever Ready, boosted the marketing, booted
out the old management and its overblown hierarchy (550
staff were taken down to 75), and shifted a much slimmed
down R&D department (250 people down to 60) onto
alkaline batteries, where Ever Ready had been weak in that
growing segment. Selling off the marginally profitable
European operation and investing in better production
facilities all helped to transform Ever Ready's profitability
and its ability to compete successfully, though it took it out
of the international league. Most of this occurred within
months of the acquisition.

Nor do firms the size of ICI always move slowly. The
Stauffer US agrochemicals company was acquired by ICI in
1987 and an immediate strategic issue was how best to serve
a relatively conservative market, given the different approaches of the two firms. ICI had been operating with 75
sales people dealing with 40 wholesaler/distributors.
Stauffer had 150 people selling to 400 distributors. It has been
reported that the two salesforces were amalgamated into a
combined salesforce of 107 people selling to 48 distributors
within nine weeks of the purchase: 77 per cent of staff
changed jobs and 30 per cent were relocated (not all within
the nine weeks). Despite enormous organizational strain,
sales went up in the acquisition year to more than cover the
volume that had been going through the other distributors.
Implementing strategy does not have to be protracted.

The issue thus becomes one of deciding in what circumstances, if any, rapid change is feasible and it can be argued
that there are nine distinguishable conditions that can meet
that test:

1.   Organizational crisis
2.   Irresistible external pressure, be it from new owners,
      predators, competitors, capital markets, legislation, etc.
      (which may create an organizational crisis)

3. An unintended effect from an action by a major stakeholder, such as a shareholder selling a significant stake or a bank calling in a loan, thus jeopardizing the firm's future
4. The spin-off or buy-out from an organization (which can also arouse crisis-like conditions)
5. Entry into a new market or setting up a novel kind of operation in the company
6. The introduction of a visionary, power-holding, new top management team, or even just a new CEO
7. An entrepreneurial organization with power concentrated in the hands of a decisive individual or small coterie
8. An appropriate shift in the organization's structure and in its reward motivators
9. A persuasive new vision which causes key people to rearrange their perspectives and their behaviour (what in one company was delightfully cited as 'the managing director has been rearranging his experiences').

A tenth sly addition would be the deliberate creation of a quasi-crisis, but that can only work if the manufactured crisis has at least some elements of plausibility and carries not too much risk that it will spin out of control into a real crisis. Many organizations have thought that a smart way to galvanize people would be generate a drama, only to find that they had opened a Pandora's box and created a full-blown fiasco.

The first seven of these conditions are likely to involve a concentration of power in the hands of the few people who bear ultimate responsibility for the success or failure of the venture. The speedy implementation of strategic change in an organization under pressure depends substantially on the effective marshalling and use of centralized managerial power. The eighth may involve persuasion and negotiation and may or may not require the use of managerial power. Only the ninth requires people to accept and support voluntarily a new view, which then leads to altered behaviour. Even then, that new view is likely to have originated from a small and senior group of people in the organization.

Rapid implementation in many circumstances is evidently practicable. Speed of adaptation is increasingly viewed as a competitive weapon, driven in part by high Japanese rates of product and process innovation. Companies and consultancies have discovered the value of time-based competition, in which you adapt faster in order to wrong foot your competitors and, perhaps, gain first-mover advantages. You may well choose to adapt earlier too if you are more confident of your ability to effect change both quickly and competently. Implementing a chosen strategy need not be a lengthy or difficult process if the management of an organization can agree to devote sufficient energy, urgency, resource and commitment to the work that will be involved.

Of course, not all the evidence supports this book's contention that the difficulties of implementing a strategy are often exaggerated. It has taken years to transform British Telecom. However, this is not too disheartening, since the size of an organization and its internal interdependencies may have much to do with the difficulty of shifting the organization's habits and attitudes. BT has had almost 240 000 employees. Furthermore, it has been heavily unionized with a very large inheritance of rules, procedures and formalized practices. Given this high viscosity, the likelihood of being able to introduce rapid strategic change into British Telecom has not been high, although to its credit many of its attitudes and practices did alter materially through the 1980s and, in the early 1990s, it has become lively and resourceful.

Similarly, a major 1985 study of ICI, the world's fourth largest chemical company, found that strategic implementation had been difficult and lengthy.[6] Yet even then it was not entirely obvious that implementing a new strategy needed to be such a big affair. Lots of things did not change. After all, ICI was not attempting to turn itself into a dog-food company or a bank; it just sought to turn a chemical company into a better-organized, better-performing chemical company. Afterwards, naphtha, salt and polythene were still being made, often by the same processes, on the same plants and with the products serving largely the same markets and customers. If an organization does not change quickly, this may be because its management does not choose to change it, rather than because they cannot do so. The pace of change at ICI increased rapidly once Hanson had bought a small shareholding and criticized its management.

Naturally, there are circumstances when a major change takes a long time. Yet some delays are found, on inspection, to have been quite unnecessary, having arisen from managerial disagreements, lack of understanding of what was involved, absence of commitment to provide sensible resources, or from plain managerial incomprehension or torpor.

If the organization is ossified for reasons other than size, then the scale and scope of the required change can create an awkward situation in which the act of gearing up for the transition can become a substantial and draining task. Creating movement in an sclerotic system can be both painful and difficult because of the slothful nature of some management processes. For example, in the late 1980s, the British Broadcasting Corporation took just over a year to consider a report that detailed urgent organizational and management deficiencies; at the board meeting which eventually considered the report, it was clear that some board members had not even read the summary, let alone the report. It then took a further 18 months to address the first of those topics and the central issue began to be dealt with almost four years after the problems were highlighted. It could all have been done inside six months if any coherent will had been applied to the unarguable needs. The lack of urgency, lack of concerted leadership, diffidence about disturbing the insular, complacent consensus—all contributed to the laxity of action. That organization was in turmoil soon afterwards, much of it having been quite avoidable.

Hence it can be seen that even an otherwise lively organization like the BBC can have grave impediments to change. If, for instance, there is a climate of

- failure (why bother to change, it doesn't help)
- entrenched interests (we'll only change if it suits us)
- myopia (we can't see any reason to change)
- self-deception (the present system is working well)
- immobility (we should stay as we are, it's quite comfortable)

- impasse (there are opposing views of equal power)
- weariness (we've seen it all before)
- inertia (the task is too great, it's futile to try)
- confusion (we can't decide what to do)
- timidity (we just can't wind ourselves up to act)
- disorder (we can't get ourselves organized properly)
- poverty (we do not have the resources to make the change)
- cynicism (don't bother; it will blow over; a new fad will be along soon)
- mutiny (undermine it, they are trying to exploit us; they don't know what they are doing; our views are better)
- disinterest (forget it, I'm retiring soon)

then change will take longer than when it is seen to be

- of low or unavoidable risk
- within the firm's capabilities
- exciting
- necessary or even vital
- historically and intellectually expected (if we're not changing, we're slipping)
- a needed stimulus to sustain commitment
- normal.

However, provided that top managers are not approaching retirement and so seeking a tranquil exit, and provided that they are not so lacking in confidence and skills that they prefer to duck the challenge, it is likely to be the firm's top management which wants to make brisk improvements in the organization's performance. They will want to create a beneficial impact. They will not want to wait passively around and then retire before the effects of their policy decisions bear fruit. How many CEOs would embark on a strategic change where the costs may be immediate but the benefits will only emerge long after their period of glory in office? Speed, force and direction—impetus if you prefer—are all vital factors in driving commercial organizations forward, because it is through such progress that the firm (and its board) will be gauged by the outside world and will earn a continued place in the market for its outputs. Firms cannot

wait until every last element of a projected change programme has fallen into place; corporate life is too short. The
organization may have to be prepared (and, indeed, may
have no option) to countenance imperfections and casualties
in the drive for commercial victory.

CHERISHING THE ASSETS

Fortunately, as in the ICI case, major strategic change rarely
requires everything to be rejected and replaced. Nor would
you necessarily want to discard all of the past. If you did, it
infers that the existing organization has become worthless,
has no accumulated value and contains nothing to cherish
and retain. That would be odd at a time when British
companies capitalize intangible elements like brands onto
their balance sheets as assets. Good leaders will want to
conserve and build on the best elements of what is already
there, so the continued existence of some unchanged features
does not necessarily indicate an untoward elapsing of time or
an attempt to avoid change, but more a deliberate preserva-
tion of the valuable parts of the organization's heritage. Nor
would one want to remove all the existing props to people's
current performance. As Charles Hampden-Turner has said:
'You need change *and* continuity. Otherwise people panic.'

Hence, the firm's administrative heritage is simultaneously
an asset to be nurtured and a constraint to be overcome when
abnormal change is needed.[7] Demands for the ditching of the
past are often symbolic exaggerations made for galvanizing
purposes. The adjustment can usually be made without
complete eradication of memory, experience and learning.
What is required is usually an adjustment, not a transubstan-
tiation. And is it so obvious that such adjustment must take
ages?

IS IMPLEMENTATION SO COMPLICATED?

In support of a more confident view of the prospects for
rapid change, it is worth remembering that if all these

troublesome possibilities were inevitable barriers to implementation, they would inhibit all but the reckless from attempting to make rapid changes to the way an organization is run. But some rapid changes do work well. For example, assiduous corporate acquirers do seem to know a thing or two. It is not normal for companies acquired by, for example, Hanson or BTR to collapse in disorder, let alone collapse in profits. Perhaps outsiders don't spot the bodies in the hedgerows, but what we can usually observe in such companies is a transformation of returns on the assets acquired and an enhancement in profits that is not due solely to accounting ingenuities.

Hanson's technique for the absorption of a new acquisition is the rapid imposition of an unchanged Hanson culture (if you can call a set of rules and criteria a culture) onto the culture of the acquired firm. In those first few critical weeks the injected Hanson team has rapidly to lift the morale of the workforce from the anxious level of the bid period. Speedy change in the acquired firm goes hand in hand with immutability of the Hanson culture. The culture of the acquired company is altered through the introduction of new criteria, new rules and procedures, new processes and habits. Rapid change is achieved. The acquired firm is forced to introduce the ground rules of its new host. It survives and usually prospers. The fact that *force majeure* may be involved is scarcely relevant; rapid change has occurred.

We have to reconsider the notion of the organization as a delicate and fragile organism that can be shattered by firm handling. Perhaps an analogy for the ability of an organization to absorb shocks should be the toughness of Tonka Toys rather than the delicacy of Meissen porcelain. Now it can be argued, as with transformations resulting from M&A activities, that rapid changes come generally from the use of power and are coerced transformations. But if, nevertheless, they are transformations, then it can no longer be generally claimed that rapid change is impossible, but only that it occurs in certain forceful circumstances and might not be self-induced in the absence of externally applied pressure. Managerial power and urgent necessity are prominent features in the determinants of the pace at which change can be effected, and strongly influence the conditions that make rapid change feasible (see pages 26–27).

CAN POWER BE USED?

Galvanizing the organization is a key responsibility of the firm's top management. After all, if those below can see that their leaders are not really interested, why should they trouble themselves? Those below want to be sure that the people in charge know what they are doing. Followers take a lead from leaders, even in daunting circumstances. Leaders have power and it is their responsibility to use it wisely. But can power be used?

Throughout this book there is an underlying tension about the best methods of making strategic changes in an organization. On the one hand, there is the explicit proposition that the possession of power helps and enables; and that the exercise of power can be fruitful and speedily effective. Some industrial sociologists may find this theme particularly unpalatable as a reminder of the coercion that can accompany the use of power. Power has been defined as the capacity to influence others with or without their consent, whether that power comes from position, expertise or the ability to reward and punish.[8] Authority comes from legitimate power, and the willing acceptance of the authority of others can be observed in many organizations, particularly via the calls for 'leadership', 'action' and 'decisions' that arise when employees become frustrated by an organization's drift. The exercise of power is frequently necessary in order to make progress towards goals held in common by leaders and followers—or to enable the views to become common— by focusing employees' attention on goals that management is determined to pursue. The application of power may appeal to the employees as an inspiring evocation of decisive leadership which, they hope, will transform the firm's situation.[9]

Alternatively, the employees' willingness to accede to the power of the boss may be calculative in that they may be prepared to give up power (and usually, let us remember, responsibility) over the work part of their lives and let the boss do most of the worrying. It can also result from the followers' gloomy recognition that the present organization is immobilized and that only by ceding extra power to a trusted leader can the log jam of inaction be broken up. In extreme cases the followers may not even trust the leader(s) but conclude that, whatever the probability of failure, there is no realistic alternative but to give him or her the necessary power to act in the hope that he or she will pull the organization through. And even where vivid leadership is absent, in many drab situations the use of power may be a great relief to the followers—as long as the power is exercised in a manner and for a goal that does not clash overtly with the followers' basic beliefs. The use of power in such circumstances may well create agreeable progress; not, perhaps, the maximum that might occur if leaders and followers were both united in their commitment, but progress nevertheless.

Such a perspective can be difficult to adopt. Too many of us over-accepted the more democratic behavioural beliefs of the 1970s which implicitly allowed that involving everyone in important decisions was the answer to late twentieth-century organizational problems with humans. Under the impact of their people-supportive assertions, the exercise of power—or even just the possession of power—thus became associated with coercion and exploitation so that, consequently, voluntarism and egalitarian procedures were lauded. The idea that more democratic systems at work might be less effective was barely canvassed. Even now, the view that, in some circumstances, teams perform less well than a hierarchy, cuts across the popular ideology of cooperation.

The underlying assumption was that employees, liberated from the oppressions of power exercised over them, would flourish and, through some behavioural equivalent of the benign hidden hand, would blossom into high-energy and high-output fulfilment. Equality, democracy and egalitarianism would be the key ingredients of organizational success. Power got a bad name.

Unfortunately for these theories, managerial power continued to work in many organizational situations.[10] The shifting political assumptions of the last decade in industrialized countries have also reflected the growing recognition that egalitarian approaches had handicaps too. When an organization does not already run on high-involvement lines and is faced with the need for urgent action, democratic processes will take time that the firm cannot afford.

PERSUASIVE LEADERS

Yet the tension remains, because it is also clear that power holders who attempt to use power, regardless of the views and values of those over whom it is exercised, find that it has limited efficacy. Organizations have changed. The proliferation of specialist professions has created ever-growing sets of people who will commit themselves to goals that they accept, but who resist being pushed around. Organizations, large and small, are often filled with talented people who have a robust view of their worth and cherish the legitimacy and utility of using their own independent judgement.

Leaders now have to be persuasive to an often lively set of skilled and potentially mobile professionals. A lack of credibility on the part of the leader can readily cause disorder and demotivation. Should these debilitating factors persist, the best followers will leave, for one definition of professionals is that they are people who have options. They are not trapped by circumstance or through building up non-transferable skills. Their very professional expertise confers transferability. Typically, they don't have to stay in a given place, since self-employment is possible in most skilled pastimes and, except in dire economic circumstances, they usually have other employment opportunities. The best professionals rarely stay very long in a dispiriting situation, as they have no desire to erode their reputation or their all-important self-image.

Hence, one result of the growth and proliferation of professions and numbers of professionals is that personal autonomy in commercial organizations has grown, though it is never entirely clear whether this is a cause of, or response to, the desires for self-control on the part of people whose skills are in strong demand. Nevertheless, autonomy at work has expanded for several reasons. The shift to a service economy has usually meant that the size of each organizational unit has reduced, for example, because shops are generally smaller than factories. In addition, the advent of lean and flexible production systems, and improved information systems, has eroded some economies of scale in favour of economies of responsiveness, while the rigidity of labour behaviour in large Western plants has reduced the appeal of gargantuan production units. At the same time, while manufacturing organizations in particular have found growing interdependence between their units—and thus a growing need for coordination—each unit is likely to have been awarded more self-government in order to foster unit accountability and unit efficiency. Hence, in modern organizations, units are not only smaller relative to the output of the firm, but it is not unusual for each unit to manage its own affairs within a broad policy framework. This encourages, or even enforces, unit autonomy.

These developments have depleted the power of organizational tyrants. Under autocratic leaders, the professionals too often just depart. The result is that autocratically-run firms increasingly need to be led by an unusually perceptive despot or they will lack talented people who have enough independent self-confidence to act incisively without reference to the leader. Such organizations may become overendowed with sycophants, clones of the leader and cynics who will bend to the vagaries of the leader's whims. Devoid of an alternative perspective, once his or her judgement slips, they all slip as the organization's performance spirals down.

Thus, most managers in organizations who have any sensitivity about implementing new strategies would have qualms about the blunt use of organizational power and a healthy concern that they should carry their independent-minded professionals with them in any significant changes. Empowerment is the vogue word to describe the desired state in which skilled employees are imbued with the mission of the firm, through which they internalize its values and, in consequence, shoulder authority and unsupervised responsibility for representing the organization in everything they do at work.

Yet there are limits to such autonomy. While companies certainly desire that employees be invigorated, it is not always obvious that self-managed initiative is so attractive. The Russian engineers at Chernobyl were using initiative when they ran the unauthorized experiments that led to disaster. This suggests that there is a need for power to be legitimated in order to combine authority with as much autonomy as is practicable. It is this need to combine legitimating systems together with invigoration through autonomy, which underscores Waterman's attempt to square the circle when he writes of the need for *direction and empowerment*.[11] Even in professional workforces, the need for leadership does not evaporate. Professional partnerships have managing partners to set the strategy, oversee the administration and persuade partners of the merits of particular courses of action. Any idea that high involvement means non-management would be erroneous.

DELEGATION, DRIFT AND DISSIPATION

A second fallacy is that of thinking that implementation can be delegated to lower level employees in the belief that, once defined, strategy implementation is just an operational matter. Sir John Harvey-Jones claimed that 'if the strategic objective has been worked out together and agreed, and the right conditions have been created in which people can be switched on, the "how" of what is to be achieved is a matter of delegation'.[12]

One can argue that, even if people are persuaded of the need for change and are committed to jointly agreed objectives, it manifestly is *not* a matter of delegation. In that way lies inadequacy and disappointment. Perhaps it does take years to change attitudes if implementation is seen as a delegated operating routine. If top management delegates (or should one say abdicates?) implementation to low levels in the organization, that certainly has the merit of involving people lower down in strategic matters, but is it a sensible or effective method of implementing strategic change? Other writers are adamant that, in such circumstances, top management must be seen to, and must continue to, lead from the front with all the commitment, visibility and symbolic pageantry they can muster.

The notion that implementation is a delegated operating routine must have a certain charm for top managers and strategy advisers. After all, it eliminates their need to visit, let alone become embroiled with, the organizational battlefield. Like HQ staff in the First World War, if they do later visit the organizational carnage, they can disclaim responsibility for the mess. They can also insinuate that the impediments to smooth change are caused at the operating level rather than through anything that emanates from their own spheres of responsibility. They can then express frustration that their well-designed plan has been put at risk by defective subordinates.

But is theirs a fair judgement? The issue at stake may be what should or should not be delegated. There is general agreement that, if practicable, people at several levels in the organization should be involved in the gestation of a programme of strategic change. That is not so much delegation, but sharing—sharing of the distributed expertise, of the detailed knowledge of opportunities and impediments that exist lower down in the organization which will help or mar an implementation activity. That should reduce the chance of the organization trying to do the wrong thing. Even then, it is still easy to fail to implement the plan properly when the senior managers leave the implementation judgements to junior managers. It is instructive to note that, a few years after Sir John Harvey-Jones's striking campaigns at ICI, Hanson took a stake in ICI and strongly criticized its management for failing to make sufficient improvement in its efficiency. ICI subsequently has had to make further major changes in order to improve its efficiency, eventually de-merging into two separate companies. Similarly, the convulsions at BP between 1990 and 1992 seem to have resulted from discord between the hard-driving architect of change and those delegated to carry out the changes, with the result that he was forced out of the organization.

The Harvey-Jones perspective gives a clue why it is so difficult for managements to delegate rapid strategic change successfully. They are delegating to the reluctant. Indeed, their motto might be 'Delegate, Drift and Dissipate', because that is what is likely to happen. The middle managers to whom implementation is delegated are the most threatened and most troubled by change. They are likely to be the ones brought up and imbued with the ethos of the organization's past: undertrained in change management techniques; possibly lacking in the new technical skills that are now required; at the crossroads of communication needs for themselves and for their clamorous and rattled underlings; previously not required to be particularly resourceful except within the standing limitations of their job; at risk of being de-layered out of their jobs, if not their careers. Their handicaps are legion; their underpreparation and suspect morale are likely to be crippling.

Delegation is only going to work well when it liberates people who are confident, relevantly skilled, adequately resourced and clear about the objectives—which they share. Otherwise, having decided to make changes, announced them and then moved on to other issues, managers who delegate tend to overlook the work that is necessary to ensure that people have been briefed and equipped properly for the task of making the changes in an effective manner. The senior managers may then close their ears to the muffled sounds of wrath coming from below, interpreting them as indicating resistance to change rather than a distaste for the particular changes being introduced, and so failing to understand the irritation of minions who are being asked to undertake tasks without proper resources, without management backing, without agreement about the scope and limits of their autonomy, and without the organizational systems that would be appropriate to give the changes a good chance of success.

Indeed, the very fact of the senior managers' interest having moved on may well have contributed to the waning pace of the strategic change. It is not surprising that the impetus slackens when top management involvement has begun to evaporate. No longer obviously backed, nor driven on, by the top executives, the signal to staff is that commitment has declined and, perhaps, that the staff's own efforts should switch to even newer priorities. The necessary dogged persistence—a hallmark of sustained organizational purpose—has wilted. The management's misguided delegation has failed, except in the political sense that the top managers have found someone else to blame. Good managers do not just initiate changes and then move on. They keep at it—leading, cajoling, demonstrating care and interest in the successful continuance of the change project, for which they continue to take responsibility.

MANAGERS' IMPLEMENTATION TACTICS

The need for sustained management involvement is not just logical but demonstrable. In a fascinating study of implementation tactics, Nutt[13] categorized four types of implementation tactic: edict, persuasion, participation and intervention. These tactics varied in the use of power and, crucially, in the amount of management involvement. The least successful was edict, in which the manager simply issued directions about what was to happen. While that required the utilization of substantial managerial power, it used little management time, and was least successful because it bred resistance to the edict and so successful implementation was both problematic and lengthy. (This may have been due to the checks and balances in the public service organizations which Nutt studied. In a takeover by Hanson, edict can work effectively and rapidly.) Persuasion, in which the manager first sponsored experts who determined what should be done and then used rational arguments to sell the plan, took as long but had a better success rate. Again it took little management time. Persuasion lacked authority and edict lacked legitimacy for those below. In neither case was the strategic manager heavily involved in the process.

Participation had a similar success rate to persuasion and took almost as long, but it required large amounts of management time to be invested, not just by the sponsoring manager but by those who formed the team of representatives to which the implementation project had been delegated. Complete delegation to all staff was rare and was costly both in managerial involvement and in needing much larger process budgets. Participation was less effective than complete delegation to all because of the need for delegates to persuade their constituents of the merit of the implementation plans. Intervention by the manager championing the implementation was the most successful tactic, and implementation took about half the time of each of the other three tactics. As with delegated participation, it involved the sponsoring manager extensively as he or she progressed the justification for change and the plan to meet the opportunities and needs of strategic change. In intervention, the sponsoring manager was the change agent and the visible, committed, action-oriented leader.

Given that managers are the key process actors—even in highly participative implementation processes—it should not be a surprise that implementation success was strongly associated with active and persistent involvement by the sponsoring manager.[14] Implementation failure was mainly due to low involvement by managers. Worse than that was the indication that managers *preferred* low-involvement tactics (as with Sir John Harvey-Jones's preference for delegating implementation) because nearly all the implementation projects that failed to use the most appropriate tactic, appeared to be using an inappropriate tactic that minimized the involvement of the manager. This tendency to be expedient in conserving the manager's precious time, led to strategic managers delegating to a staff expert or issuing an edict when intervention or participation would have been more appropriate. Overall, in 93 per cent of the implementation failures, tactics that appeared to be minimizing the strategic manager's involvement were applied.[15]

Apart from this reminder that senior managers cannot abdicate their lead role in strategy implementation, the doubling of the time taken when intervention was not used indicated that, where speed of action is a competitive consideration, managerial intervention is a valuable tactic. Participation is more appropriate for professional and collegial organizations where the manager's power to intervene and lead so aggressively would be impractical or counter-productive. Where managers do have the power to intervene and lead, the indication is that the manager should do so. In particular, an organization with an urgent need for strategy implementation would be well advised to have its managers lead the charge. The fashion for embracing participation may be overdone.[16]

THE SPARTACUS CHALLENGE

The fruitful impetus for change is thus likely to come from the top. Indeed, there are consultants and experienced managers who say that they have *never* seen major strategic impetus start from the middle or bottom; it *always* starts at the top.

> I have never seen it done except by either one person or a very small group of people. You've got to have momentum and you don't generate momentum terribly well in a bureaucracy or in a democracy. And I don't see it coming up from below, because people don't have the broad view, the overview. You have to have people who are not only in a position to have that overview—most bosses are in that position—but they also have to have the capability to take an overview. There is a limited number who can generate a strategic overview and retain it under pressure. You've got to be able to impose it downwards and have the energy to do that as well as the will to do it and the endurance. You never get anywhere by milling along in the middle of the throng. In the case of the British National Oil Corporation, Frank Kearton had the drive and the vision. He had two people as an extra left and extra right hand, but it was his vision and drive. He was a man who would deliberate a long time carefully before he did something. Once he had, he did it with furious energy and he proved that if you're going to do something, you'd better do it well and keep doing it until you've won. Its a simple lesson. With a good strategy, do it with a lot of energy and keep doing it until it is done.
>
> (Sir Alastair Morton, co-chairman, Eurotunnel)

If you dissent from the notion of top-down initiative, then set yourself *The Spartacus challenge*. Name one sizeable modern commercial organization that has carried out a major strategic change as a result of a successful revolt of the slaves. Product and process ideas, which may later have strategic connotations, may well have come from below, but where are examples of a coordinated, well-considered reconstruction of the organization's strategy that has emanated from beneath? Where are the examples of a bottom-up revolution in an organization's strategy in which those below introduced a new strategy, as opposed to successfully resisting a strategic change initiated by top management, such as might occur in a professional firm where the vital expertise is held by technical specialists who can resist unwanted change success-fully? Of course product ideas, market insights and customer initiatives can all come bubbling up through an alert organization's ranks. But a major strategic change? Very occasionally, it would appear.

The only exception is in a decentralized firm where the corporate centre commits itself to devolved autonomy for its units and then refrains from issuing edicts about how those units must act. The units have the freedom to design and execute a change within the overall remit from the top, although the local champions of that change will want to receive the blessing of corporate management to demonstrate support for their local power and to protect themselves from later recrimination if the change does not work well. Even then the local champions are usually the unit's managers, not the staff.

The conclusion is that rapid strategic change can occur in an organization, particularly when its leaders use their power and influence to orchestrate the forces that press upon the firm. They cannot duck or delegate that responsibility if they want to implement strategy effectively. Delegation can only work in a context where top management remains symboli-cally and practically involved, championing the change process and encouraging those below. The top management will need a clear plan—not an exact, detailed blueprint, but something akin to that classic, laconic Western film dialogue in which the follower asks 'Which way should we go?' and gets the answer 'Keep the herd heading West'. Lacking that, a management whose best advice is 'Do what you choose and

don't involve us' should resign to make way for managers
who have a decent clue about the firm's purpose and
direction and who are prepared to demonstrate their judgement by leading the organization along its chosen route.

REFERENCES

1. Sandra J. Hale and Mary M. Williams (eds), *Managing Change*. Urban
   Institute Press, 1989.
2. Robert H. Waterman, *The Renewal Factor: Building and Maintaining Your
   Company's Competitive Edge*. Bantam, 1988, pp. 291–3.
3. John W. Hunt, Stan Lees, John J. Grumbar and Philip D. Vivian,
   Acquisitions—The Human Factor. Egon Zehnder/London Business
   School, 1987; Anthony F. Buono and James L. Bowditch, *The Human
   Side of Mergers and Acquisitions*. Jossey Bass, 1989.
4. Stuart Slatter, *Corporate Recovery*. Penguin, 1984.
5. Tony Alexander, Chief UK Operating Officer, Hanson plc, *Financial
   Times*, 23 August 1990.
6. Andrew Pettigrew, *The Awakening Giant: Continuity and Change in ICI*.
   Blackwell, 1985.
7. Christopher A. Bartlett and Sumantra Ghoshal, *Managing Across
   Borders: The Transnational Solution*. Harvard/Hutchinson, 1989, pp. 35
   and 41.
8. John W. Hunt, *Managing People at Work*, 3rd edn, McGraw-Hill, 1992,
   p. 65.
9. James MacGregor Burns, *Leadership*. Harper Collins, 1982.
10. Jeffrey Pfeffer, *Managing with Power*. Harvard Business School Press,
    1992; Kenneth E. Boulding, *Three Faces of Power*. Sage, 1989; Henry
    Mintzberg, *Power In and Around Organisations*. Prentice-Hall, 1983.
11. Robert H. Waterman, *The Renewal Factor: Building and Maintaining Your
    Company's Competitive Edge*. Bantam, 1988, p. 7.
12. John Harvey Jones, *Making it Happen*. Collins, 1986, p. 72.
13. Paul C. Nutt, Selecting tactics to implement strategic plans, *Strategic
    Management Journal*, **10** (2), 1989, pp. 145–61; Paul C. Nutt, *Managing
    Planned Change*. Macmillan, 1992, pp. 152–4.
14. Paul C. Nutt, The tactics of implementation. *Academy of Management
    Journal*, **29** (2), 1986, p. 233.
15. Nutt, *op. cit.*, 1989, p. 160.
16. Abraham Zaleznik, The leadership gap. *Academy of Management
    Executive*, **4** (1), 1990, pp. 7–22.

3 Planning and a new model

- **Memories of the future**
- **The merits of planning**
- **The value of opportunism**
- **A new model**

In order to champion the change process, top management must have an idea of the strategic route it wishes the organization to traverse, and some idea of how to traverse it. It is not that the plan will be perfect; nor will it remain unmodified by events. But the lack of a plan is negligent. As Denis Healey has put it, from his long experience as Foreign Secretary and Chancellor, 'My great lesson ... is that all plans go wrong, and yet you can't work without a plan.'[1] Unfortunately, in business, planning has become an object of disdain for too many careless managers, and for three principal reasons.

The first is that, too often in organizations, planning has been used as a control device connected to the treadmill of short term budgetary pressures and so managers have become reluctant to commit themselves to targets in case they are then held to have promised to deliver them. If, in addition, the plans are linked to rewards, then games start to be played in which the managers gauge the prudence of putting forward ambitious targets, while the top management exhorts them to be more ambitious in order to fill the shortfall between plans and corporate aspirations.

The second came from economists' belief that large corporations could plan and control their futures through market domination. This belief has not been borne out by events. Whether the upsetting factors have been the discord of international conflict, the consequences of commercial battles, the growth of international competition aided by deregulation and anti-monopoly legislation, diseconomies of scale or the vagaries of economic fluctuation—as with the oil price shocks—a firm's ability to smooth its future has been severely tested over recent years. Grandiose plans have come to look pretentious. In a turbulent world, the value of detailed long-range planning is not so obvious when events can readily make them wrong.

The third reason is that, over the last two decades, firms have devolved management responsibility from corporate centres to business units. Closer to their fluxing markets than the headquarters, the units have tended to plan more informally, with the corporate centre acting in a more limited capacity; advising units on the planning format, seeking consistency of planning criteria and pressing unit managements to be more ambitious and causing irritation as it intruded upon the units' supposed autonomy. Units have come to resent both the intrusion and the hostage to fortune which explicit, quantified plans offer through giving the corporate centre a stick with which to beat them.

Given these reasons, it is scarcely surprising that grandiose planning became discredited, though it is worth remembering that the ideology of decentralization does not apply to all situations. There are many centralized companies that have been effective, such as Coca Cola and successful, leading Japanese firms.

But planning itself is vital; the idea that organizations should not bother is ludicrous. Strategic thrusts rarely just occur, uninfluenced by corporate purpose; the thoughtful organization does not simply react to some circumstance that emerges from time to time. Good strategies are worked on with intelligence and anticipation; they do not just emerge. Nor is the world so chaotic as to make planning pointless. There are immense stabilities in life—business and organizational life included.

MEMORIES OF THE FUTURE

Everyone who can do so, anticipates the future in order to rehearse prospective actions and responses to possible circumstances. It may be the queries of: What if we moved to the country? What would I do if my partner left me? What might happen when I leave college? What would we do if we came into money? What should I do if my car broke down on a deserted road? How should I respond if I win this prize? What would I do if, on a dark night, I saw three menacing figures walking towards me; should I cross to the other side of the street?

Anticipation through planning provides people as well as organizations with that crucial asset—memories of the future. Fascinating work has been carried out by Ingvar and others into people whose brains have suffered some lesions or degradations, and he termed the capacity to remember and be conscious of concepts of future events 'memory of the future'.[2] People have concepts, ideas and hypotheses of anticipated future events as well as memories of past events and consciousness of current events. This capacity for developing an inner future, to make up alternative action plans, to programme anticipatory goal-directed behaviour and cognition and to be able to recall short- and long-term plans for future behaviour and understanding, helps to solve problems about ways of reaching future goals.[3] Scenario and catastrophe planning are forms of anticipating the future, and are often used in military, governmental and business circles.

People with certain types of brain damage cannot readily rehearse the future and so, faced with unexpected circumstances, their reactions are slow and hesitant. They would only seek to react to a menacing situation when it was encountered. They would be trying to deal with the problem, if there was one, on the spot, lacking any preconsidered contingency plan. As Ingvar wrote, they 'suffer from inadequate concepts about the future ... and unawareness of the future consequences of behaviour ... such symptoms all represent interference with the long range purposive concepts about the future which normally form an integral part of the intellect.'[4] Most of us have known people whose motto does appear to be 'live for today', and whose discounting of future costs in favour of current gratification is disconcerting to anyone who plans for the future. As Ingvar concluded, 'it is only by access to serial plans for future behaviour and cognition, i.e. access to our "memory of the future", that we can select and perceive meaningful messages in the massive sensory barrage to which our brains are constantly exposed'.[5] This is what gives value to planning.

THE MERITS OF PLANNING

Planning has two main roles: the more intellectual element of thinking through the issues and their implications, which leads to the second, more practical activity of delineating resources that would need to be assembled to carry out the plan. Whether as a process, or for its content, or for its strategic logic, or for its early warnings of mismatches and inadequacies of resources, planning provides an intelligence system—a coherent map for management. A proactive approach to planning seeks to anticipate outcomes, to identify potential risks and problems and to plan to avoid or circumvent them. It is a discipline which orders ideas and options and gauges them against the practicalities of making them work. A good plan provides guidance to avoid indiscriminate backing for unruly ideas, and focuses on the qualities needed by the organization in any strategic initiative it might take.

It is an integrating mechanism for the parts of the enterprise; it also helps to create a team effort and to provide an anchor against the swirling currents and day-to-day gusts of navigating the company. Planning is a management tool. As Weick wrote: 'Plans are important in organizations, but not just for the reasons people usually think. Plans are symbols, advertisements and excuses for interaction.'[6] A planning process also has the merit of defusing emotion by augmenting opinion with some dispassionate, fact-based truths. It also helps strategic thinking because the process and outcome of planning informs the strategic debate.

Effective change can rarely happen without a plan. Much

of the purpose of sensible planning is not to produce an exact blueprint, but to highlight errors of assumption. As the old military maxim states: 'Plans sometimes may be useless, but the planning process is always indispensable.' Military strategists know that there is no point in developing a plan to move troops 200 miles in a day if, in the event, they find that there is no fuel for the trucks. Planning also helps to develop a shared rationality among the participants.[7] 'Strategic planning is a precursor to superior performance. We need a sense of direction and purpose. The will to win is necessary; but the will to prepare is vital' (Neville Bain, group chief executive, Coats Viyella).

Hence planning has a number of virtues. It should help to:

- induce a change of attitudes;
- discriminate between the merits of alternatives;
- foster openness and debate;
- augment opinions with more facts;
- liberate people from previously unchallenged assumptions;
- refine the objectives of the change
- destroy unfounded optimisms;
- converge support for the chosen plan;
- indicate needs for new resources and capabilities;
- draw attention to major impediments and contradictions;
- encourage factions to work together as a team;
- indicate timescale, cost and value;
- create a mind-set of preparedness for change;
- show how the change will be managed;
- anticipate the consequences before the event;
- reduce the stress of enforced change;
- prepare the key people for rapid, united action when required.

Can a sensible planning process be avoided?

Provided that it involves line executives and is not merely a cerebral abstraction carried out by staff analysts crunching data in a department disconnected from the businesses, the planning process helps the firm to prepare itself for the future. There needs to be a way of mediating between the options that might come from the outside world and the wish of the firm to gather and focus its energies most fruitfully. It may be that the strategy has to be adjusted because of deficiencies or implausibilities that are revealed by the plan, or by the original plan's inability to attract endorsement. A good plan will help to build support.

In some circumstances there may be no choice but to have a clear plan. The more active stakeholders there are, the more an organization will have to persuade them of the merits of a strategic change. It is unlikely that a government department could initiate a major change without prior explanation and negotiation with its key stakeholders. Unplanned change and opportunistic behaviour could provoke a damaging reaction.

Hayes wrote of developing capabilities first and then encouraging the development of plans to exploit them.[8] Yet that is just as judgemental as planning, in that it requires a prior view about what would be appropriate capabilities. Capabilities are only useful if you have some early idea of the goal you might pursue once they are in place. Otherwise, how would you know which capability to develop?

How much planning is useful?

Too much focus on planned strategic change will leave the organization unfit to meet unexpected circumstances. If there is insufficient focus on planned strategic change, the organization won't have a coherent, cohesive plan. Planning helps to confirm or disprove the plausibility and practicability of the chosen strategy and the pathways by which it might be actioned.

This does not mean that the plan has to be exact into the distant future. If you plan an implementation strategy step by step then it is going to be trumpet-shaped—wider at the later stages, because of feedback to be gained on the efficacy of the earlier stages, from evidence of developments in the market over time, by finding new and better insights and by learning about what might be more appropriate. The later stages will look uncertain. So it is helpful to predetermine your boundaries of acceptability. What is inviolable? What is the bottom line of options? If the implementation progresses within those boundaries, should the management mind how the organization evolves as long as it adheres to certain goals?

Planning gets discredited when it is too detailed since it inevitably becomes short term, because only then can the detail be accurate. Predictably, the attempt to put accuracy and defendable numbers into longer-term plans simply leads to the extrapolation of existing data as those responsible try to limit their forecasting risks. Consequently, detail becomes self-defeating and gives planning a bad name. Good top managers recognize this and actively seek to avoid visionary plans being emasculated through becoming coupled to detail and rigour, for they know that that will destroy the vision. As Mike Bett of British Telecom put it: 'Don't confuse things between a one-year plan and a vision which would be eviscerated by an interlocked plan. The conversion of good vision into a spurious plan is pointless. Planners order your thoughts but you've got to remain light on your feet to react to events.'

Grand Metropolitan's directors believe that the combination of preparedness and mutual understanding is important, since making strategic moves is affected by

the possession, or lack, of credible and imaginative long-term market scenarios. Most firms have extrapolated plans, done by accountants. Our strategy process is both top down and bottom up. The vision strategies are done at operating company management level and they attempt to project ten years ahead. There are ideas only—no numbers and only two pages from each business. Our four-year business plans do have numbers, but they are not as detailed as in the annual operating budgets. The details of our strategy, the infilling of what the vision means, these require a two-way dialogue—almost daily exchanges that hone the process. Your dialogue must be with people who understand the vision. Dialogue with our Drinks sector has been two-way for two decades, but the Foods group was not involved in the purchase of Pillsbury. That is changing as we develop the Foods sector. When you are making strategic moves, it helps when everybody has a good understanding of what the game is beforehand.

Pascale concurs: 'Planning is as essential as opportunistic behaviour in the evolution of successful strategy.'[9] Planning, therefore, is part of the indispensable minimum of organizing coherently and it can be reconciled with a loose texture that enables creativity, initiative and opportunism to play their parts.

THE VALUE OF OPPORTUNISM

Companies, therefore, should balance planning and opportunism by remembering Louis Pasteur's remark that 'Chance favours only the prepared mind' and by being poised for uncertain but anticipated opportunities to arise. This is a better discipline than pure opportunism, where there is a great temptation to distort the analysis to make the opportunity fit the strategy—like being overenthusiastic at an auction and buying something on a whim. 'It's amazing how often companies buy something that they don't know how to manage.' Given managers' inclination towards action, a planned strategy has the merit of reducing the chance of impulsive behaviour. Yet it should not be too difficult for a firm to discipline itself and still be able to be opportunistic. That cautious strategist, Lord Weinstock of GEC, is clear about this: 'Of course we're opportunistic. You can only take advantage of opportunities; you can't take advantage of non-opportunities.'

As Robert Waterman stated when extolling the virtues of informed opportunism:

> Renewing organizations set direction for their companies, not detailed strategy. ... They know the value of being prepared, and they also know that some of the most important strategic decisions they make are inherently unpredictable. ... They often see more value in the process of planning than in the plan itself. ... They assume opportunity will keep knocking, but it will knock softly and in unpredictable ways. Their ability is to sense opportunity where others can't, see it where others don't, act while others hesitate, and demur when others plunge. They behave as informed opportunists.[10]

An analogy for the organization's needed mixture of flexibility within a constancy of purpose, might be that of the improvisations of a jazz group around a melody—neither sticking rigidly to the written score, nor roaming off into the discordant wilderness of free-form.[11]

Planning is manifestly not implementation. As a result of a planning activity, all the firm knows is what it would need to do if it ever chose to do anything in line with the plan. Indeed, this poised readiness can mean that years can separate the formulation of the strategy from its implementation. For example, the Rank Organisation finally bought the Deluxe film processing laboratory in Hollywood in 1991. It had decided that it wanted one of the big processing laboratories there, having already had a good processing business in Britain for some 50 years.

> The decision was made in 1984. We had an idea of where we wanted to be and why we wanted to be there. We didn't deviate from what we were trying to do and we discussed it continuously for six years until it finally fell into place. We were very persistent. There were only three significant film laboratories there and we made serious approaches each time their ownership changed, which happened several times during that six years. But we couldn't get what we wanted at a price we wanted to pay. We became known as the buyer of last resort.

Similarly, the joint venture between GEC and Alsthom occurred five years after they had first talked about it. Some of the prospective deals that GEC presently has in its corporate mind may not be feasible within ten years. It depends on circumstance, personality, the attitude of key customers, anti-trust policies and, unless the firm is prepared to make a knockout bid (so could it ever make the acquisition pay?), some strategic moves just have to wait for the confluence of factors to become favourable—much as one has to do in personal life ('We've always had our eyes on that house').

There are so many such circumstances where formulation and implementation are inevitably or prudently separated that the view that you can just formulate and implement strategies as you proceed without any serious attempt at planning to cope with the consequences is plainly defective. The twin notions, popular in academic circles, that strategy emerges out of the actions of the firm and that strategy formulation and implementation coincide, do not describe the normal process of major strategic change. Plans may be developed iteratively, but they have to be laid out in a rational form in order to paint a meaningful picture to the subordinates who will be involved in their consequences. People can only make sense of complex, challenging, fresh information by summarizing and simplifying in order to permit logical thought in an otherwise confusing situation. Those below are likely to lose faith if those at the top appear to be making up strategy as they go along. Focus and guidance are vital; good planning is where preparedness meets opportunity.

A NEW MODEL

So what are the links between strategy formulation and strategy implementation? The traditional view of the strategy process showed the two phases of formulation and implementation as a straightforward sequence of the two separate stages. A less primitive version has formulation followed by a design and planning stage, followed by the implementation phase, in a sequence flowing generally in one direction— though there are feedback loops between stages as the formulation, plan and design elements are modified by changing circumstances and fresh learning, as in Figure 3.1.

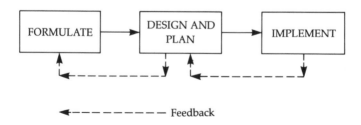

Figure 3.1   *Traditional planning model*

The feedback loops show that strategic action is a process as well as an event, so that the total separation of formulation and implementation is unrealistic. The feedback loops enable strategy to evolve, but this model indicates nothing of the crucial need to obtain backing from the organization's inhabitants for the strategy, for the plan and for its implementation.

Figure 3.2 provides a further illustration of both the separation of stages and the accent on action, but it also elaborates the intermediate stage between formulation and implementation. Its main feature is the addition of the development activities of selling the strategic change to those who will be involved and of assembling the resources to put the plan into effect.

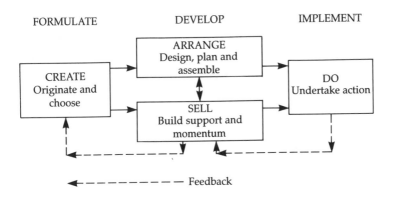

Figure 3.2 *Enhanced model*

Create

This element involves the origination and choosing of a new strategic route from a range of alternatives that have resulted from analysis. There may or may not have been a widespread debate in the firm in order to get to that point, depending on the circumstances. But this is where the new strategy is formulated. The two elements shown as simultaneous processes then follow.

Arrange and sell

In the upper strategy development process of 'arrange', the implementation of the chosen strategy is planned and designed and the resources that will be required begin to be specified and assembled, be they physical assets, financial budgets, specialist devices and staffs, employee skills or coordination mechanisms. This process may well lead to modification of the strategy, as impediments to the original plan are uncovered.

In the parallel development element of 'sell', commitment is sought through communication, persuasion and the offering of rewards (and perhaps sanctions) in order to build support and momentum and also, in so doing, to obtain feedback from employees (and perhaps suppliers and customers) about the proposals, in order to further refine and develop the strategy and the plan. Designing, planning and assembly go hand in hand, as do gaining support and building momentum. Both arranging and selling activities interact with and influence each other. Together they form the phase in which the strategy is developed into the thrust for action. It is the critical stage of endorsement, when those who are to be involved support the proposed changes and gird themselves for fresh action.

Do

The final element begins when the buttons are pressed to turn the plan into successful action.

Yet this model does not capture the overlap that occurs as strategies are developed and modified. Despite the fact that it includes feedback mechanisms to avoid the complete separation of elements, the model can give the impression that overlap between the elements does not occur. Yet because the stages overlap and intermingle in practice, Figure 3.3 has been developed to illustrate the elements that typically occur in the strategic change process. There is a general flow from formulation via planning, assembly and endorsement to implementation. It is not that movement cannot occur in the

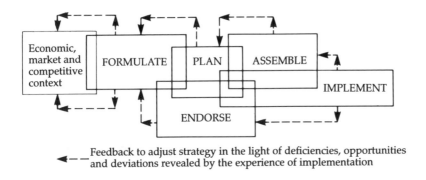

Figure 3.3 *New model*

reverse direction—as feedback affects perceptions, plans and actions—but, as with prevailing winds, the sequence is more likely to run from left to right than to flow in the opposite direction or to have the elements jostling together in inchoate turbulence. The presence and amount of overlap between the phases in Figure 3.3 is illustrative only, because the exact configuration depends on the specific situation, and the elements will float and overlay each other to fit the particular strategic change circumstances.

Figure 3.3 indicates why many analysts claim that implementation is a lengthy process. What has been commonly called implementation is often nothing of the kind, but is usually the development phase—the intervening stages of planning, endorsement and assembly. These are the periods of getting organized: preludes to the action of implementation; a gathering of the forces; persuasions of the mind; crystallization of the plans. Once the desired strategy has been delineated, the method and process of its introduction needs to be tested for feasibility and modified in the light of judgements about practicality, acceptability, time-scale and cost. It is the time when people are being persuaded about the action that is to ensue, and resources are being assembled to help the strategic change to proceed. Of course those intermediate stages include some action—

the activity of persuading people what changes should occur—but that precedes implementation, i.e. the making of those changes.

Successful implementation

Those intermediate stages are crucial elements in the translation of a formulated strategy into the actions of strategic change. The key to successful implementation (assuming that the chosen strategy is sensible) rests in those intermediate stages, particularly that of endorsement. The valuable role of planning has already been discussed. The assembly stage is a more technical matter—one of physical and intellectual logistics. If the endorsement phase is the gaining of commitment and understanding, the assembly phase is the gathering of those committed personnel, together with the logistical and financial resources to turn the plan into action.

This limited discussion on assembly is not meant to be cavalier or to ignore the problems of bringing resources together. The resources can be acquired, but that may take time. It may not be easy or cheap, but without the necessary resources the plan will probably not work. A firm, however, can usually sense when its members are being asked to make bricks without straw, and the single most important process is bringing the needed people together—uniting on goals, cooperating in action, utilizing their skills creatively, and positively motivating them towards a concerted campaign of strategic change. This is why we need to concentrate on the endorsement phase.

REFERENCES

1. *The Guardian*, 15 May 1993.
2. David H. Ingvar, Memory of the future: an essay on the temporal organization of conscious awareness. *Human Neurobiology*, **4**, 1985, pp. 127–36.
3. Ingvar, *op. cit.*, p. 133: see also F. T. Melges, *Time and the Inner Future. A Temporal Approach to Psychiatric Disorders*. Wiley, 1982.
4. Ingvar, *op. cit.*, p. 132.

5. Ingvar, *op. cit.*, p. 134.
6. Karl E. Weick, *The Social Psychology of Organising*. McGraw-Hill, 1979.
7. George A. Steiner and John B. Miner, *Management Policy and Strategy*. Macmillan, 1977, p. 174.
8. Robert H. Hayes, Strategic planning—forward in reverse? *Harvard Business Review*, November-December 1985, p. 118.
9. Richard T. Pascale, *Managing on the Edge*. Viking, 1990, p. 65.
10. Robert H. Waterman, *The Renewal Factor: Building and Maintaining Your Company's Competitive Edge*. Bantam, 1988, p. 6.
11. Lee Tom Perry, Randall G. Stott and W. Norman Smallwood, *Real-Time Strategy: Improvising Team-Based Planning for a Fast-Changing World*. Wiley, 1993.

4 Endorsement: the growth of concerted will

- The meaning of implementation
- Resistance strategies
- The principle of least action
- Confusion on the board

Change does not just happen; it needs endorsement—the growth of concerted will. In strategy implementation, endorsement is the pivotal element in the process: the stage between deciding how to do it and doing it; the period of negotiation, of people reconciling themselves and girding themselves for the actions for which they will be responsible and which they will have to back. It is the process of arousing and engaging support and of building up momentum behind the change process. It begins when the proponent(s) of the new strategy—in the interests of generating impetus to implement it—seek to unite among themselves and then to extend that unity to as many people and factions in the organization as can be persuaded to agree, with the minimum condition that the united group must have enough positive force to make the changes successfully (and therefore ensuring that those outside the group have insufficient, coordinated, counter-vailing force that could thwart or seriously weaken the process of putting the new strategy in place). The objectors may have substantial power available to them, but if they can't or won't combine, then their latent power will remain ineffectual. This is what makes it imperative to overcome any confusion on the board, for if its members are not jointly committed to the new strategy, the signals to those lower down will be puzzlingly, perhaps disablingly, confused.

During the endorsement phase, the promoters of the plan are entreating with the rest of the organization in order to extend acceptance of the new strategy until, perhaps modified by the discussions, it provides a sufficient basis of support for effective implementation of the strategy. The key point is that prospective backers are enrolled, enlisted, their allegiance is checked off, fealty is called in, their mind-sets are modified and their agreement and support are obtained as they accept the new strategy for principled or expedient reasons. It is a period of negotiation, influence and reconciliation as people come to terms with the desirability of the proposed changes or the inevitability that the situation is going to alter in some way. Whether the uniting, positive factions are induced to agree to pool their forces through negotiated exchanges or are persuaded of the uplifting appeal of the new strategy without exacting a price for joining the group, will vary from circumstance to circumstance.

Getting the whole group lined up in the right direction is certainly part of it, but just lining up in compliance could betoken sullenness—as with circus lions, where one cannot assume them to be committed to what they have to perform. Endorsement is more positive and has an air of concordance, agreement and harmony.

The endorsement stage has several purposes. Their order of priority will depend on the circumstances in which the promoters of the newly formulated strategy are exploring the practicability of their chosen strategy, the feasibility of their chosen implementation method, the support they will receive and the contingency plans they might need. It is a stage of

- testing/exploring
- judging/gauging
- negotiating
- cultivating (of people's views and support)
- influencing
- converging
- informing
- feedback
- refining

- proselytising
- cajoling
- offering benefits and disbenefits.

There may well be uplifting visions of a moral imperative as to what the organization should do; yet there will also be calculations of threat and promise. Not all the informing and negotiation will be sweet; some will involve argument, recrimination and the painting of unappetising pictures to 'persuade' the reluctant.

Nor does endorsement mean just lip service. The growth of concerted will is not merely the mouthing of convenient phrases, as might occur with a politician who finds it expedient to go along with sentiments with which he or she disagrees. Public commitment is valuable; rules about collectively binding decisions also entrap would-be dissenters—as with the collective responsibility of members of a government. The discoveries of the endorsement phase could lead to actions such as the removal of obdurate members of the change team. It is the period when the unenthusiastic reconcile themselves to the likelihood that the new strategy will be endorsed by the majority and that, if they do not agree, they may have the plan foisted on them or even be exited from any positions of power or from the organization itself. Endorsement may also require gaining the support of key suppliers and customers whose own activities will be affected by the forthcoming changes.

But is this not part of the implementation process itself? Well, no; it cannot be, unless the process of endorsement is completely empty—a plain sham, a mask for coercion. One cannot claim that the endorsement stage is part of implementation because, if one is already implementing, that would indicate that endorsement was not necessary. If the strategic change is going to be forced through regardless of whether it is endorsed or not, then endorsement is superfluous, though it might be useful to go through the motions to improve commitment.

The test of whether endorsement can be part of implementation comes if one asks what will happen if the formulated strategy *isn't* endorsed? If you need commitment and consensus in order to implement then, by definition, the process of endorsement cannot be part of implementation, otherwise you would be conceding that the process of persuasion was hollow and that, even if the reception to the proposed changes was unremittingly hostile, you would still go ahead with the strategic change. If, on the other hand, you would cancel the proposed strategic change if it met great resistance, then the process of discovering objections through the consensus building (or, in that case, the discovery of the *lack* of consensus) cannot be part of the implementation since, given the resistance, you no longer are going to implement anything, pending a regrouping round a different scheme. The activity of endorsement is not effecting the changes; it is agreeing that they should occur.

THE MEANING OF IMPLEMENTATION

There seems little room for dubiety about the meaning of implementation. Implementation is action. It is not planning to act; nor thinking about acting; nor clearing the organizational decks for action; nor persuading others to back your proposed plan; nor even just deciding what action should occur and how it should take place. It is the action itself, whatever it is and however it is occurring, with all its attendant elements of error, frustration, turmoil, expense and confusion.[1]

The conclusions are (a) that planning, a logical form of anticipation, is vital for all thoughtful people in organizations, so that they can be as poised and ready to take advantage of opportunities as they should be; and (b) that the most important element of preparation for implementation is the gaining of endorsement from key personnel for the implementation plan and its objective. The very essence of gearing up for implementation is the management act of managing and orchestrating the growth of concerted will in order to overcome organizational inertia and resistance.

RESISTANCE STRATEGIES

The stage of overcoming organizational inertia and resistance is probably the most vital early facet of converting strategic ideas into productive action. It is not that organizations are inert; indeed most people in organizations have an inherent restlessness which produces continuous adaptation. The issue is one of galvanizing the firm when that natural, normal pace of change is not enough and when extra momentum needs to be created or a change of direction is required—and the restlessness needs to be channelled in a particular way.

An organization will often have the potential to achieve significant improvements in its present practices and in its competitive position. Yet the concerted will of the organization prior to the mooted change is oriented towards its present practices. Abandoning them is a perturbing prospect and one not readily relished unless the organization's members have become frustrated with its present habits. There will be scepticism, if not resistance, to the proposed changes, whether these be fully defined or generally sketched and, before considering the sources of resistance and what can be done to overcome them, a brief word about resistance strategies is needed.

Resistance to change is probably at its most acute in old religious organizations, which tend to have high anxiety about the loss of traditional habits. Not far behind are public bodies and government administrative departments, replete with their world-weary recognition that today's political fad can be reversed by one election, by one change of minister. Elegance is often the hallmark of their resistance strategies.

Most business organizations, by comparison, are a model of responsiveness when they are in a competitive market and so lack the torpor that can afflict a monopoly. Yet they are not devoid of politicking, for once you define politics as the struggle to obtain, hold and use power and influence in order to pursue goals that you deem to be worth while, then every manager who is competent is, like it or not, a politician to some degree. In business, the range of resistance strategies is narrow compared to those available to public bodies that are monopoly providers of service and where the complexity of public accountability is ever-present. There are four basic reasons for this:

1. The business goal is more straightforward and there is greater convergence of commitment in the more single-minded circumstances of a business.
2. The range of constituencies that have to be considered is narrower than in the political domain, though it has been growing as the range of vocal stakeholders has expanded.
3. The need to obtain public funds from other places is usually absent. Imagine Ford having to make a bond or stock issue every time it needed funds for investment or working capital.
4. A company in a competitive market has to be more responsive because it has less control over its arena than does the monopoly supplier of government services, since its competitors provide an alternative benchmark against which to judge performance. There is no galvanizing benchmark competitor for the average government department.

The result is that the focus on narrower goals and the concentration of power typical in a commercial organization undercut any attempt to build an alternative power source and so give business leaders far more unchallenged authority than is typically available to a public administration, harried by the media and its political opponents. In a public administration, dissent is legitimate and expected. The dissenters belong to a different party or interest group. No such independent basis is afforded to dissidents within the commercial organization. Whistle-blowers and resisters are less well regarded and are likely to be disadvantaged, or even fired.

The comforting aspect for business organizations is that they are much more inclined to change than government departments. Government officials are keener to conserve, to cling to nurse for fear of something worse, to see new policies as threatening existing schemes that are still being refined. Business leaders want to be remembered for impact and progress and they have the advantage that, unlike civil servants, there are no politicians eager to claim all the credit if the results of change are favourable. Business executives' own drives towards growth and profit are powerful, as the organization's leaders seek their place in the company's pantheon of achievement.

Yet business managers—who typically sneer at the flexible attitudes of politicians—are not immune from political pressures and the opportunity that those provide for rivalry, revenge, a search for advantage, and sheer challenge. Almost any significant change offers the chance for politicking to become aroused, since the act of change is itself a dislocation from a previously stable state. Politicians like the flux of change, for, in the fog and smoke, opportunities flourish and dirty deals can be done unseen. The result is that new opportunities arise which the combatants can exploit as they seek to achieve their personal or departmental goals. It is prudent to recognize the existence of these motives, for ignoring them can prove fatal to the chances of successful implementation, given that change in business organizations is a political process.[2]

Whatever the inclinations of the top management and their expressed distaste for organizational politics (despite the likelihood that they got to the top as a result of their own politicking), it is difficult to demonstrate that a particular line of argument or action is basely motivated. Nor is it easy to detect subtle political manoeuvres until they have begun to work, by which time it may be too late to counter them. The only political choices then open are (a) to negotiate with critics on the removal of their objections or (b) their immediate and brutal removal from either the organization itself or from any position of power they may hold within it.

The advent of a proposed change will be seen by both prospective advocates and critics as a device for pressing their own interests, particularly if the existing situation is one of stalemate. This new catalyst can be harnessed by the change's promoters to create winners and losers, which should shift perceptions about the merits of the proposed change. The difficulty for the advocates is judging which of the objectors' concerns are valid criticisms and which are politically based. What if they are right? Self-interest may have been an underlying motive. Yet it is just as plausible that their resistance will have arisen either from different perspectives and values or from different judgements about the merit and risks of the new proposals. It is a necessary precaution to seek to understand the logic of the critics' objections before concluding that they are a form of sabotage.

There is also the problem that if the organization has decentralized feudal power to its divisions or units, the divisional barons will only introduce something when they think fit; their hesitance is not necessarily resistance or ill-will, but merely a continuance of their autonomy. Trying to galvanize action in a decentralized organization can be a nightmare, compounded by the inhibitions at the centre. How can a head office insist that the divisions and units are responsible for their own actions and then interfere, without damaging the whole logic of decentralization?

Any management contemplating a major change could prudently spend time trying to gauge the likely sources of resistance and organizing to deflate them through policy adjustments.

Sources of resistance

•	*Ignorance*	Failure to understand problem
•	*Comparison*	Solution is disliked, alternative thought better
•	*Disbelief*	Feel that solution will not work
•	*Loss*	Has unacceptable personal costs
•	*Inadequacy*	Insufficient rewards from change
•	*Anxiety*	Afraid of coping in new situation/fear of being discovered
•	*Demolition*	Risks destroying existing social network
•	*Power cut*	Erosion of influence/control
•	*Contamination*	Distaste for new values/practices
•	*Inhibition*	Low willingness to change
•	*Mistrust*	Disquiet about motives for change
•	*Alienation*	Low shared values/high alternative interest
•	*Frustration*	Reduces political power and career opportunities

Failure to do this can have chronic effects. One extremely costly British dock strike was occasioned by loss, inadequacy and demolition when working practices were altered. Despite a wage rise for workers, the employers—through lack of basic analysis—had failed to grasp that they were requiring dockers to work much harder for an unchanged income, while destroying their cherished social network. The dockers had worked it out as soon as the proposals were made. The employers thought that resistance was just a self-serving obstruction and had ignored the dockers' complaints. Had the employers gone down the check list and played devil's advocate by taking the dockers' perspective, their proposals might have altered to tailor them to the circumstances.

There are many reasons why organizations and individuals prefer not to change, be they concerned with the self, the rewards or the stability of the work. Ways of countering these causes of resistance include education, reassurance, skill enhancement, social, technical and financial support, reconfiguration of the proposals and timing adjustments, but the mix of treatments will depend on the nature of the resistance as well as the circumstances of the change. For example, if the prospective losers from change have the power and the technical skills that the organization needs, then change will be obstructed, probably successfully, and the losses will need to be reduced. It matters greatly whether resistance is passive (and a subtle form of passive resistance is to embrace the changes with a deadening lack of enthusiasm) or active, undermining through frontal assault or guerrilla warfare. Frontal assault is often the easier to face because at least the campaign and the combatants are obvious. Guerrilla warfare is more treacherous because its effects may take time to surface. In a professional organization, guerrilla action can take the form of psychological withdrawal, where participants go through the motions but their hearts are elsewhere and they make little more than the minimum effort required to keep the system ticking over. They comply, but they do not commit.

Not all resistance to change can be shrugged off as inevitable by quoting Machiavelli's famous dictum:

There is nothing more difficult to take in hand, more perilous to conduct or more uncertain of success than to take a lead in the introduction of a new order of things because the innovation has for enemies all those who have done well under the old, and lukewarm defenders in those who may do well under the new.[3]

Even if one accepted Machiavelli's warning, it would be feeble to assume that no impact can be made on the prospects for smooth change. It can be vital to neutralize likely critics before the event; to wrest or cajole resources away from the domain of a manager who will resist their effective deployment; to persuade a senior sponsor to give visible backing and credence to the proposed actions in order to avoid resistance delaying the triggering of change; to enhance the skills that are needed but absent; to eradicate inefficiencies that will slow it down; and to head off efforts to de-energize the change through the resistance strategies already described.

In dealing with implementation resisters, there is a hierarchy of appropriate techniques.

1. Convince the critics of the (selfless) validity of the chosen strategy. If they can be brought on side without having to pay them a price, then that must be most cost-effective, if it works.
2. Show that the behaviour you want will have a track to the top and that it is in their interests to clamber aboard.
3. Buy their support and/or flatter them—as with the health minister who, when asked how he would obtain the support of the complaining medical consultants for the inception of the National Health Service, replied 'We will stuff their mouths with gold'. And it worked.
4. Marginalize the critics and extract their skills for the benefit of the rest of the organization; they can later be exited if they remain a nuisance.
5. Neutralize or exit them (which may be the only way to neutralize them).

But we must not overstate the likelihood of great resistance to change. The notion that people don't want to change is deeply insulting to members of organizations. They don't want adverse change, change that might not work, or change that will disrupt fruitlessly. But to not want to improve? To not want to be more successful, admired, heroic, rich, secure? Why would people not want these things? The resistance problem is often one of divergence: between sections of the organization, departments, sites and levels; between, particularly, senior management and the main ranks of functional managers and specialists; and between the winners and losers from the changes. They may agree on the need for change, but not the changes needed. For the most part, however, resistance is likely to be dormant until roused by the worrying prospect of a change that people do not fancy.

The pressures for change in an organization have to contend with the forces of inertia that will resist any significant displacement of the status quo. Those ready to resist will include people who want the organization to change, but not in the direction that has been chosen. They may also be fearful. As Lord Weinstock, managing director of GEC, said: 'Almost by definition you have found fault and want to make things better. If you want to change, then there must be some people faults—so they are fearful.'

THE PRINCIPLE OF LEAST ACTION

There is a universal principle of physics—the principle of least action—which states that whenever anything changes it does so in such a way as to minimize the effort. e.g. a moving body will travel in a straight line rather than zig-zag, which would expend additional energy to create the changes in direction.

If one accepts that this principle has relevance to organizations as well as to physical matter, the conclusion that emerges from the principle of least action is that people in the organization will themselves seek to minimize the transformation necessary to achieve enough of a result to be deemed satisfactory—unless they intentionally zig-zag in order to delay and confuse. At its best, least action is efficient, but it may not create the transformation designed or desired by the top management. Employees may have a more modest idea of the necessary shifts compared to top management. If the management is right about the scope of the needed changes, what the employees would choose to do may be an enfeebled version leading only to an ineffectual result. In that case, the instigators of the strategic change would have to dramatize the need for change—in case the undramatized version was too subtle or too modest to be taken seriously—or would have to use their power to drive change along.

The stratagem usually embraced by managements is to endeavour to warn their staff of the full dangers of the organization's present state and the actions needed to improve it. The problem with this candid approach is that a new, contradictory, consequence can arise—particularly in a low-trust situation. The staff, while aiming off for what they deem to be managerial exaggeration of the problems, will nevertheless become alarmed at the possible implications. Defensive behaviour will then ensue, even if the management itself has not already recoiled from telling them the whole truth for fear of spreading panic. Yet the threshold of awareness must be reached if the staff are to become sufficiently aroused to change.

The lesson that the principle of least action teaches for organizations is the predictable one: the less you have to change, the easier it will be. The advantage is that the search for the least action option should locate the least costly and least disruptive method of getting from A to B. A management bent on implementing change should always be seeking the least action option that will result in the desired change. The challenge for management is to find a level and style of change that will be both sufficient and economic in requiring minimized efforts. Otherwise critics will complain of 'change for change's sake'.

An example of a least action decision might be the purchase of new computer equipment that is compatible with the old equipment—even if the change is not technically optimal—in order to minimize the transition costs of moving from the old to the new. Another would be an airline that has standardized on Boeing planes and Rolls-Royce engines and will therefore be inclined to buy again from those makers in order to minimize the costs of technical diversity such as retraining and having to hold additional tools and spares, even if other makers' products offer cost savings. It follows that strategic alterations that go beyond the minimum necessary should only be made if they have the effect of galvanizing action that, without the symbolic visibility of the additional thrust, would cause insufficient change. All prospective changes should be gauged beforehand by asking oneself if the chosen change is the least action device that would achieve the desired result. As one strategist remembered their implementation choice: 'It wasn't better than the other strategic choices, but it was the one we knew we could do.'

An inference of the principle of least action is that a subtle alteration in the organization's recipe might have extraordinary effects if it is seen as innocuous and demanding little action or response while, at the same time, altering people's perceptions and behaviour in the desired ways. Achieving such serendipity may be difficult, but the gearing effects of a small but influential adjustment make it highly desirable that such a potent intervention should be discovered.

A simple equation would suggest that, when organizations are in a reasonably stable state, the forces for change are roughly countered by the forces resisting change. Only when the forces for change have a material advantage will a transition occur. This might seem to be a statement of the blindingly obvious, but it is strange how such simple matters are overlooked by those who assert that organizations are always changing, or others who claim that people in organizations can be relied on to resist any proposed change.

The question for managers bent on changing their organization is how to tilt that equation in the direction of change with the minimum disruption, effort, cost and delay. The style with which they approach this task will partly depend on their own inclinations, experiences and talents, but it will also depend on the nature of the pressures for change on the type of organization and on the advantages/disadvantages held at the outset by the key participants. These parameters will vary with the type and state of the organization facing the prospective change.

Sole proprietors have only one key player and, in a calculative sense, that person may need to consult nobody else, provided that none of his or her personnel is crucial to the plans. It might be prudent, or perhaps ethically appealing, to involve the employees in the debate and decision, but it is only essential to do so if they have power to thwart the key player's moves. On the other hand, CEOs usually require board approval; dictators need to guard against coups; leaders of professional practices need to carry their partners with them. The minimum condition is that the instigator can put into place what he or she sees as necessary with the tacit approval, compliance and trust of the employees, or can act fairly in the knowledge that subordinates are powerless. If the organization is a professional practice then consensus among colleagues will decide the acceptance or rejection of the proposed changes. In that case the promoters of change will need to capture the assent of most of those in the organization and, given the workings of professional organizations, probably the key clients too, since they may become worried if their service seems likely to be affected. In other circumstances it may be that the technocrats are the key group in making the new strategy work properly. Finally, there will be organizations where, in the absence of the support of the mass of employees, little effective change can be achieved, whether the workforce is unionized or not, because the massed workers can obstruct the changes or the dispersed and lightly supervised field staff can just fail to alter their behaviour.

The questions then are: how can one change the odds towards success? and Where does one start? The answer to both questions must be: Start at the top. After all, if the top management doesn't fully support the changes, why should anyone else? If the board is disunited, what signal is being proffered to those below? Hence, the starting point has to be that of the endorsement of the board. A simple thing, one might suppose, given its members' non-sectarian role as guardians of the overall interests of the organization. But that would be to underestimate the politics of boards.

CONFUSION ON THE BOARD

It is all but inevitable that the group initiating a strategic change will either be the board or a group of senior executives who work together and who face a shared issue. We are talking about the implementation of a newly agreed strategy and, while the board may not have originated the idea, its members would almost certainly have been involved from an early stage. Unless the strategy is obviously flawed, and not likely to work (in which case, why have they endorsed it?), they will want to be seen to be in charge of its evolution. Their power over resources also makes it prudent that they be kept involved for the sake of their patronage and support. Whether the initiating factor has been a gathering storm that has been detected, an opportunity that has manifested itself, or the possibility of a new juxtaposition of forces that will alter competitive conditions, it is at the board that the arguments are likely to start. Indeed, they are to be expected. Peter Drucker once said: 'When the board is unanimous, delay the decision'. His point was that a board without dissent is a board possibly too lethargic for the company's own good. Vigorous, rigorous questioning is a necessary goad to a flabby board which would otherwise allow proposals through too easily.

However, thoughtful unanimity on the board is not usually the problem; either excess deference is given to the dominant top person, or dissent remains suppressed rather than resolved. There are rivalries, territorial considerations, power struggles, concerns about damage to what exists, differing views on what would be prudent, conflicting criteria, genuine scepticism about the outcomes of the proposed changes, fear, ignorance, misunderstanding, and concern about a threat to what has been seen as the firm's heritage. There are also stalemates, feelings of personal inadequacy and vulnerability, arguments over facts as well as over their implications, divergent views about what should be done even when the problem is agreed, issues of timing, an urge to wait for some other matter to work itself out, squabbles about what should be the interconnections between elements of the overall business (which are typically 'turf' issues disguised as matters of logic) and reluctance to face up to unpalatable facts. Turf issues are normal; almost by definition, those who have reached the top group want to run things—and if they cannot run everything, they will at least try to run their own fiefdom, with an unspoken mutual agreement not to question or invade matters associated with the territories of others. A board whose members represent near-independent baronies will be more difficult to unite than a board with more convergent interests. Senior people are rivals as well as colleagues.

Getting the board on side for a major company-wide initiative is a major task for the chairman and chief executive (assuming that *they* are of one mind), particularly if the board members are accustomed to operating in such a federal structure. It can require the advent of a new chairman or CEO from outside before the independent heads can be influenced—or knocked together effectively.

One world-renowned organization had to wait to replace its dictatorial CEO before it could change its divide and rule style. He had led from the front and had never let his most senior directors meet. The new CEO invited the firm's worldwide top 50 managers to an away-day strategy meeting. Senior executives in their late 40s were shaking hands because, although they had spent almost all their careers in the company, they had never met. So unused were they to cooperating and being asked to generate views that, when placed in small groups in one conference session to think through strategic issues, they asked, 'What are we supposed to do now?'

Philips suffered for several years from a power stalemate between its divisions and its national organizations. Neither was strong enough to overcome the veto power of the other, but each was powerful enough to exercise its veto power. Lacking a common view, the group at the top was not a team and, with both factions represented on the board, there was an intense amount of dissent. The chairman was an enabler rather than a leader and so, lacking board agreement on what should be done, results were no better at the (enforced) end of his reign than they had been at the beginning. Without consensus, there had been nothing to enable. His successor had a mammoth task because he inherited a firm then several years further adrift.

A current example is the multinational organization in which the charismatic chairman is partnered by a short-termist profit-seeker as chief executive. Exhorted by the chairman to seek international and cross-business liaisons in the face of the chief executive's scepticism, the business unit managers did their best to balance the competing demands, though cynicism was rife and the short-term goals always took precedence. The international links remained flimsy and its overseas performance ranged from erratic to doleful.

A strong bond between chairman and chief executive can withstand intense factional pressures.

> With André Bénard as the chairman of the board, we work as one. We don't just cooperate. We always support each other. If you have two bosses, they must not fall out with each other. So that the whole thing can operate as one, there must be personal chemistry. (At Eurotunnel) we were condemned to get on well together—or fail. The fact is that we got on from day one and nobody has ever succeeded in separating us by pressure.
>
> (Sir Alastair Morton, co-chairman, Eurotunnel)

In less impressive circumstances, again and again one sees in-fighting between factions at the top of the firm. Sometimes it is a rivalry between contenders for the top job, where decisions can be gauged by their effect on the struggle as the organization all but seizes up through the resulting hiatus. Or the last lame-duck period can prevent either the top manager or the successor from acting incisively. Organisations are sometimes driven, if not riven, by emotional, personal perspectives as much as they are by the logic of their competitive market positions. There may be genuine differences of opinion and judgement that neutralize each other to create an inability to act, and neither the CEO nor the board will decide.

The difficulties within the board can be substantial. Iain Mangham has captured the agonizing process that can occur in an executive team.[4] 'Team' is perhaps a misnomer to describe the squabbling group he studied as they dealt with unwelcome information by

- ignoring the feedback
- deleting sensitive and critical bits
- identifying the critics' 'misunderstandings' and recriminating with them.

He pointed out that the failure of the top team to get its act together had consequences and quoted Alonzo McDonald:

> If the power center at the top is in chaos, what hope has the rest of the corporation for constructive action? Business cannot go on as usual. Limp, anxious and vulnerable, the organization is unable to react effectively to new threats. As the contagion spreads, even distant departments are soon infected with pettiness, personal rivalries linked to different leaders, and arbitrary rulings of little logic or importance.[5]

This is not to say that all dysfunction is inadvertent or regretted. Dysfunction may be quite rational—a spoiling tactic, a delaying device, a political tussle or a way of pursuing a displaced goal. But the extent of disunity, often deplored by all individual board members, is astonishing. As two colleagues have written:

> In almost all the companies with which we have worked, top managers have difficulty in communicating their strategies between themselves. The communication of strategy down to the line managers is correspondingly muted. ... Under these circumstances, it is unlikely that the strategy will be properly implemented because few of the participants have a shared vision of what the strategy is supposed to represent.[6]

Andrew Kakabadse found that nearly two-thirds of general managers believed there were serious problems in their top teams which prevented their organization from attaining its objective.[7] Yet the top team of any purposeful organization eventually needs to appear united and to be fully conversant and able to explain what is proposed because, if not, that signal of disunity will reflect itself further down, confusion will occur and people will be half-hearted and not quite sure whether what they are attempting to do will later be countermanded. Resisters will be heartened by the ambivalence; even supporters will realize that the proposals may not be serious and give up for fear of looking foolish when the new strategy is overturned. If the middle managers' support has not been captured the strategy won't succeed anyway, and probably won't deserve to succeed.

The disunity of the top team is perhaps worse when the board consists of functional managers in the company, with no leavening of less-involved external directors. There is no point in expecting functional executives to disregard the importance of their own function and to act completely dispassionately in the interests of the entire organization. There is a tension between the need to see the organization as a whole and the need to back one's perspective. If your title is production director, and you are the top person in that function, who else are the production staff going to look to to represent, protect and reward them and to put forward their production perspective—which is a wholly reasonable view as they see it?

Unity on the board has another function. The source of strategic change is important. A change which 'only comes from personnel' is not going to receive as much credence as a change backed by the whole of the unified board. It is not seen as valid or as representing the power blocks in the organization. Hence the recipients of the policy for change will reserve their position, warily wondering if it is serious and what the top person thinks of it, and be alert to signals from other departments that 'nobody consulted us; our area hasn't agreed this'. It is in such situations that strategy consultants are often required to mediate between functions and factions in the organization's political maelstrom.

Sir John Harvey-Jones highlighted the critical job of transforming ICI's top executive from a collection of rival advocates into a cohesive body of directors in order to release greater resources for ICI's growth businesses.[8] It seems then, that the first task of the endorsement phase is to unite the board. Only then will the new strategy stand a chance of being actioned. As one chairman put it: 'What helps the change to work is the strength of will and unity of the board. If the board isn't pushing the change all the time and driving it and has great will to achieve the change, it won't happen.'

Ambivalence on the board

Ambivalence can easily grip a board. This usually emerges through arguments about the balance of advantage for changing as opposed to not changing, or for one change compared to another. The difficulty is that a balance of advantage debate, of its very nature, legitimizes resistance to change. As Smith and Berg pointed out: 'The supreme difficulty for an executive group is that it must expose differences, enhance rather than inhibit conflict, *before* it can attempt to reconcile different positions, but, in promoting differences, it fears that it will cease to be a group.'[9] The problem is accentuated by the need for a common purpose for which they hold themselves mutually accountable. Katzenbach and Smith found that top teams were the most difficult to make effective.[10]

As the new strategy is developed and considered by the board, there may be sceptics among the power holders—including some with counter-proposals—and their dilemma is whether to become involved or to stand aside, exerting only negative influence and placing themselves in a position of having neither a positive role nor the oppportunity to gain any credit for supporting or being party to the changes. They also risk being marginalized to the point of removal from the organization if their behaviour is seen as dysfunctional by other members of the board. Such discordance has to be faced, preferably, by building the unassailability of the case in which certain inferences are inescapable. At its most dramatic, an executive resistant to change may chant the John McEnroe cry of 'You cannot be serious'. Back may come the passing shot of 'Yes, we are. You're fired'. As one major organization put it: 'If a manager won't buy in to what has been decided, in the end he goes. We do it nicely; but we do it.'

More productive top management groups are able to embrace diversity, to cope with open debate, to unite behind a decision that not all may have favoured and then to sustain that unity even if the decision turns out to have been flawed. The board then has to debate and unite behind a strategy modification that will get the firm out of the mess. The more effective groups can channel their individual ambivalences into a concern for the good performance of the whole top team—not by suppressing conflict but by transcending it in order to make progress because 'denying the tensions and emotions serves to hold the group in place, for ever marking time, unable to move on. Addressing them threatens the very existence of the team and, paradoxically, simultaneously enable it to truly become a team'.[11] It is the very diversity of opinion that enables alternatives to be considered when facing a novel, ill-defined issue.[12] Denying argument in a spurious display of unity can be exactly the wrong recipe for making good decisions. The need for board cohesion is not just to provide an example to those below but to ensure that a high-quality debate leads to a sensible strategy being adopted. The board is the critical group that must drive the company forward. If its members are fearful, the move will flounder.

> It's a major problem when the board members cannot stretch to the new vision. Everybody has to be aware of what they are getting into; if it's going to be controversial and prone to publicity, then if people aren't happy, the board should back off immediately. It can require a lot of talking and allaying fears with individual board members. If there is an absence of will, it won't happen. The form of the analysis and the presentation is important—the way the firm should react to its strategic challenge. You have to get the whole board to agree that these moves be made. A lot depends on whether the chairman and chief executive are able to handle the arguments intellectually. If they are woolly, you just go round and round getting nowhere. It's not easy to get a firm to do something new when nobody knows much about it. If it's an overseas expansion, it's not all about strategy; it's about expert power—who is going to do it? Who is going to get on the aircraft? Is anyone familiar with the country, the people, the industry?

Demb and Neubauer[13] found that

> developing a strong board is like building a bridge. There is no universal design which will fit every case. It is a matter of balancing the opposing forces and stresses to suit a particular situation. In a board there are three main sources of tension: (1)

management autonomy versus board control; (2) commitment and involvement versus detachment and objectivity; (3) good teamwork versus the judgement and initiative of individuals.

Demb and Neubauer questioned 72 executive and non-executive directors of 11 large corporations based in eight countries. Data came from two-tier and unitary boards, state-owned and private businesses. They found that, regardless of the board structure or the industry, nearly all the directors faced the same kinds of issues of establishing strategic direction, securing top management succession, controlling and monitoring management, caring for shareholders and allocating resources.[13] They also found that every board, regardless of national setting, faced the same challenge in defining its portfolio: to distinguish a reasonable and productive threshold between the responsibilities of the board and management.[14]

The power of expert knowledge helps a firm to tackle an external uncertainty, but there are internal uncertainties too. Conflict on the board produces internal uncertainty because, unless there is a dominant board power source, managers below cannot be sure of the board faction from which it would be prudent to take a lead. Board members typically have considerable power as individuals—be it over structures, jobs, promotions, tasks, via information or through the control of resources—and, the greater those powers, the greater their control over the actions of others.[15] Furthermore, as the uncertainty of the strategic challenge increases, there will be fewer procedures for dealing with this within the firm, and the powerful, previously successful and charismatic individuals will more probably be listened to and followed.

This puts a great responsibility on the board members to unite; to use their valuable variety of perspectives to improve the quality of debate and decision; and to agree and to support a coordinated goal that they can articulate with clarity and conviction. The agenda and processes of change in the firm are largely in their hands. They need to connect with each other, to develop cooperative links and to resolve dilemmas if they are to give a coherent lead to their puzzled, perhaps fearful, subordinates. In the end a board has to back its own decisions. One member of a board, which had made a questionable strategic move, incensed the other members by complaining endlessly about the decision until the exasperated chairman finally told him, 'Look, we've done it. Just stop going on about it and help us to make it work.'

Board members in companies that find radical change difficult to embrace, let alone implement, typically do not spend enough time together. The more they quarrel, the more formal and limited become the contacts. There is insufficient meeting of minds and the problem gets worse. That is why a perennial proposal from consultants to a riven board is to suggest that they clear time to go away, facilitated by a considerate process consultant, in order to work out their agendas far from the harassment and inhibitions of the office. Informality can unblock the strategic knots that bind them and the use of outsiders as catalysts is a well-established way of creating productive convergence. There are other ways. One board managed— and still does—to remain innovative and united by the simple expedient of having its eight members work from adjacent open-door offices. The better performing boards know that the maintenance of their group cohesion is both important and is the responsibility of the chairman, whose job is primarily to manage the company's external face with its shareholders and to run the board, while the chief executive runs the business. Chairmen with an executive role will obviously have more of an operational role in the company, but persistent tension between chairman and chief executive, or neglect of the uniting of the board, are usually strong signals of a board in trouble.

The way a board can become united will be heavily influenced by its circumstances and the power relationships that exist between its members. In the first of the six types of organizational change that follow (Takeover change), the way in which the board unites is likely to be a defensive one, in an attempt to fend off its own probable removal. The uniting of a professional practice (Partnership change) demands much more subtle skills.

REFERENCES

1. Danny Miller and Peter H. Friesen, Momentum and revolution in organisational adaptation. *Academy of Management Journal,* **23** (4), 1980, pp. 591–614.
2. John W. Hunt, *Managing People at Work.* McGraw-Hill, 1992, p. 262.
3. Niccolò Machiavelli, *The Prince,* translated by G. Bull, Penguin, 1967.
4. Iain L. Mangham, *Effecting Organisational Change.* Blackwell, 1988, p. 165.
5. Alonzo McDonald, Conflict at the summit: a deadly game. *Harvard Business Review,* March–April 1972, p. 60.
6. Alex Roberts and Simon Pitt, Strategy implementation: a dynamic process guide. Working Paper, London Business School, 1990.
7. Andrew Kakabadse, *The Wealth Creators.* Kogan Page, 1991.
8. John Harvey Jones, *Making it Happen.* Collins, 1986.
9. K. K. Smith and D. M. Berg, *Paradoxes of Group Life.* Jossey Bass, 1987 (quoted in Mangham, *op. cit.,* p. 160).
10. Jon R. Katzenbach and Douglas K. Smith, *The Wisdom of Teams.* HBS Press, 1992.
11. Mangham, *op. cit.,* p. 147.
12. A. C. Filey, R. J. House and S. Kerr, *Managerial Process and Organisational Behaviour.* Scott Foreman, 1976.
13. Ada Demb and F. Friedrich Neubauer, *The Corporate Board: Confronting the Paradoxes.* Oxford, 1992; review by Bernard Taylor, *Financial Times,* 24 March 1992.
14. Demb and Neubauer, *op. cit.,* p. 66.
15. Sydney Finkelstein, Power in top management teams: dimensions, measurement and validation. *Academy of Management Journal,* **35** (3), August 1992, pp. 505–38.

PART II
Change and its contexts

5 Six contexts of change

- Takeover change
- Injection change
- Succession change
- Renovation change
- Partnership change
- Catalytic change

Since all analysis begins with a categorization scheme built on distinctions, we need to specify the circumstances of organizations that undertake major changes.[1] The achievable rate of strategic change will vary greatly from firm to firm, depending on the general preparedness of each organization and on the power concentration that can be brought to bear on the change process. That power concentration, in turn, depends substantially on the way in which the senior personnel have reached the top and on the kind of organization it is. Changes affect people in different ways. A radical reorganization will generally have high impact on management—though not necessarily on all functions and units—but may leave the truck drivers unaffected. With the focus mainly on management, a number of alternative change contexts are relevant.

The first is that of *Takeover change* where a change of top management arises from the firm being taken over and a new top person/team installed. The second is *Injection change* when the firm's owners or the board decide that an outsider should be brought in to become chief executive. The third is *Succession change* when the top person, or perhaps the top team, is replaced from within as the old controllers retire or move on. The fourth is *Renovation change* when the existing top team realizes that a new strategy is required and itself seeks to shift the organization into a new mode. Then there is *Partnership change* where the organization is not so obviously a power structure but more a collegial, federal body of autonomous equals who can only be persuaded to change, but not instructed. This is typical of a professional service organization. Finally, and in a different style to the other five contexts, there is *Catalytic change* in which an agency, typically a set of consultants or advisers, intervenes on behalf of one or more stakeholders, usually the management.

A detailed look shows a general gradient from context to context, from power to persuasion, as the power available to the change initiators dwindles (Figure 5.1). Of course, powerful people may choose not to use their power; they may prefer to cajole even when they can issue edicts that would be obeyed. Their power then remains latent, but it still lurks as a hidden source of intimidation. Some partnerships do have quite strong power hierarchies.

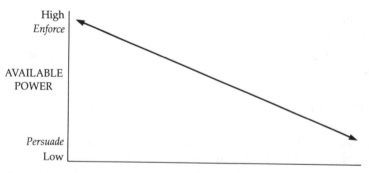

Figure 5.1 *Power gradient*

TAKEOVER CHANGE

The location of resistance to change in organizations depends greatly on the circumstances and focus of the particular changes that are being faced. If the firm is being taken over, the resistance tends to be from the board and the external threat may unite its members. (Will anyone break ranks and side with the incomers?). Board members are those more likely to lose their power, their perks, their reputation and, maybe, their jobs. After all, it is those in the top positions who have the most leverage, the most power, the greatest visibility and who are the symbolic role models for those watching anxiously from below. It is usually those at the top whom the new owners will try to change. Reconstruction of the top echelons is all but mandatory for an incoming regime—otherwise how is its arrival to make any difference? The only circumstances in which the existing management is likely to remain untouched are: (a) where the existing management is competent but has lacked some vital resource that the new owners bring, such as money, access to better distribution, better technology; (b) where the new owners transform the behaviour of the existing management by altering the criteria of performance, reward systems, organizational structure, etc.; and (c) where the new owners decide to behave gently in order to reassure the acquired firm's people that no brutish alterations are intended.

It is scarcely surprising that top managements often resist takeover, for they are faced with a difficult choice if they are unable to negotiate a 'business as usual' deal with the firm's buyers. Should they abandon what they have believed in and acquiesce in the new management's plans and habits? Or should they fight to the last for what they had been trying to achieve, and then go? This is a galling choice if the old management had already been trying to change things, had been doing that well and yet the new owners have timed it so that they arrive just as matters are getting better, but before the old regime has proved its competence. This problem is even worse if the target company has been under takeover threat repeatedly, for its management will have become so wearied and distracted by the unceasing fight that they either cannot change faster or do not have the spare resources, manoeuvring room or confidence to make the necessary adjustments.

The middle managers in a firm being taken over often have a more ambivalent attitude. This is not because they are necessarily enthusiastic (though they may be if the departing regime has been a frustration for them), but for three central reasons. Firstly, they may have fewer immediate options for alternative employment. They will likely have a higher ratio of personal commitments to personal wealth, given that they will be younger, building up their family and assets and will not have lucrative service contracts, significant shares or stock options. At least as important will be their hopes, as they see that a clear-out at the top will free up some interesting promotion possibilities for their own cadre. Secondly, they will also hope that the new regime will be more supportive of their frustrated plans for the business. It is quite normal, as with Grand Met's experience in buying Pillsbury, for the acquirer to laud and utilize the middle managers in the acquired company while doing without most of the top brass.

The third reason for the middle managers to be more acquiescent is that they are not organized. They will not be in trade unions; they may not have met before; they will have only defensive shared goals and no mechanism for converging in a hurry. Provided that the acquiring company is speedily clear about its overall goals, good at communicating them and willing to listen, and that a few key winners from the process appear quickly, the middle echelons can probably count on being sufficiently advantaged that resistance will not be a serious problem—unless they think that, under the new owners, they will not be able to cope. So a key goal for the incoming owners must be to reassure the middle ranks of managers and specialists, help to train them and to guide and support them in making the necessary transition. Their support for the new regime is important as a powerful reassurance for the blue-collar masses beneath, not only as exemplars, but for the messages transmitted to staff by the immediate line managers.

The existing top management can, therefore, count on little

support from their subordinates and staff unless they can convince those below them of a threat that faces them all. That can be done if those below fear that they will be savaged under the new regime. Faced with a takeover by Hanson, many workforces would feel uneasy and might become aroused to united resistance. A community as well as local trade unions may also become involved in fending off takeover, such as York with Rowntree (unsuccessfully) and St Helens with Pilkington (successfully). The chance of gaining support from institutional shareholders in an Anglo-Saxon stock market is poor; they will typically take the money without protracted sentiment, and run. Indeed, the old City adage about the consequential costs of takeovers is utterly simple: 'Accept the bid; sell the bidder.'

The new regime therefore starts with a mix of disadvantage and advantage. The disadvantage arises from the new owners' unfamiliarity with the entrails of the organization they have acquired, though if they are from the same industry and if they have done their due diligence checks well, they should have some idea of the situation, of what is wrong and how it might be rectified. What they will not know in detail is who in the acquired organization is any good. A further disadvantage is that rumour and speculation will have spread in advance of their arrival, particularly if the defending management had focused on the grim fate facing the organization if the bidders are not repelled. Unless it has been a friendly takeover, the new owners are likely to start off in deficit, unless the old management had been so awful that the pent-up desire for change means that almost any new regime has the chance to start off in surplus. However, the deficit can be eliminated, for those inside the organization will want to believe that things are going to get better, not worse. This all suggests, as was argued earlier, that the new management needs to make its mode of running the acquisition immediately, clearly and decisively obvious, so that there is no doubt about their intent nor is there much opportunity for confusion, rumour and disorder to fester.

Yet many new owners do not need to engage in immediate, unremitting brutality. The new mode of running the company may indicate a delicate set of actions on the part of the incomers. For example, the takeover of Verkade by United Biscuits in 1990 resulted from an approach by Verkade because, while it was an important company in its domestic Dutch market, it was insufficiently so for increasingly international market conditions. The logic for bringing both companies together was compelling. United Biscuits had long wanted to develop more in the European market and with its strong brands and low production costs, the market wisdom and distribution systems of Verkade fitted well. Acknowledging Dutch sensitivities, the new owners made it more of a partnership than a takeover. A more forceful approach might well have been notably less successful at achieving those gains.

Whether the takeover style is delicate or forceful, it is the clarity of the new mode of behaviour that is vital, together with the rapid communication of the new ground rules. For example, a valid statement when absorbing an acquisition may be the simple 'here are the two things you need to understand in order to know how it works'. If the two things are that the mode will be of continuing independence of the acquired units, coupled to the mandatory reporting of a specified monthly financial data pack which has to be at head office within seven days of the month end, then the acquired units can see that operating autonomy and financial accountability are the two key working rules.

If, on the other hand, the whole logic of the acquisition rests on the integration of the two firms, then the two ground rules might well focus on the way the united group is to operate and the criteria by which they are to be brought together. It is odds-on that, if these two matters are to have an effect, their introduction may be a shock in requiring the organization to adapt rapidly. Yet you have to push them in quickly so that people soon know, don't fret from uncertainty, realize that change is serious and have no time to organize alternatives and defences because you have introduced the new rules at the moment of impact of your arrival.

> The most successful are where you have a team of people who have done these things before and who know what to do. If you have done acquisitions before, you do have power because you have confidence, and the people in the company which you have

bought know that you have experience. It's meat and drink to merchant banks and acquisition advisers and, added to your own team of managers, everyone knows what has to be done in the first few days. There's almost a list. Who handles the cash; who sanctions investment, who takes what levels of decisions; the parameters of running the acquired business; sorting out the top appointments. Financial controls are not usually as tight as in the acquiring company, that's often a reason why the takeover occurred in the first place, and the acquirer is usually better run, both financially and in having superior marketing skills. You have to decide quickly because people in the acquired firm are waiting for things to happen. There will be a period of great uncertainty. If you leave things too long, you may lose out and not be able to do it. In a larger or more public acquisition, it can take longer because you may have given assurances in the offer document and you have to honour these.

This points up the need for incisive action and gives an indication of what kind of skills are being introduced into the acquired organization. Haspelagh and Jemison,[2] in their study of acquisitions and mergers, distinguished three types of strategic capability that may need to be transferred between the two organizations. Firstly, there are general management skills, such as those of financial control and resource allocation, be these skills transferred by edict, as in the example above, or quietly introduced by persuasion over a period. Operating resources are a second form of strategic capability, covering the tangible components of the organizations. As in the earlier example of ICI and Stauffer, this may require the amalgamation of assets and activities to cut out duplication. Closing one head office, merging the salesforces, rationalizing the factories or branches, and coalescing the distribution systems will all have organizational as well as financial consequences. The third strategic capability is what they called functional skills: this concerns one organization's methods of operation that are deemed useful for the other to adopt. To this one could add a fourth: architectural skills— the way of shaping the new combined organization to best fit with its new, united purpose, i.e. the structure of the organization.

Obviously, the most appropriate approach to melding the

two organizations together will be greatly determined by the savings and advantages from rapid amalgamation, the urgency of the situation, the motivations and inclinations of the key staff and the level of autonomy with which the two firms could continue compared with the level of useful interdependence. While the extent to which individuals and departments are affected varies enormously, Haspelagh and Jemison concluded that a number of simultaneous actions needed to be taken whether the two organizations were to be fully integrated or more loosely associated: the instillation of a clear sense of mutual purpose which went beyond immediate, short-term objectives; the surfacing rather than the repressing of potential problems; and the establishment of a formal interface (preferably via one dedicated representative of the acquirer) to channel linkages between the two organizations in order to avoid one side dominating the other and to reduce the chance of mixed messages and multiple communication channels causing confusion. They pointed out that one problem in executing these tasks is that the interest of the top managers in the merger peaks at the time of the coming together, and a leadership vacuum can then ensue as those managers move on to the next strategic drama.

An example of the failure of that lax policy came from the Bridgestone takeover of Firestone. Bridgestone had already bought and turned round a Firestone lorry-tyre plant in Tennessee by concentrating on production methods while leaving the American managers to handle the workforce.[3] It had sent 35 management advisers from Japan to Tennessee. In 1988 it bought the whole of Firestone: 20 tyre plants, 20 other factories and 53 000 employees. It would have needed 700 Japanese managers to repeat what had been done in Tennessee. Not being able to spare that number without crippling the Japanese factories, Bridgestone adopted a velvet glove approach, and lectured the Americans about quality—who then did not internalize the lessons but instead hired 500 quality control experts when the Firestone headquarters staff already totalled 3000. Bridgestone allowed its acquisition to stick to its old ways and so retain the defeatism that had set in at Firestone during the 1970s. Firestone's continuing losses then dragged Bridgestone down for years until the chief executive was replaced and the company was reorganized by a top Bridgestone manager, who duly became president of the parent company in 1993.

This points up, yet again, the perils of assuming that implementation is a delegated matter not worthy of top managers' continued attention. The post-convergence period is critical. It may be that the assumptions of the merger or acquisition turn out to have been wrong and, if top management's attention has moved on there will be a tendency to continue as though the assumptions were right, because the underlings are left with only the original prescription for sorting out the situation. This emphasizes one of the enduring messages from strategic change programmes; namely, the need for sheer persistence as well as consistency of attitude, action and commitment from the top team in the organization.

Before amplifying what a new regime *should* do, it is necessary to consider the other five circumstances of organizational change in order to see what, in practice, are any differences in action approaches in differing types of situation. The next, Injection change, while lacking the raw power that can be available in an externally forced change, is not as different from Takeover change as one might suppose.

INJECTION CHANGE

Injection change occurs when a new top manager—typically the chief executive or the executive chairman (perhaps both)—is parachuted into an existing organization. This is a slightly less dramatic process than Takeover change (but more forceful than the third type of change, Succession change). Injection change implies that powerful stakeholders no longer have faith in the adequacy of the firm's existing management. Assuming that the injected executive has the backing of the chairman, the non-executive directors and the shareholders for any changes that he or she may introduce, the initial manoeuvring room will be substantial. The injection may indicate little about the attitude of the other executive members of the Board, but injection usually occurs when the previous management team has been persistently unsuccessful (as with the appointment of a new chairman and chief executive at the Rank Organisation in 1983), when the chief executive retires and the board or shareholders decide that new blood is needed, or when a new project is not getting off the ground. The very fact that the top person has been brought in from outside should indicate something about the views of these powerholders, since it also infers that no internal candidate was deemed to be satisfactory. It also raises a question about the state of the organization's morale. Injection is not a takeover in the sense of an ownership change but, if the power given to the new CEO is substantial, it might as well be, for he or she can act firmly and, indeed, may need to do so, for in those circumstances the top manager may be making a strategic change under duress.

As another example, consider the new board recruited for British Telecom at the beginning of the 1980s. Several key executives were brought in, not so much because of the inadequacy of the previous incumbents, who had worked satisfactorily under the old public sector regime, but because the move towards a competitive market required BT to be run by managers who knew how firms worked in such markets. It was quicker, and a vivid signal of the new circumstances, for a new top echelon from the business world to be injected than to hope that the incumbent executives could adapt in time to meet competition for the first time.

The injected CEO is likely to be either fairly young, ambitious, and not wanting his or her career to stall here, or a highly experienced older executive who is brought in to put the organization back on its feet and who will not want a discordant swansong or an epitaph bearing the sound of a raspberry. Both types of injected CEO will want to get it right. This is feasible, though not easy if the firm is still doing well. In an unthreatened organization it takes an unusually inspiring leader to convey a sense of urgency by lifting, from latency into consciousness, the feeling that change is required, can be mapped out and could be introduced successfully.

Installing a sense of urgency

Apart from a few early symbolic acts which trumpet that incisive change has begun, the new leader nearly always announces that 'We need to change' and 'We are going to change'. This is not done to create a crisis but to initiate a sense of urgency and anticipation and to raise the stakes for both leader and subordinates. It pumps up the adrenalin and the drama and, like burning the boats behind you, indicates that retreat is not an option—only success or failure are now on offer. For those who injected the new leader, it shows that he or she is gearing up to meet their expectations. For subordinates, it demonstrates urgency and raises the stakes. Either they have to back the leader publicly or reveal that their loyalty to the leader's ideas is suspect. This has an advantage over a more stealthy approach, where resistors may only become visible a long way down the track after the foliage has been cleared and after their sabotage has gained a considerable hold.

To find time and space, the smart injected manager will have indicated to those who injected him or her, that the situation will get temporarily worse before improvements can come through. While the new leader will be expected to undertake early and incisive action, he or she has the advantage of already having their support and does not need to convince them of the need for change, and perhaps of the need for additional resources; indeed a mandate has already been given to take strategic initiatives in order to improve the firm's performance.

'A culture of change was created at the top in the first week and it began to permeate the organization. An outside appointee with relevant experience is able to energize the company; people become excited—even those whose jobs haven't changed. The problem is maintaining that energy.' This tapping of any latent desire for corporate renewal also helps the injected executive to assess the existing in-house talent and to gauge if they are up to it, if their loyalty can be depended upon, or if the situation is of such urgency that there is an immediate necessity to recruit people from outside who know how the executive works and who, having been appointed by that person, will be loyal since they will all sink or swim together. Their arrival not only dilutes the original management team, which makes it less likely that it can overpower the new chief executive, but it also ensures that the old team cannot return to its original configuration.

If the new executive does decide that additional support is required, then he or she will bring in people who can be trusted—usually previous colleagues who can be relied upon to work constructively within the team. This typically happens quite soon after the executive has surveyed the company and its senior management, and before there is any possibility of being captured by the day-to-day operating requirements and enfolded and absorbed by the old regime and its old ideas. The executive will usually bring in trusted associates once the firm's management has revealed a glaring gap that cannot be filled from within. To avoid reaction in the company the new executive probably 'has to get the door (of change) swinging first' so that the incomers are seen as useful and not as bagmen and intruders.

Studies in minicomputer firms by Tushman, *et al.*[4] found that major strategic changes were more likely to be successful when accompanied by changes in the entire top management team than when only the CEO was changed.

The introduction of supplementary talent from outside is not always necessary. It may be feasible to redirect the existing key personnel to suit the new circumstances and, unless the cost of so doing is prohibitive in time or money, it would seem sensible to retain the accumulated experience of as many executives as practicable, and kinder to give them the chance to show their talents. The previous mess may not have been their fault. When the new top duo at the Rank Organisation took on the task of galvanizing the firm (in 1983, Rank's managed businesses had made pre-tax profits of £5 million on capital employed of £750 million) they kept virtually all the operating managers. The galvanizing signal was the chief executive's rejection of over 90 per cent of the unambitious budget plans. The goals and performance criteria were changed; the managers were not. As with Takeover change, the middle managers are seldom bad; they are just badly led.

Except in the most demoralized organizations, the injected manager will usually find that pent-up frustration is waiting to be released. Just asking the question 'What's wrong round here that hasn't been fixed?' can trigger a torrent of ideas. The new CEO of Campbell Soup, David Johnson, put it plainly,

> I don't bring anybody with me because I maintain that . . . talents want to be released and have so much to give me. They know the organization backwards. They've been there. They know what's good and bad. So I ask 'What's non-strategic, what's diseased, what's underperforming?' . . . And guess what? They rally and work and burn the midnight oil.[5]

However, that kind of confidence is unusual. Typically, the injected manager does bring in other new people. The injected manager is not part of the old team; and as its not his or her team, it can be changed more easily. (The replacement of significant numbers of the top team can also occur with Succession and Renovation changes, notably when the new top manager is materially younger than the other members of the top team. When an insider succeeds to the top job, that must be less risky, for at least he or she knows the business; whereas if an injected manager makes too many new appointments from outside, the risk of a major error must be higher since the injected manager also lacks in-company experience.)

Orchard or minefield?

The injected executive brings mystery, the opportunity for a new style and the evaporation of some previous assumptions, and so, during the honeymoon period, bold initiatives can be taken. The executive will likely be different enough to have a licence and a perspective for innovation, while wanting to be reassuring enough to be respected for his or her relevance. Although the executive has great initial freedom of manoeuvre, he or she may not know enough about the current situation to act with confidence. Is it an orchard with ripe fruit waiting to be plucked, or a minefield with every step a potential hazard? As we shall see in Part III, there are ways of turning some minefields into orchards.

Nevertheless, the appointment of an outside top manager is inherently more risky than a succession change from inside. The first risk is that the board will not know the person nearly as well as they will know the inside candidates. The second risk is that the appointee will not know very much about the firm and his or her actions must stem from a smaller, narrower base of knowledge and experience. The appointee will have to listen very carefully and question incumbent executives closely, for they will know the history and the context of the firm's practices and they will need to explain the rationale in order to strengthen his or her insights and judgements. The key is to appoint someone with highly relevant experience from elsewhere. After all, the decision to appoint an outsider reflects a failure on the part of the firm to generate plausible inside candidates and the board, needing a high degree of strategic change in the company, feels that it is not going to get that from inside. The third risk is that, prior to the injected manager settling in, it is difficult to forecast that the chemistry will work between chairman and chief executive. One public company chairman spent considerable time investigating this link; both he and the incoming manager took batteries of psychometric tests to check their compatibility. The imported executive departed quite soon when it was evident that the chemistry had not worked as planned. However, assuming that the chemistry within the top team is good, the injected manager has substantial power arising from prior experiences (that helped him or her to gain the job) and from the circumstances that led to his or her being 'imported'. The fourth risk is that the new executive may wait too long before deciding on and implementing his or her intended changes, so that the expected difference between the new and the old guard dwindles and the executive's mandate becomes dissipated.

Power and confidence can be increased if the new executive already has wide-ranging prior management experiences. By definition, the new executive's entire career cannot have been spent in the company he or she has just joined; and the wider the executive's multi-functional, general management, multi-industry experiences, the broader is the perspective that he or she can bring to bear on the new strategic task. This wide experience also demonstrates the executive's own proclivity towards learning and change[6] and can be traded off against the narrower, but more intimately knowledgeable experience of his or her new firm, which is possessed by a succession manager who has been appointed from within the company.

SUCCESSION CHANGE

Succession change comes when an executive who has been in the firm for some years succeeds to the top operating office. That person will have less mystery, less power than in either the external or the injection change circumstances. What the person will almost certainly possess is intimate familiarity with the firm he or she now heads. The question is: Why was that person appointed? If the appointment was designed to provide a smooth continuation, business as usual, then an accentuation of change may not be a primary objective and, for the purposes of considering rapid change, might seem to be something of a non-event. That may well not be so, because 'there are things which tend to adhere to a regime which has been going on in the same way for a long time'.

Yet this third context should be relatively tranquil because no direct imposition of change has occurred. In its calmest form, the incumbent board has planned and agreed the person who is to take over—usually because of the retirement or departure for another post of the current chief executive. The question is whether that serendipity is justified. The retirement or departure may have been assisted—that is, requested or demanded from other board members. An internal succession does not automatically signal that all is well. The issue is whether the new office holder is expected to change things or to let the organization operate much as before. Even in the latter case, the appointee may well want to alter some features of the organization in order to make a mark, to bring forward supporters, to sideline opponents, to secure his or her own position and to demonstrate that a new era has begun. You could say that Succession change is intended to be a more delicate version of Injection change.

Discomfiture can readily occur with succession appointments. The board may have made the appointment, confident that the new person will get a grip on the failures of the old system—but that doesn't happen. The pre-appointment promise remains unfulfilled. Alternatively, the board members fondly hope that the new executive won't disturb things, particularly themselves, but then an axe starts to swing and the new executive becomes evidently more radical than they had wanted.

The previous chief executive may not have thought that certain practices needed changing, or perhaps couldn't be bothered as his period of office was coming towards its end. It might be that he let an operation continue to be overstaffed and have poor productivity, since restructuring would have involved redundancies and redundancy costs. He would not have wanted his regime to end with a poor set of results because, and while a major change might have been absolutely the right thing to do, it would have adversely affected earnings in its first year. He may have taken no action precisely because he had no desire to bow out with a blot on his final phase. He would want the smooth growth to persist and would be reluctant to risk it plummeting as he exits.

This leaves the firm with a problem, but gives his successor a clear opportunity. The succeeding manager may not have been appointed to make that major change, but the conditions are ripe. The company is already known and the new appointee will not be inhibited by any ignorance of the situation, as might be the case for a manager injected from outside. The successor will want to act quite quickly—some people say that most of what a new top manager does is carried out in the first year—and get the bad news out of the way in order to gain the benefits later and so start his or her own smooth climb in company earnings.

You know what you want to do because you've been sitting there and you know the business well so that all these things

tend to happen pretty quickly. Its important to act reasonably fast and not let it go on. While the injected manager may have more licence, the knowledgeable succession manager can move as fast. If you are new in the top job, you are going to bite the bullet pretty quickly—so long as the result isn't so awful or drawn-out that you cannot stay to enjoy the fruits of the change. If you don't act, that sends a signal to those in the business who are watching you, waiting to see what happens.
(Dominic Cadbury, chief executive, later chairman, Cadbury-Schweppes)

If those actions are taken early, they give the new chief executive space and time to improve and develop the business. In addition, early action infers that the deficiency being corrected was the fault of the departed top manager. If it is only tackled three years later, people think it is the newcomer's fault that it has been allowed to fester so long. The new appointee from inside the business will know of frustrations that have built up over the years and can have a wonderful honeymoon period tapping those frustrations and making the easy changes which stand out for action, and so harness the latent motivations in the company.

One key facet of Succession change is the amount of manoeuvring room available to the new appointee. This is partly a question of the severity of any need for change, including the awareness of the board that change is needed at all. The other factor is the extent to which the new executive can remain distant from the previous regime.

The factor of age is important. If the age gap is significant, then it is more like appointing someone from outside. The change will be much less if the board is of the same age and people have come up together and been subject to many of the same influences and participated in many of the same decisions. I came in aged 15 years younger than my predecessor and hadn't shared in the development of the company the way he had or been party to the main decisions. Selling Jeyes and the Foods businesses was fairly easy. It cleared the decks, took away the drag on earnings, reduced the management distractions from the two core businesses and it meant that you didn't have to squeeze those so hard to make up the performance. If I had been, say, the previous finance director and party to the decisions to buy into those other businesses, I would have found it much more difficult to make changes.

(Dominic Cadbury, chief executive, later chairman, Cadbury-Schweppes)

The other key facet is timing. The ideal succession time is when a mood has grown in the company that the time has come for some material changes; that the organization's performance is below its potential. A surge of energy can be released by appointing a new top manager who embodies those concerns and who has both a view about desirable changes and the capability to make them happen effectively. The inference is that the new manager should have an approach that contrasts with his or her predecessor if the pendulum of relevant style needs to swing over. When people who hold new values get into power, they change the norms of behaviour. This happened vividly when Sir John Harvey-Jones took over at ICI.

This indicates that, outside the stressful circumstances of a crisis, the most desirable appointment is where someone comes through from inside, who has the advantage of knowing and being known in the organization, but who is sufficiently of a different generation that he or she is going to bring some real change into the place. 'That person is going to be pretty senior because the board isn't likely to appoint anybody from inside who hasn't been close to the board for a reasonably long time.' The age difference is not absolutely essential, except as a signal, because it can be feasible to appoint a near colleague of the previous incumbent—provided that the board knows that he or she will change things and has been frustrated under the previous regime. Not every successor is inhibited by their association with the previous regime. As Dominic Cadbury indicated, it is also easier for a new chief executive who has not been part of the previous board to act dispassionately and without regrets in changing elements such as senior people, as well as changing contracts and business links, if he or she has never known the other partners.

Being younger has both helpful and hindering features. The helpful feature is the ability to be unencumbered by responsibility for the present situation and to be relatively detached from the habits and assumptions of the old regime. The handicap is that

> you take charge of an executive team where you have previously been, and are seen to have been, significantly junior, so that you have more work to do to persuade the board that you know what you are doing when you propose significant change. Someone who is older on the board will have worked for longer with it and external board members will have more confidence in those older executives—even though the non-executive board members were party to approving the decision to appoint the young chief executive.

It seems that one of the most difficult tasks for the new chief executive, particularly when young and when other board members have residual qualms about the wisdom of their choice, is deciding how and when to dispense with the services of other experienced senior managers who are in the way of strategic change.

> The biggest impediment to making major changes is almost bound to be the people factor. Shifting one or two key people who were a brake on change was difficult because they were very senior in the firm and had been in it for a long time. Persuading a board that you need to make those sort of personnel changes is rightly a difficult task. Even very good companies have barons who control successful parts of the business. They are well known and respected and have good relationships round the firm, but they may well be preventing you from exploiting bigger opportunities because they control an area of the business which they want to keep separate. It is always about the group versus a part of the operation. Each baron has been successful, so you are getting rid of somebody who has a good track record and you can't just do that; the board knows he has been achieving results. So what are you doing getting rid of somebody who has achieved results? The barons may well become even more difficult with a new incumbent because they probably found it easier to get along with his predecessor and they want to establish their authority straight away with a new appointee. Yet, if you don't make those changes, you are not going to establish your own authority and

there is the danger that others will follow suit and resist your strategic changes.

To get board support for removing senior people, you have to establish the evidence that you have been thwarted from doing what may be vital in getting the new strategy to work. You cannot be seen to be acting impetuously, even if people will acknowledge that you are right. You have to build up support on the board and you have to do it over a longer period of time than you would wish—even though you know from day one that you need to do this. You have to control the quite understandable impatience to get on and do it. Otherwise what grounds have you got, other than your prejudice? You could be seen as over-ruthless if you remove some senior people very quickly because, almost inevitably, you have been quite pally with those people, so you are removing these members of the team that you were meant to be working with; that's rougher.

An example of the need for evidence would be United Biscuit which, in 1992/3 removed the manager who had been running its Keebler cookie/biscuit business in the United States. It had taken the recently appointed, younger chief executive a couple of years to do. The departing manager was on the board and well regarded by the previous top management, and for the younger new man to come in and remove someone who had been on the board longer, must have been a difficult job. It required evidence built up over a period—even though that period must have been frustrating.

The lesson for a succession manager is, therefore: the more initial licence that can be obtained to make changes, the better—because it gives manoeuvring room and the confidence of having power delegated from the board. The managers being dealt with know that too, and are duly inhibited from mounting overblown challenges.

Compared to a succession manager, the outside appointee can act more quickly and not be seen to be impetuous because he's been injected into a company with a board mandate to shake it up. He then brings his own people forward quickly to make up his team. Because the existing team wasn't his, he has more licence. If you are an insider you are supposed to be part of that team anyway, so what are you doing suddenly removing members of the team of which you were a part?

The changes go a bit wider than simply moving a couple of people; there is also a natural movement of people, such as retirements. You are then going to pick, as replacements, people who have been somewhat frustrated and want to move ahead, so you are going to be bold and appoint new people to bring about more change. The guts of producing progress really comes down to getting the people right and having the people motivated and on your side and, if you can establish that, you have got a lot going for you. Bringing on the people you feel confidence in, particularly if they are of your own generation, means that they can be more energetic, more aggressive and they will be more loyal to you, the person who promoted them. Most people welcome a new appointment, provided you are not talking about a ridiculous changing of people every year or two. If the firm has had a quite a long period of the same man, there is the same style, he has done whatever he was going to do and most people welcome a change. There is always a degree of optimism and renewed energy around when you get that change.

I have come to the conclusion that, in any organization when you have had a leader for a considerable time, you can be quite sure that when you make the change that a lot of other people changes become inevitable. The team will change substantially and the board had better understand that when it changes the top person it is also, in effect, changing probably half of the top team, who will leave, for whatever reason. They don't like the new chief executive; he regards them as an obstacle; they are getting closer towards retirement; they want the top job so they say, 'I'm not going to make it, I'm going to go.' So his team will change pretty comprehensively. That could be quite an important consideration for the board because it isn't as simple as just changing the typewriter. When you are changing the chief executive, you are effectively saying that the rest of that team may change too, so it should cause the board to weigh it up. I could imagine when you change the top guy and you have got two or three very able people on the board who are doing a good job with the company, you may be signing their departure from it as well, and the board may say, we don't want to lose those three chaps because they are delivering very well for the company. I would look at that as a member of the board.

Succession change, while having less power than is usual in Takeover or Injection change, nevertheless contains a prospectively fruitful blend of change and continuity, of novelty and familiarity, of insight without (with luck) excessive entrapment by the past. The conclusion is that a succession manager can have substantial power to alter the organization—not as much as a takeover manager perhaps, but nevertheless enough to change the firm significantly, even though he or she may deem it prudent to take some actions softly and after a period of time. The danger is that a Succession change may result in the appointment of a chief executive who is highly socialized within the firm and will only do what he or she knows the organization will accept rather than what is required by external circumstances. The travails at IBM under John Akers might be a salutary example of the limitations of Succession change. An Injection change can show similar shortfalls if the incoming executive has been chosen not for any innovative perspective but for a similarity to those already in the organization. An internal succession combined with top team stability mean that team tenure is likely to be long, and this has been found to impact negatively on the firm's performance when the situation in the industry is turbulent. Long tenure is more appropriate in mature and stable industries—but how many of those still exist today?[7] The injection of an executive with a different perspective seems to be of higher added value unless the succession manager has a wide perspective and some pent-up desire for change, shaped and focused by intimate knowledge of the firm and its markets. It follows that an alert Succession change executive will want to make early changes in the top team, for if he or she can see, and was appointed to deal with, growing turbulence in the firm's markets, then rejuvenation of the top team will be a necessary prelude to the carrying out of strategic changes that go beyond the reach of the existing long-serving team.

The fourth circumstance is materially different from, and more subtle than, Takeover, Injection or Succession changes—even if the top group introducing the Renovation change has substantial power and discretion.

RENOVATION CHANGE

Renovation change occurs when the existing managers conclude that the firm needs to alter and that they, the same team as before, need to make the transition and manage its outcome. This can be difficult for them, particularly if they have changed the firm already when they first took up their appointments. To gird themselves up again, sometimes to solve again the problem that they thought they had solved the first time, is daunting. What makes it the more difficult for them is that they have been, indeed still are, responsible for the existing orientation of the firm. Now they have to agree a course of action among themselves and persuade subordinates to alter their habits, views and work. Unlike the new top managers of the Takeover and Injection changes, they cannot claim to have arrived with a different perspective or with a fresh mandate given to them by those introducing them into the company. They cannot, as could be done with Succession change, point to the beginning of a new regime. Instead, they have to justify their change of course to people they have, until now, urged to behave in the existing ways. They have to have a persuasive case, and the power to move things along in the likely event that they are not persuasive to everyone. If the organization faces a difficulty, it makes a difference whether that difficulty is outside the company (such as an adverse change in market conditions) or inside (as a result of the organization drifting from its original competence). The latter condition is trickier, for the drift may have resulted from the top team's failure to detect it and there will be an understandable reluctance to accept that remedial action is necessary.

It is rare for a long-standing team to initiate a major change unless forced by external circumstances, including a drooping performance by the firm when measured against its competition. 'People don't accept that they are not quite up to it or that there is a need to change.' The question the management team will be asked by those below, and which they therefore must ask themselves, is: Why change? 'People are conditioned by their experiences and unless you can counter their historical experiences with high drama or compelling logic in the way you present things, people will find it very difficult to change.' In order to effect successful strategic change, the top managers must become united behind a valid case or the discordance from mixed messages and unconvincing claims will torpedo their plans. All that will be left will be the coercive elements of power rather than widespread commitment. There might just be enough management power if employees were neutral about the changes, but not enough to take the organization through a forced march to an unappealing goal. The case for change has to be persuasive.

If you accept that the source of strategic change is likely to be top-down, then the first condition is that successful Renovation change requires the board to be, or to become, positively united—not a condition that can always be assured (see 'Confusion on the board' in Chapter 4). However, assuming for the moment that it is united, the board has four principal levers for changing the organization's activities: (1) the power it wields over resources, appointments and job specifications; (2) the middle managers who control the operations; (3) the deployment of incentive and control systems; and (4) the impetus (or resistance) that the board members create through their statements and actions. Examples of successful Renovation change occur repeatedly in larger and more stable enterprises such as Unilever, where the idea of appointing an executive chairman from outside would be unthinkable, given Unilever's durability, sustained success and careful grooming of executives at all levels of the business. Very few large corporations have found an equivalent formula that is efficient for changing their business and its strategic fit.

This places a heavy responsibility on the firm's management. The stakeholders are rarely given the option to replace key individuals. (It *can* happen, however. Regulatory authorities, financial institutions and major customers have been known to threaten retribution if the firm does not change certain personnel.) The managers usually have to make the strategic shifts themselves. This process typically starts when a key executive experiences a shock, sees a new vision or is aroused by some startling possibility. The changes in

Unilever Europe were triggered for its European Regional Director when he was washing up the dishes one Sunday night, listening to a radio programme about the aftermath for Europe of the Second World War. He handed the washing up over to his wife (what an excuse for not washing up), walked to his study and dictated a memo to his chairman. He had connected the post-war inertia of the winning nations to the galvanizing, renewing effect of devastation on the losers, while realizing that you didn't need to wait for devastation to enforce renewal. He changed his mind-set, reinterpeted Unilever's position and prospects and came to some new conclusions. He found that other Unilever directors were also beginning to ponder the same issues and so the groundswell for change commenced. Unilever had previously felt that it was well prepared for the single EC market in 1992. After all, had it not been in almost all these markets, in almost all its product categories for upwards of 70 years? The shock was the realization that with all that history and with 240 factories in those 12 European countries, it was a company ideally set up for the 12 independent national markets, not for an unifying region of integrating nations.

The trigger event or insight can come at any time. A holiday hotel chain curtailed its expansion plans in semi-tropical countries when its managing director noticed young women in California carrying parasols to protect themselves from the sun. The trigger event happens when a thoughtful manager wakes up one day to a fact, a trend, a confluence of strategic factors (which is why it is more likely to be a manager than a shopfloor worker), which cause a reassessment of his or her assumptions, the inferences for the firm and the consequent need for change. Whatever the source of the impetus, one day something clicks into place and the thoughtful manager realizes that 'We cannot go on like this'. The stimulus can be reading a report, attending a conference, talking with a friend. That is why effective managers are voraciously curious and open to signals. It is amazing how many managers do not even read a serious newspaper each day, saying that they are 'too busy'. No wonder that unexpected events are, for them, so unexpected. Good managers build networks outside the firm, outside the industry, outside the domestic market, as well as inside those familiar domains.[8] Organizations which perform well in volatile circumstances usually have a high information-processing capacity and so they respond well to signals.

The source of inspiration for good managers may have been an event or a gradual process that changed a number of factors in the firm's strategic position. But processes are often triggered off by what is described as an event; perhaps a trauma, a discontinuity, a rapid sequence of occurrences which creates the opportunity or necessity for profound change. A prepared management, alert to signals and shifts in its environment, is not then wrecked by a trigger event, for it will always be conscious of Montesquieu's caution: 'If a particular cause, like the accidental result of a battle, has ruined a state, there was a general cause which made the downfall of this state ensue from a single battle.'

Changing an existing business from inside demands most from management because it needs to achieve success with a new strategy while avoiding the destruction of the existing business. What is being changed is a complex relationship between management, the individual and the existing cultural systems, and these have to be compared with the projected new system in order to determine what needs to be changed. The insider is part of the past, has responsibility for the past, knows the people, and was party to those old decisions. It needs a jolting factor event or sudden insight for the cosy group to realize that it cannot go on as before.

> I've never known a case of spontaneous combustion where the old guard has pulled itself together without the introduction of a new factor. You need a considerable degree of humility to overcome the refusal to recognize mistakes. Consensus is an impediment to change because changes are often offensive to the original culture and they conflict with the unspoken aim of keeping everyone happy. Someone has to arrive or come up through the business; something has to startle the organization into revising its behaviour.
>
> (Lord Weinstock, managing director, GEC).

A Renovation change has difficulty in succeeding unless there is a riveting reason and a symbolic event of significance. Some managers believe that for a radical switch of strategy—from retrenchment to growth for instance—the appointment of a new chief executive is the essential signal that occurs with Injection and Succession changes, but not with Renovation change and hence the difficulties with getting Renovation change to work.

Whether the impetus comes from a person, an external pressure such as the actions of a competitor, a new insight, a change in technology or an impediment to existing strategy, the proposals and processes of Renovation change demand great intellectual clarity and persuasiveness. Several of the factors discussed in the ensuing chapters are particularly pertinent for Renovation change.

PARTNERSHIP CHANGE

The above four contexts—Takeover change, Injection change, Succession change and Renovation change—all presuppose a power relationship in the firm, strongest with Takeover change. But different considerations apply when the organization is a professional practice. Partnerships are much closer to the academic world of a quasi-voluntary organization in which people buy in if it suits them and where there are few immediate personal costs if they don't. Influence is important in a group of peers, for who can exercise position power or resource power in a group of equals? Expert power is not readily available to the leader, for there is a perception of intellectual parity by other professionals. His or her expert power has to rest on having greater experience and performance track record. Yet the differences compared to commercial firms should not be exaggerated. In a large business, with quasi-autonomous divisions, those seeking backing for particular policies still have to entreat with senior executives who have a range of options to which they can give time and from which they must select for their concentrated attention. Equally, most professional organizations have some hierarchy, some pecking order of senior partners, with junior staff undoubtedly lower in the power and autonomy stakes.

There will almost certainly be a ruling coalition of managing partners and heads of important sections of the firm. Those trying to buck that system would have to be very sure of their ground, of their support and of their ability to achieve positions of influence. After all, only in dire circumstances would the ruling élite be likely to make a dissident the managing partner. Accidents do happen, of course. An apparently 'safe' appointment can turn out to be more revolutionary than was anticipated. But a ruling élite will normally appoint a supporter of the status quo unless its members are feeling radical, in which case they will appoint someone who can be trusted to shift the firm's strategy in an agreeable fashion.

In professional practice, the problem for the leader who seeks to make significant changes is how to obtain agreement; how to satisfy enough of the firm's factions that the changes can be implemented. The organizational dynamic which the leader has to address can be called 'multiple minorities'.

Multiple minorities: the conflict within

The logic of 'multiple minorities' is well known in politics for, whatever their common front, all political parties and governments are coalitions. The question is only whether the coalition is contained inside the party or whether it encompasses outside interests. The factions come together because it suits them. When the amalgamation no longer seems productive, coalitions tend to break up. The Israeli Government has been a vivid example of multiple minorities in action. These only arise when no dominant element can succeed alone and when it needs the predictable support of some other faction(s). The problem for the leader of the leading faction is how to stitch together a durable amalgam of discordant interests. As fast as the leader offers one wing of the coalition further favours to keep it from bailing out, the opposite wing is likely to resent such offers—even to the point of departing from the coalition. It is no wonder that leaders of political parties hate such deals and will do all they can to avoid them.

In professional organizations, the more key factions there

are, the more any policy alterations will have to be negotiated. Even if there is a leading speciality profession which sets the overall tone of the practice and which generally decides the strategy, there will be a need to entreat with the other factions which, should their support be withheld, could cripple the strategy because of their vital role in its execution. Trying to alter health care management without the support of the clinicians is perilous, but without the backing of the nurses the clinicians would be hamstrung. Financial services dealers may set the rules, but if their back office staff are mutinous, it will not advantage the dealers. Whether they be lawyers, computer specialists or actuaries, the need for agreement across the interested groups is necessary. When there is no dominant hierarchy, each needed faction has veto power. Any single group can blackball a proposal and, without its support, implementation will be risky, if not doomed. Smaller professional organizations will suffer less from these effects because people can see the contribution of other factions.

Weak power structures

In a partnership organization the aggregation of power which helps a business leader to lead is absent. The consequence is that relationships, negotiations and favour-trading are far more important in professional firms, coupled to the likelihood of the organization being structured in a looser way so that the tensions of coming together are reduced by having cushions of quasi-independence between what might otherwise be warring factions. Partnership organizations are weak power structures.[9]

This makes the issues of strategic change in professional service organizations significantly different to those of straightforward commercial enterprises (or even to other service firms such as retail banks and hotels) because, not only is power more evenly distributed than in the typical business power structure, but it may be further fragmented if there are many, scattered, autonomous offices all belonging loosely to the same firm in what are essentially federations.

Professionals tend to regard aggregations of power as a potential threat and are duly suspicious. Quite a proportion of professional firms are more like federations than centrally managed enterprises. This may well be good for local motivation (and reward) but it does make the problem of concerted change rather difficult. Indeed, professionals tend to see 'good' decisions as those that give them more autonomy and more money to do the things they want to do without much supervision or accountability and through which they get support for their individualistic goals.

The consequence of this is that the organization's style has to be highly consensual in both decision-making and decision implementation. In partnership organizations, it is more difficult to disentangle strategy formulation from strategy implementation since they coalesce. Strategy emerges from gradual agreement, through the winning over of doubting personnel, from the emerging example of an idea working in practice. Endorsement of a strategy comes not from acceptance of a detailed plan installed by a powerful top management, but from the gradual absorption of a list of options offered delicately in the hope that some will find favour. That delicacy also avoids the risk that the managing coterie will be rebuffed since, in proffering the choices, they have not put their own chosen plan on the line. If the partners choose a particular strategic change, they are demonstrating some commitment to that course of action. The process of strategy agreement has a profound effect on the ease of implementation as it focuses attention on important matters and accrues support. The gradual consolidation of a desire for specific changes is the process of endorsement at its most delicate.

But endorsement by whom? Subtlety in making changes is the hallmark of effective leaders in professional, partnership organizations. In terms of multiple minorities, the issue is whether the support of a recalcitrant minority can be captured or whether the objectors can be faced down. The objectors have a problem too. It may be that they have a prospective veto, a blackball to throw. Yet they have to be careful. There have been numerous instances of the members of a tightly-knit group overplaying their hand in the fond belief that they were vital to the organization. Fired by the belief in their indispensability, they learned that the firm could dispense, bypass or replace them with little effort. Whether it was the striking computer technicians in British Telecom or the air traffic controllers who took on Reagan, professionals need to be very sure of their value (and of alternative employment prospects) if they are to obstruct an organization that is determined to make changes.

A sane partnership organization would hope to avoid such damaging confrontations. One subtle way is to find a vehicle or topic or issue which evidently requires action of a kind that all can agree within their existing mind-set and where the evidence which supports action can be made obvious to one and all through a process of exposure to it. One such device is for the managing partner to claim to be asking for help (i.e. inferring that he or she does not have a solution and so the request is not seen as hollow) and he or she sets up steering groups or working parties or task forces to address the issues. Each group should contain a reputable member of all relevant factional interests; this will help the group to be recognized as valid, and to have its remit accepted by all relevant parties. This minimizes the risk of any working party being undermined as being unrepresentative. The use of several groups prevents the process and recommendations from being captured by one faction, which could happen if only one task force had been formed. The elements that the managing partner has under his or her control are (1) the membership of each group, (2) the terms of reference and (3) the timescale, so that power rests on that ability to specify the tasks, the personnel and the deadline in order to influence the outcome and reduce prevarication. This was the device used by the consensual head of the BBC in 1991, when he set up numerous task forces to advise on the future shape of the BBC, as it faced political and commercial pressure about its role and efficiency.

If such initiatives are accepted by the key personnel, as they were in the BBC, then the facts and their inferences will lead on inevitably to better understanding of the pressures facing the organization and on to alterations in approach, habit and attitude of the kind required as the respected task force members act as ambassadors for change. In particular, the collection and analysis of data—notably external, market, competitive data about facts and trends, and internal data about costs and revenues—will alert task force members to the strategic context without the managing partner having to load his or her values onto their interpretation. Nevertheless, to sustain the task forces' 'ownership' of their proposals in order to gain their commitment, the senior partner needs to be open to a variety of suggestions about the methods of achieving results. He or she will hope that the inferences will become obvious and that the members will become sensitized to the logic of the need for change.

The central sublety is that of starting by persuading reluctant people to accept an innocuous looking initiative which, in reality, is the first step on an irreversible journey. For example, in a recession, when partners are finding it difficult to market their services in the traditional, uncoordinated, personal way, it should be easier to persuade them to agree a more coherent, more coordinated scheme, without their realizing that the subsequent logic would lead to the introduction of a professional marketing function. A harmless looking staff attitude survey can be the first step to questioning the management style of the heads of the various offices and departments. Letting people discover the facts for themselves and argue out the inferences may be the only sane way forward in a partnership organization.

It is important to get the vital factions to accept the process. If those who are to be involved in the consequences of the change are not sufficiently part of the generation of the change plan, they may, out of politeness and a wish to avoid conflict, give misleading signals to the champions of the change. If they agree radical proposals without much contention, then be prepared for limited commitment to what has been accepted. It may have been accepted, but not agreed. Those apparently acquiescing in the proposals may even feel that they were being helpful by not voicing their concerns. It would have been better if the proposers of the changes had encouraged them to speak out so that their reservations could have been taken into account. Failing that, the suppressed objections will tend to seep out, contaminating other apparently uncontentious matters and so undermining changes that would otherwise have been acceptable. Their concerns then become not just suppressed but damaging in a way that is difficult to diagnose. The managing group may find that it has to stop and investigate the underlying malaise in order to stop the firm going backwards.

Most partnership organizations try to build on involvement and positive encouragement and, when the trading situation becomes threatening, they have an advantage over firms with long lead times, big order books or lengthy contracts. Market signals reach the partnership organization relatively quickly. If clients are still coming in, change may not occur—but, in that case, how necessary is it? On the other hand, if new client work becomes less plentiful or more difficult to win, those signals reach the partnership personnel very quickly. The signals that are more difficult to spot are the structural shifts in the partnership's market; that is, when the compartmentalized specialists cannot spot a change in the way services are being affected and so do not respond to new forms of market demand for their skills.

While it is not sensible to use 'hard' managers when managing professionals, because the professionals just melt away—withdrawing psychologically if not materially—it would be wrong to delineate partnership change as a maverick condition, outside the range of factors which permeate successful changes in the other change circumstances. What have to be considered are the social inclusiveness and the ties that bind people together in the partnership organization.

The professional firm cannot operate while those below are mutinous, but the blunt fact is that the need for consensus is largely restricted to the partners. Convince them of the merit of a strategic change and much else will fall into place. The partners are the equity holders and risk takers and, apart from their attachment to the quality and integrity of their work, they become concerned about two core matters: the profit-allocation system and the risks attached to changes and developments in the practice. One affects their income, the second affects their financial exposure. It is they who decide whether to invest in, say, information technology, or to open an overseas office and carry its losses until it becomes self-standing and begins to contribute to practice profits. Non-partners and the salariat have no such direct financial risk and may get no bonus or profit share either. That will depend on the firm and the profession's habits.

The big dilemma then is what is to happen to that office's profits. Is the whole practice 'one firm', like Arthur Andersen, in which all revenues are pooled and then disbursed to partners on a universalistic basis throughout the firm, with limited regard to local performance? Or is it a federal structure in which each office, perhaps each identifiable element in each office, is responsible for managing its own affairs, including its financial risk and reward? Some practices have little more commonality than the practice name. The 'one firm' practice has a much higher chance of cross-selling, personnel transfer, team assembly for given projects and mutual cooperation—including the transferring of knowledge, skills and experiences. The 'one firm' system does not halt feelings of inequitable rewards, but these are muted when the firm does well as a result of its close cooperation. In order to absorb the stresses of compensating poorer-performing offices by better-performing offices, there needs to be a high level of mutual regard and trust. The federal structure, on the other hand, encourages parochial thinking and actions. It is not unknown for a partner in a loose federal structure to ignore a sales lead that would provide a major benefit to the firm overall—but principally to another office—in favour of a far worse prospect locally.

Even in federal structures, change is possible. If partnerships were thoroughly flat and democratic, with every faction staffed by individuals who could withhold their commitment to change, very little could occur in the way of strategic moves except at the lowest common denominator of consensual agreement—which is what often happens in worker cooperatives.[10] But partnership enterprises solve this problem by introducing hierarchy. There will be senior partners, partners, junior partners, associate partners, and fee-earners and salaried staff who are not partners (though aspiring to become partners); there will also be administrative staff and executives.

The hierarchy works by stratifying the organization and introducing a promotion route which suppresses dissent. The aspiring professionals enter an apprenticeship of articled training where they have to work hard, prove themselves, gain qualifications and keep fairly quiet to avoid upsetting their mentors (who are the partners) who will determine when and whether they will be allowed to join their ranks. An example would be the junior hospital doctor, putting up with chronic overwork in order to gain promotion. The aspiring young professional grumbles quietly, puts up with indifferent working conditions and is then chosen or exited.

Typically, partnership firms change their thrust, their orientation, via selective recruitment and selective termination in order to switch the emphasis into a growth area. Selective termination may not mean firing many people, given the significant labour turnover. It is more problematic if the surplus people are in the ranks of the partners. Then the ease of making changes depends on the exit arrangements. Do new partners have to buy their shares or do they accumulate them through taking subnormal remuneration until they build up their equity stake in the firm? Then, do they get capital appreciation back when they leave, or is that a legacy to those remaining and to future partners—just as they themselves had benefited in their time from the exertions of previous partners?

The consequence of these singular features is that some of the normal corporate management tools are not practicable in a partnership and, even when the partnership votes for and installs a board of management, scepticism and concern about loss of partner power continue. The task of administration is often thought to be inferior to the exercising of professional skill on behalf of the partnership. It helps when highly respected partners are put onto that management board because, reassured, the other partners' resistance to board proposals dwindles and the managing partner will be given more backing for changes. Yet it all remains a delicate balancing act of influence and leadership by example, needing subtlety and sensitivity to move the firm along. Running a partnership firm is not as gruelling as herding cats, but the very intelligence, professional autonomy and self-esteem of its inhabitants lead to a situation where a command structure has little hope of working. The professionals delight in finding loopholes and ways to undermine unwanted change. The managing group has to find ways of blocking up some loopholes and enlarging and utilizing others.

The chosen path is almost inevitably cooperative rather than coercive and only in high-stress, high perceived threat circumstances would even a charismatic partnership leader be allowed his or her head without enfolding colleagues in the decision process and in the acceptance of the strategic change. Without that stress and urgency, change will be incremental as well as collaborative as partners are persuaded of the need to adapt. The style will be one of participative evolution.[11]

Typically, the positive appeal will be based on what are hoped to be commonly held motives. The deal on offer from the top group would claim that, by making the changes, we could be more productive with less hassle; we could make more money; we could do more interesting work; our future could be made more secure; we could be happier in our work; we could be more of a cooperative community. These form the basis on which a partnership leader can hope to persuade colleagues that a strategic change would be fruitful.

There is a different set of dynamics when the partnership extends beyond the confines of the firm. In a joint venture, consortium or similar multiparty collaboration, there may be no single power source that can acquire the dedicated loyalty of all parties, since they have loyalties to their own firm as well as to the joint venture. This wider topic deserves a fuller treatment than space here allows, because the central focus of this book is on the implementation of strategic change within the one organization. But a brief aside is relevant, for the multifirm venture is a growing phenomenon and contains many of the same features as do multiple minorities inside a single-partnership firm; i.e. weak power structures, a spectrum of relationships which ranges from mutual trust to contractually explicit obligations and the need for mutual persuasion. Indeed, in a multiparty venture the absence of a controlling faction can be vital to the ability to sustain a collaboration when divided or conflicting loyalties tear at its fabric.

> You had to keep any one group from acquiring a veto power. Our achievement was to hold them at bay, even though we had no strength whatever because we did not have our own treasury and so were not in control of the situation. Everyone was part of a minority—four agent banks, 218 other banks, two groups of five contractors each who did not control each other, two governments, each with several departments involved, the Inter-Governmental Commission, the collection of disciplines in the Safety Authority. It took an enormous amount of time, effort and legal expense to keep this collection on the road. You simply have to maintain interlocking or interacting pressures. And he who gets the most pressures together, wins the round—and the losers are there to fight another day. Nobody ever gets killed off.
>
> (Sir Alastair Morton, co-chairman, Eurotunnel)

Firms that have become involved in partnerships with other powerful enterprises, such as GEC with its joint venture with Alcatel-Alsthom, have learned that there are necessary factors which affect the success of this type of venture, such as:

- You have to communicate with your partner a great deal. You cannot afford to surprise or shock each other.
- If an early dispute in seeking agreement is 'Who is going to control it?', head for the door. If you cannot agree about that, what are you going to do when something important comes up?
- The venture must have room to grow and not be hemmed in by either partner's other interests. There will be more progress if neither partner has reserved some of its own activities in prospective competition with the joint venture.
- The venture has to have its own identity as a business and not be an airport ('get through quickly and don't get stuck in it') where managers pass through to and from their parent company.
- The parent companies' views of themselves have to evolve to see these new ventures as normal and acceptable.

- The venture's managers must have access to senior executives in the parent companies if decisions are to be made quickly and the venture is not to be relegated to the sidelines.
- Avoid having a partner that is monolithic and used to doing everything itself. It will never agree to anything that has not gone through its internal (jealous?) equivalent for appraisal, and the concept of sharing, as with power in a joint venture, will be alien to it.

Clearly, the systems for handling divergence and dissent in a major joint venture will be different, more protocol-oriented and contract-based than would be the case in a single firm of partners—particularly if, as with the building of the Channel Tunnel, most constituent parties have other activities and if, for some, their active involvement is limited to the construction period. Yet, whether the glue that binds them is one of contractual obligations or convergent interests, the parties, even in a single organization of partners, face unusually subtle management challenges.

CATALYTIC CHANGE

This is not an independent type of change but an adjunct to all the above five types of intervention. Catalysis is as likely to be associated with Injection change as with Partnership change and it may or may not accompany changes in the top team of managers. The catalysis comes from the introduction of an agency—typically consultants or advisers. There are many motives for bringing in consultants and the following list presents 24 reasons:

1. As initiator of debate and attitude change
2. As catalyst to initiate action
3. To structure a problem so that it becomes more amenable to analysis and action
4. To enhance impetus
5. To augment in-house resources temporarily
6. To provide expertise and relevant skills

7. To bring in experience not available within the organization
8. To crystallize existing internal views
9. To give legitimacy to internal views
10. To adjudicate between internal factions
11. To confirm/validate an internal decision/perspective
12. To endorse a new management's proposals
13. To minimize management's guilt by shifting blame; to act as scapegoat for unpopular actions
14. To endorse unpleasant action
15. As a sacrifice, to be disowned and exited quietly if their proposals meet overwhelming hostility
16. To show seriousness of intent
17. To defer action while investigation occurs
18. To trail a coat: to produce terrorizing prospects so that management can get their own more modest way with relative ease
19. As decoys, to divert attention from other painful matters
20. To reconsider a decision that has already been made
21. To implement a decision that has already been made
22. To provide believability through independence; to deliver a message that would be rejected if it came from the firm's own management
23. To provide a quality check by assessing the worth of the strategy process and content
24. To create a surrogate form of threat in order to induce change.

Whatever the motive(s), the introduction of the catalytic agent is designed, as with all catalysts, to improve the process of transformation. It also strengthens the process of change when it becomes the second element of a double-acting mechanism. The first element is the advent of the new top manager(s) with the new vision. The second is the impetus given to the top manager's vision by the intervention of the catalyst. Most consulting assignments have the effect of stimulating managers to face up to factors that they may have previously ignored, overrated or discounted. Consultants' ideas are not always right but, like all challenges to one's deeply held convictions, they force the recipients to decide just what *is* right.

The change agent is aided by coming from outside the organization, because he or she has not been indoctrinated and immobilized by the firm's existing mind-set. Lacking a thorough appreciation of the firm's habits, the consultant may be, in one sense, naive. Yet that can be offset by his or her having insights gained from many other consulting circumstances. An experienced change agent with good influencing and manipulative skills can ask the innocent questions and have a licence for candour, able to coax, cajole and jostle people towards the strategic goal without disabling the organization or alienating those involved.

But why bring in a catalyst? 'Almost invariably there is some adverse symptom in the organization, something is hurting and the CEO or the head of a business feels it and needs to act' (Faith Gibson, Gemini Consultants). While the underlying problem may not be quite what the key executive believes, he or she has become aroused enough to realize that something is amiss that will not respond to the normal interventions of day-to-day management. Furthermore, the incoming executive cannot carry all the burden, and there may not be enough other managers in the firm who are readily able to handle the transition process. The company cannot run itself like an American football team and take the previous top team (the defence) off the field and temporarily replace it with another team (the offence) instead. If the firm has to make a strategic change using most of the existing management team, it may be feasible for the key executive to lead the charge if he or she is particularly adept at coaxing radical change out of others; but the management is more likely to need its skills augmenting with acquired specialist help. Furthermore, if the incoming manager believes that there is a major gain that could be attainable, the strategic change will be viewed as an investment, and the sooner the payback can begin, the better. Consultants have a significant role in the speeding up of strategic changes.

The introduction of catalysts is not restrained to Succession, Renovation and Partnership changes, although consultants are used extensively in such circumstances when the new top management wants to augment the firm's skills or to galvanize the firm's existing managers. Takeover and Injection change managers also typically bring in consultants too. One reason is that, despite the powerful mandate that they possess from those who appointed them, when they arrive they do not have a reliably loyal and effective power base inside the firm. If the new appointee has qualms about the capabilities of the firm's existing management, he or she will want to obtain a second opinion and have a closer look at what needs to be done and who is capable of doing it. The new manager will want to obtain reliable information quickly.

Additionally, if a restructuring is likely, the new appointee will not want to leave it to the existing managers in case they let the good people go in order to protect their own positions—a strong possibility if it is their lax behaviour that has led to the need for restructuring in the first place. Consultants can also be valuable in helping to transform a business after it has been restructured and the necessary pruning carried out. The new managers may not be as good at developing the underperforming business as they were at rectifying the organization's faults. Whatever the combination of reasons for introducing catalysts into the firm, the driving force comes from a realization that the firm cannot make the improvements it wants, in the timescale needed, with only its own resources.

The consultants have two main problems in helping the firm to effect useful change. The first is that the organization inviting them has, in all probability, already decided what the problem is and has chosen a consultancy firm that is renowned for solving that type of problem. If, on investigation, the issue is found to be markedly different, the consultant's skills may be of little help in catalysing the situation effectively and it is a noble consultancy that will then say: 'We can't help you with this problem.'

The second is that the rest of the organization may be suspicious if the consultants are too exclusively associated with the new top management; the consultant's credibility will be low. This might not matter too much if the consulting assignment is concerned with competitor and market analysis and hence largely outside the firm. If, as is more likely, the assignment is concerned with transforming the internal workings of the firm, then the consultants have to involve themselves throughout the organization and they need to demonstrate their independence of judgement and neither become entrapped by the organization as a whole nor just take on the singular perspective of the top management. The closer the introduction of consultants is to a recent organizational trauma—such as a harsh downsizing reconstruction—the more guarded will be the employees. It can be difficult in such circumstances for the consultants to pick their way past the organizational booby traps and gain the confidence of those in the firm.

So the question now is what, in the light of the six change circumstances, should managers in commercial firms *do* in order to make the organization respond and change fruitfully?

REFERENCES

1. J.-C. Spender, *Industry Recipes: The Nature and Source of Managerial Judgement*. Blackwell, 1989, p. 14.
2. Philippe C. Haspelagh and David B. Jemison, *Managing Acquisitions: Creating Value through Corporate Renewal*. Free Press, 1991.
3. *The Economist*, 7 September 1991.
4. Michael L. Tushman, William H. Virany and Elaine Romanelli, Convergence and Upheaval: Managing the Unsteady Pace of Organizational Evolution, *California Management Review*, **29**, 1986, pp. 29–44.
5. Leaders of corporate change. *Fortune*, 14 December 1992, p. 94.
6. Arvind Bhambri and Larry Greiner, A conditional theory of CEO intervention and strategic change. Strategic Management Society Conference, San Francisco, October 1989.
7. David Norburn and Sue Birley, The top management team and corporate performance. *Strategic Management Journal*, **9**, 1988, pp. 225–37.
8. John P. Kotter, *The General Managers*. Free Press, 1986.
9. Geoff Mulgan in Stuart Hall and Martin Jacques (eds.), *New Times: The Changing Face of Politics in the 1990s*, Lawrence Wishart, 1989, pp. 347–63.
10. Tony Eccles, *Under New Management*. Pan, 1981.
11. Dexter C. Dunply and Doug Stace, Transformational and coercive strategies for planned organisational change: Beyond the O.D. Model. *Organisation Studies*, **9** (3), 1988, pp. 317–34.

PART III
Fourteen factors of change

6 Purpose and initiative

- Factor 1: The pregnant executive
- Factor 2: Single goal
- Factor 3: Clarity of purpose

It might be expected that the differences in strategic change practices between Takeover change, Injection change, Succession change and Renovation change would be substantial, let alone different from Partnership change. Fascinatingly, and a touch surprisingly, the similarities between the change circumstances are more marked than the differences.

Discussions with senior executives who have been involved in extensive, sometimes dramatic, strategic change processes, reveal a number of common factors that apply to most of the change circumstances, despite the fact that each company and industry has specific characteristics that cause the particular conditions and prescriptions to vary. Furthermore, the similarities do not seem to reduce markedly for different elements of the strategic change process; whether it is a change of goal or a change of route to the same goal, the execution process shows similar characteristics. 'No matter what problem we identified, the solution was the same, it was changing people's behaviour and attitudes' (Geoff Gaines, KPMG). One respondent concentrated on a single factor: 'There is only one factor and it is will' (Lord Weinstock, chief executive, GEC). For most executives, there were several interlinked factors which they saw as crucial to making economical progress with strategic change campaigns (see Figure 1.2, page 12).

This did not require that the specific content of what was

done in different circumstances was unvarying. Each situation had its own context, its own particularities, its own situational dynamics and processes. But analysis of all the experiences and insights did yield 14 factors that were widespread enough to be termed general. Their use does not guarantee success in changing the firm's performance, since the links between strategic change and performance are difficult to gauge in complex circumstances. Where, for instance, is the reference point? You cannot be sure of what the performance would have been without the change. Nevertheless, the 14 factors come from extensive analysis and from managers and organizations that have been generally successful.

FACTOR 1: THE PREGNANT EXECUTIVE

There has to be a champion who embodies and lives the new dream.

First, as already noted under the Spartacus challenge (see Chapter 2), the impetus for change manifests itself at the top of the organization. This does not mean that ideas and pressure for change cannot come from below, but short of revolution in the organization, it is the top that actions the requirement for change. Indeed, it is usually the case that there is a small coterie of key people, or perhaps one key manager alone, who drive the strategic impetus along. These individual prime movers are vital.[1]

As Doz and Prahalad[2] found in their studies of large complex organizations:

> Impetus was unlikely to come successfully from the ranks. Although individual product managers, and managers within subsidiaries, could occasionally become aware of the need for strategic redirection, they lacked access, influence and data to put their position forward, and usually did not find receptive ears in their own hierarchy. Status quo endured. In all the successful cases of strategic redirection that we observed, the status quo was broken only by the appointment at a senior position ... of an executive pregnant with a different vision ... a change of single key executive usually has an impact in less than a year.

Similarly, Pennings observed that a high degree of chief executive turnover coincided with the onset of strategic change in the organization.[3] This should not surprise us, since the widest vision should be at the peak of the organization and Takeover, Injection and Succession change all raise the likelihood that a new top person and the onset of change are intimately connected. Raw ideas may have been plentiful down in the organization before his or her arrival, but it requires broad vision to fit ideas into a context, to cultivate their appeal, to assemble resources and to back an idea with power in order to implement it.

In the absence of someone at the top with the power and commitment to make the necessary changes, the likelihood of action is much reduced. If there is a power stalemate, the organization is in trouble. Then the questions arise: What will break the log-jam? Will it be an outside impact, a suicidal insider, the leaving of a key, disgusted executive, a stakeholder revolt, an employee initiative—or what? Usually it is the intervention of a new leader or a well-placed person with vision who kindles support for a particular initiative. One experienced executive is convinced of this requirement. 'Our young graduate managers asked me how you get change in a company. I told them, you won't unless the person at the top has a vision and an integrity of purpose.'

Mike Heron of Unilever agreed:

> Almost always there is some sort of evangelical vision at the heart of it—it may be one person, someone who believes, because without that belief, it doesn't happen. There was one board member in a division who cottoned on to the importance of Information Technology for our future and he wrote a paper saying that we wouldn't be able to do the strategic things we wanted without a transformation in our approach and investment in IT. We were nowhere near a leading position two years ago. Now we are getting quite close to being in the forefront of IT. You don't do it unless you feel it with the whole of your person.

Managers in an organization that has a leader with such an evangelical vision are usually clear about the leader's obsession. They know that he or she is red hot on a particular matter. All the actions signal and reinforce the leader's evident commitment and, being pragmatic people, they gravitate towards the same view and act in the light of his or her leadership. Some become disciples, spreading the word in their turn. If they have all been together for a long time, the leader's persistent commitment will have rubbed off on them, just as the Roman Empire knew that when the wagon train of a trained and trusted governor rolled over the horizon on his way to his province, he, without benefit of phone or fax, would carry out the enduring policies of Rome.

The leader has to show sustained commitment and long-term persistence for this understanding to gell, but a powerful new leader, such as an incomer resulting from Takeover or Injection change, can use his or her licence to initiate the same effect, once those in the organization realize that the leader is serious about his or her evangelism. Gradually, the message spreads and the leader's new insight and way of reframing the possibilities alter the mind-set of close colleagues. It may take a little time; there may have to be a couple of spectacular casualties among the management; and the early experiences may include setbacks. Yet if the leader is prudent, he or she will have warned those who have put him or her there that the situation will get worse before it gets better in order to gain space and time to succeed. Such a warning is akin to the ritual that often accompanies a new top team which loads all the costs and write-offs into the existing year's accounts in order to clear the decks for an improvement from the first year under their stewardship.

To maximize the impact the leader will act in two ways: symbolically as a role model, a rule breaker, a creator of climate and conditions which develop an awareness of the need for change; and as the organizer, using power, resources, conflict-resolving decisions, organizational restructuring and rewards to drive the changes along. It must be signalled, again and again, that the leader is serious about the changes; that inaction is not an option. It is not that the followers are looking for a hero, but searching for a leader. They have to see that the leader believes in something that makes him or her worth following.

Because organizations have finite lives, and key executives

have even shorter tenures, it has become fashionable to sneer at the activities of charismatic leaders. Yet charisma often works for long enough to achieve truly impressive results. The inspirational, transformational leader can be a valuable catalyst and stimulator for a sagging organization.[4] Repeating that impact in the same organization is more problematic. It is not easy to sustain successful change after successful change and why leaders should be expected to perform encore after encore is not obvious. We should cherish them for their achievements, not deride them for their inability to do it again and again.

FACTOR 2: SINGLE GOAL

There has to be a clear and sustained purpose to which people can commit.

It has been said of inflated mission statements that 'People will work for a sentence, but not for a paragraph'. There have been few memorable battle cries that are a paragraph in length. Keep it simple is an old motto but, in an increasingly complex world, with most major companies trying to stay on the right side of several stakeholder groups, multiple goals are difficult to avoid. The way to keep the goal simple is to have a permanent context about product quality, customer service, employee policy, whatever you choose. The context becomes a given orientation; a set of house rules to be permanently taken as read; superordinate goals, that is guiding principles and a set of corporate values.[5] The aspirations of that context then no longer need to drag down the core message with worthy but leaden sentiments. The strategic goal can become very simple. It can also evolve.

For example, Unilever has a range of guiding principles that have been built up over the years and with which its staff have become imbued. These principles are not abandoned as some new priority arises, but remain steadfast as part of Unilever's whole operating culture. They are not quite immutable, since they are gently adapted through experience, but socialized Unilever managers take them as given for as long as they are current. This leaves the firm free to focus on the potent issue of the moment, be it global cash flow, reorganizing in a continent or gaining critical mass in a region or sector through rapid acquisition.

The recent Unilever single goal has been utterly succinct: 'Grow the Core, Globally.' 'Grow' is plain enough; concentration on 'Core' businesses serves to highlight focus; and building 'Globally' evokes clear notions of transnational products. The three major parts of Unilever's corporate strategy are captured in four words. You would have to be quite dense not to know what the overall strategy was and whether a particular element fitted in. It shows a remarkable difference from the organization where a divisional director was heard to bemoan: 'We were told to focus on quality, then on customer service, then on cost reduction, later on linking our businesses together, then on creating new products and now the priority is expanding into Europe. And the year isn't over yet.' Such temporary, episodic goals breed indifference, for why commit your efforts to the current strategy if another will be along in a minute?[6]

Unilever's single goal is an object lesson to the wordy and the unfocused. Yet there are still people who believe that all you need to do is to energize the organization with a clarion call and keep people constantly on their toes—no matter that the reason either isn't obvious or changes every few months. Energy without some idea of the desirable route is going to be wasteful—like having drive without direction. Lacking any notion of path or destination, the organization will inevitably act indiscriminately and its good people will either resign or quietly give up, unwilling to continue through the aimless turmoil and shifting fads. Tom Peters seems to advocate continuous anarchy—which he calls 'purposeful chaos'—as a way of galvanizing organizations, but this scarcely seems to be sensible advice when organizations are trying to unite internally to face external pressures. Continuity and durability are valuable attributes, not just for suppliers and customers but for staff, and should not lightly be discarded.

Having a single goal and some guiding principles is practical as well as sensible. There needs to be constancy of purpose combined with flexibility of action. As Kotter[7] has said: 'Typically a vision is specific enough to provide real guidance to people, yet vague enough to encourage initiative and to remain relevant under a variety of conditions.' As he explained, 'Vision is not mystical or intangible, but means simply a description of something (an organization, a corporate culture, a business, a technology) in the future, often the distant future, in terms of the essence of what it should become.' A single goal is easier to unite behind since it can enfold a number of divergent sub-goals and understandings within its broad scope. The exact route to achieving it may not be clear; the company may have to tack towards it like a boat sailing against the wind.

That is why it is easier to build consensus round a single broad strategic goal such as 'Beat Benz' or 'Encircle Caterpillar', which sound rather more emotive than 'Raise our earnings per share by 10 per cent above inflation each year within a debt ratio of 60 per cent maximum'. It is also easier to sell to everyone in the organization because it makes more sense. The broad single goal has to have a purpose that means something valid to all sections of employees since 'objectives that have little meaning for large segments of an organization cannot be shared and cannot weld it together'.[8] As one business leader put it: 'The goal has to be credible and it must help you to focus on your resources.' In addition, the top person's capabilities and behaviour must add to the credibility, otherwise the people below will agree the goal, but despair of reaching it.

The trick for the leader is to be able to turn the broad single goal into more detailed plans and specific actions without derailing the consensus that backs the goal. He or she has to slim down many agendas and resolve the problem of priorities so that the general thrust of the chosen strategy can be translated into those specific actions. Without that translation, little can be expected to happen. It is important that strategy implementation can be seen to follow a clear path because major changes in direction are unsettling, promote unease and create a lack of certainty or commitment which can readily lead to failure. If a few golden rules that aren't open for debate are permanently highlighted with the minimum number of commands from the centre, then flexibility and initiative further down the organization are possible without diverting from the overall goal or violating the golden rules. It is not that the firm's strategic goal is an immovable rock in the swirling currents of competitive markets. Rather it is an anchor, stabilizing but capable of being moved intentionally.

Of course, events get in the way. Yet the top management and, one hopes, the remainder of the organization will keep that major goal in the forefront of their minds and it will transcend all others, even though many events will take time and attention. No management is wholly in charge of events. A young reporter once asked ex-Prime Minister Harold Macmillan what had been the most difficult thing he had had to deal with as Prime Minister. 'Events, my dear boy. Events', he replied. Yet despite the intrusion of events which, as a later Prime Minister said, 'blew us off course', the fact is that the chosen course remains the heart of the matter, and if you fail in that one thing, then the whole strategy fails, no matter how well the individual events have been handled. They are peripheral to the main challenge. As Lord Sheppard of Grand Metropolitan has put it: 'You have to have the determination to actually implement the chosen strategy and not be side-tracked by trivia or internal noise.'

> You have to have an objective, but you've got to stay reasonably flexible in pursuing it. Self-generated strategic change requires the stamina, the endurance and the resilience to just keep coming back to that strategy. You get knocked partly off, but you come back. You get knocked the other way off, but you come back. You're not going to arrive if you get diverted. If you think of situations in sports, you have to maintain the speed of the ball even though it ricochets. There is a shot in billiards where you try, with spin, to get the ball to come off the cushion faster than it went on, so that it gains speed. That is what sustaining momentum really involves and you must listen in order to hear what the real problem is, otherwise you won't so much get deflected, you will go into a sandtrap and just get stopped. You don't keep momentum if you aren't absorbing the energy of the people who are deflecting you.
>
> It doesn't do much good to win a 6 love, 6 love battle over a key player, if he ditches you the next time. You have to make

him believe that, while it isn't what he intended, it is never-theless satisfactory. It's the old story that once you get a person out on a branch, you've got to provide him with a ladder, or you may pay a heavy price for it the next time. It's not a question of being magnanimous, it's a question of making people feel part of the solution. It is also a function of retaining the sympathy of people. If they are sympathetic, you can mobilize them quickly.

(Sir Alastair Morton, co-chairman, Eurotunnel)

FACTOR 3: CLARITY OF PURPOSE

There has to be a defensible, unambiguous reason for the change.

With Takeover or Injection changes, the power of the new top management makes it less necessary, though still desirable, to persuade people lower down of the case for change. The top management's very arrival may have happened because those in the company were confused, stalled, fearful or leaderless. In that state, they are not likely to mount serious opposition to a strong new leadership with a firm mandate. They just have to be persuaded that the new management knows what it is doing. If people are not sure why they and their work have to change, confusion and resistance will ensue. There has to be a shift in perceptions if support for the changes is to be mobilized. A plausible proposal which distils the beliefs and experiences of those being led will readily gain acceptance. Giving employees a clear purpose which respects the organization's heritage and builds on the existing capabilities of its inhabitants without being too constrained by the past, seems to be the best mechanism.

Compared to Takeover or Injection change, the leaders of Succession or Renovation change require a far more persua-sive case. They cannot rely on the combination of mystery and hope that can accompany the entry of takeover or injection leaders, so that their plans have to stand up to knowledgeable, perhaps sceptical, analysis. Unilever's prac-tices have been partly formed by the need to consult in detail in both Germany and Holland, causing its changes to occur only after detailed planning and debates involving many groups of employees. As Mike Heron of Unilever has stated:

There is an absolutely prime need for the reasoning of the case to be intellectually clear. If you don't persuade senior management of the rational, intellectual validity, they won't be able to defend and promote it. With our EC 1992 changes we took a lot of trouble getting the case right and then getting our senior management on board. The penny had dropped with a number of senior people that with our vast experience in Europe, we were in danger of taking the baggage of the past into the future; that we would become like the pterodactyls—awesome but dispossessed.

The case for change must carry conviction when put under load inside the organization since, in the words of one top executive, 'It is better to have the proposal dismantled from internal pressure at the approval stage than to have your competitors dismantle it in the marketplace.' Lord Sheppard of Grand Metropolitan concurs: 'You have to know what you want to do and explain it under pressure. If it is glib, it will fall apart.'

As another organization's senior managers found, failure to build sustainable intellectual strength and clarity can lead to discomfiture.

We failed the first time with a major change because the blueprint was not convincing or worked through, so that the key managers were not persuaded. We were trying to put a large region together with several country managers who were at the pinnacles of their careers and who had enjoyed being the barons in charge of their own patch. They needed a lot of persuasion and they didn't get it; the supervisory director tried to browbeat them and that failed. It would have been pointless to try to bypass them and take the change further with the managers below them when the top people were obviously sceptical. We had to put a new director in and he asked the barons to look at the region's markets and the trends in them. The facts were persuasive and the logic became clearer. When he put the chairmen of the main countries onto the new regional board they became winners and also had to develop a wider perspective. Gradually he pulled them in and they brought young, talented managers with them and it all began to work.

It may be that the first attempt helped to soften the key managers up, but not enough to close the deal. When, in the second attempt, the central figures were co-opted into power positions in the new set-up, the impetus began to grow because the vital people had been turned from prospective losers into winners. The role of personality is important too and one would have to consider how much the better reception at the second attempt was due to a more appropriate approach by the director who was orchestrating the changes. A sound strategic plan can easily go awry if the wrong people are entrusted with it. The timing may also have been more appropriate on the second occasion.

Having the relevant person in the key position is clearly important; but it is not the complete story. The need to act appropriately goes far beyond one person. The situation described fits closely with Doz and Prahalad's findings.

> In most of the cases we studied there was no perception of immediate crisis. Performance was deteriorating slowly, for reasons that were not sufficiently clear to arouse questioning or discrediting of the past strategy. Indeed, if anything, performance deterioration led to a reinforcement of the past strategy, for instance by establishing tightly measured and strongly motivated strategic business units within subsidiaries. This only reinforced the local 'patch' orientation of operating managers in subsidiaries ... local national 'barons' had managed subsidiaries for a long time and were rather insensitive to global perspectives. Further, any departure from the status quo was likely to undermine the autonomy of the subsidiaries, on which the success of the company had been built and the careers of the most senior executives made.[9]

The second effect of having intellectual clarity of purpose is that it helps to capture the young managers who have everything to gain from change and who will be attracted by the logic of an attractive idea. To quote Mike Heron of Unilever again:

> The other important element of getting the intellectual case right is that the young managers then buy in. The group well below are the young implementers. They grasp the intellectual case, are

keen on change and then there is a squeeze, a pincer movement on any recalcitrant middle managers. It's an important process. There are winners and losers. The winners take the lead and the losers become converted—or go.

As Pascale noted: 'Change flourishes in a sandwich; when there is consensus above and pressure below, things happen', though for maximum effectiveness this does require that the pressure is in harmony with the consensus.[10] The best results come when there is visible sustained commitment from the top and a shared enthusiasm among the livelier personnel further down. Sir John Harvey-Jones of ICI summed it up: 'You have to give them a better picture of a better tomorrow.'

The heart of gaining management agreement to a strategy lies in convincing people (a) about the issue that should be faced and the need for action; (b) about the appropriateness and benefit of the solution; and (c) that the implementation of the solution is feasible. As one large company realized: 'It wasn't that the way we chose to change our strategy was better than the others. They were as good. But it was the one that we knew we could do. It was a matter of capturing the moment; we had the time and the resources and it looked like the kind of thing we already believed in.' This refers to the highly successful changes at Guinness in the late 1980s. The fact that the strategic change process was one that the management felt confident it could do and so could articulate clearly, must have reinforced its chance of success. Having the persuasive, right purpose, boosts confidence in both the managers and the managed.

The need for intellectual clarity is unarguable. In his research with CEOs on common factors in strategy implementation, Alexander[11] asked what points they had found helpful in promoting successful changes. The CEOs emphasized communication, both top-down and two-way, as a means of monitoring and analysing progress, together with the need to start with a sound concept or idea, since 'no amount of time or effort spent on implementation can rescue a strategic decision that is not well formulated to begin with'.

REFERENCES

1. Rosabeth Moss Kanter, *The Change Masters*. Simon and Schuster, 1983, p. 296.
2. Yves Doz and C. K. Prahalad, A process model of strategic redirection in large, complex organizations, in *The Management of Strategic Change* (ed. Andrew Pettigrew). Blackwell, 1987, pp. 71–2 and 78.
3. J. M. Pennings and Associates, *Organizational Strategy and Change*. Jossey Bass, 1985.
4. James MacGregor Burns, *Leadership*. Harper Collins, 1982.
5. Thomas J. Peters and Robert H. Waterman, *In Search of Excellence*. Harper and Row, 1982.
6. Robert H. Hayes, Strategic planning; forward in reverse. *Harvard Business Review*, November–December 1985, pp. 111–19.
7. John P. Kotter, *A Force for Change*. Free Press, 1990, p. 36.
8. Hayes, *op. cit.*, p. 113.
9. Doz and Prahalad, *op. cit.*, p. 70.
10. Richard T. Pascale, *Managing on the Edge*. Viking 1990, p. 126.
11. Larry D. Alexander, Successfully implementing strategic decisions. *Long Range Planning*, **18** (3), June 1985, pp. 91–7.

7 Concordance and trust

- Factor 4: The illusion of unity
- Factor 5: How open to be?
- Factor 6: Communication

FACTOR 4: THE ILLUSION OF UNITY

Don't expect everybody to back the change.

No matter how appealing the single goal, no matter how splendid the clarity of the intellectual case, the organization's members will never unite fully behind a strategic change programme. Doubters, sceptics, losers, will remain. Unity is an illusion. In fact, it would be a depressing commentary on the human condition if individual attitudes were open to obliteration through an organizational change campaign.

Hence, an organization will never be seeking change from an uniform starting point, with everyone facing the same direction, even if they might be 'singing from the same hymn sheet' as it is sometimes described—though possibly not all singing the same hymn. It would well be worrying if they were. As already mentioned, Peter Drucker has observed that, if the board is unanimous, the decision should be delayed because, for a lack of questioning is unhealthy and is likely to lead to mistakes.

Pluralism of interests and perspectives means that the cry of 'We must have complete backing. Everyone must be convinced' is illogical as well as unrealistic: if a strategy can only be pursued when *everyone* backs it, then it is wide open to failure. The most obdurate person in the entire organization has been handed the power of veto. One blackball would be enough to halt any proposal. The determinant of agreement would not then be that of the most reasonable, best informed, most intelligent people in the organization, for they will compromise to make progress. The firm's policy would instead be set by the views of the most recalcitrant minority. Nor would that change. Attitudes in a changing organization will not come from uniform values, so there is little reason to expect that initially differing values would be uniform after a change process. The search for complete backing is a recipe for disablement, where the organization, just as it needs to change, can only achieve unity by drooping to the lowest common denominator of universal agreement.

All those managers who implore their personnel to be unitedly on side should remind themselves of a central tenet of Isaiah Berlin's teachings: that absolute values are not perfectly harmonious but are irreducibly plural.[1] Managers must seek complete agreement, but not expect to get it, nor spend untoward time pursuing it. As Charles Hampden-Turner wrote: 'Consensus is a sloth-like beast of mythical properties, long thought to be of great value. In fact a consensus of any size is very hard to find and tends to vanish mysteriously. Much time and effort can be saved by not seeking it.'[2]

Hence a lack of unity would not betoken sloppiness or inattention, for the world is made up of competing pluralities and incompatibilities that have to be reconciled, not to the level of dissolving the contradictions, but by coming to terms with their inherent tensions. The central problems are those of agreeing the balance point on the spectrum of views and of deciding the basis for agreement—such as a democratic vote or through the use of managerial power. Dilemmas abound. In this organization, do we now need freedom or control; authority or autonomy; security or risk; functionalism or integration; long-term or short-term perspectives; centralization or decentralization (and of what?), specifics or generalities, separation or togetherness, competition or cooperation? One might not want the full panoply of tensions as recommended by Richard Pascale—to all those choices he would reply 'both'—but the managing of organizations is always replete with tensions and contradictions.[3]

Because constructive contention (what in Grand Metropolitan is called 'the challenge culture') causes discomfort and can be thought to be a reproach to the organization's ability to resolve differences, companies and managements are endlessly exhorted to make this congruent with that and not to make changes until congruence has been achieved. But full congruence is a mirage. Reward systems are a case in point. They may need to be company-wide for collaboration and cross-selling; but separated for focus on organizational subtasks. If you want cross-selling, you will need internal cohesion. If you want task focus you may prefer to differentiate goals and rewards. The differentiated organizational structure of a commercial bank is not conducive to getting all departments to pull together. So it may be cheaper and more effective for the bank to pay people to cross-sell rather than seek a cohesion that is spurious when it doesn't match the organizational structure or its basic reward systems. Large multi-office organizations that run a 'one-company' scheme of complete reward uniformity, face the resentment of those offices and functions that feel they are carrying the others. If it is a professional service firm, the high performers in the high-profit offices may leave to set up on their own in the hope of catching all the benefits of their efforts. Nevertheless, the one-office firm can move personnel across the globe more readily and often at short notice to service a sudden client need, because the firm gains overall and the individual offices then have an interest in high-capacity utilization rather than worrying about what the loss of personnel will do to 'their' office's results.

Who gets out alive?

When faced with calls for unity in the midst of localized rewards and performance criteria, it is useful to ask the person who is exhorting to consider the following dilemma. Suppose that you are one of a theatre audience of 1000, each of whom has been told on entry that, if fire breaks out and people panic for the exits, 10 per cent will get out alive, but if people stay seated and file out in orderly rows, 50 per cent will survive. You know that every separate one of the thousand has been told the same. You are sitting in the theatre and fire breaks out. What will you do?

The answer is that you would dash for the exits. The reason is that, although you know that this will reduce the overall chance of survival, you have no agreement with the other 999; no reciprocal deal—so you try to maximize your own chance by being the first to dash. In terms of self-preservation it is perfectly logical, particularly since you have no time to seek an agreement. The organizational equivalent is an insurance professional who will pursue a poorly paying prospect on which he or she will gain a commission, rather than sell a lucrative policy for another office in the same firm. It happens at all levels. In the days of trading stamps, you could see some employees buying petrol at expensive, stamp-giving garages rather than at cheaper ones which didn't, because the petrol buyers kept the stamps and the employer paid for the expensive petrol. So it is always prudent to keep in mind the sayings 'What gets measured, gets done' (as that is the basis on which your performance will be gauged) and 'What gets rewarded gets done' (as that is the basis on which promotion and wealth can become available).[4]

In war and crisis it can be different; deeply moving acts of bravery and unselfishness are legion. But the implicit work contract in peacetime is typically more calculative. The lesson should be that people may be selfless in moral situations, but not if they are in an instrumental circumstance and are about to gain no reward of any kind—and perhaps even pay a cost—from their selflessness. The cynical but sensible question when considering the motivation of others should be 'Is it in their interests to do this?' If the answer is plainly 'no', then one should be cautious about the persuasiveness of exhortations that fly in the face of the interests of those being exhorted.

It follows that appeals that are handicapped by disincentives and organizational impediments are ineffectual for uniting people. For example, a major electronics company, long used to the separate, arms length operation of its units, realized that the convergence of electronics technology would make it sensible for the units to work together. Cross-unit working groups were announced and managers were urged to work together to obtain economies from coopera-tion. When the senior management was asked what over-heads or costs could be allocated to this new activity since it would distract managers from their current jobs, the answer was 'nothing; though you can charge your travel expenses from visiting each other'. There would be no relaxation whatsoever from the oppressive regime of monthly head office interrogation of each unit's performance. The exhorta-tion was 'collaborate'; the indication was 'relax your focus on your own unit at your peril'. Not surprisingly, only the feeblest, token collaboration then occurred. The firm was later taken over after years of stuttering performance.

In Partnership change, in particular, it is vital to consider the effects of proposed changes on various interest groups in the enterprise, if only to modify the plan where practicable in order to make it more palatable and to estimate the likely source, attitude and strength of potential resistance. Even in Takeover change, let alone Injection or Renovation change, it is prudent to do the same. Clearly you cannot countenance conflict on everything all the time. There is a limit to the amount of productive turbulence and argument with which a company can cope, after which it ceases to be stimulating and merely exhausts the combatants. There is a domain between crisis and tranquillity that gives people a chance to act cooperatively and constructively.

So what should the organization do about any residue of deviants and resisters? The idea that they will evaporate completely is a mirage. The differing opinions need to be argued, accepted and choices made that do not leave a sullen minority uncommitted or wishing to undermine the chosen strategy. Some will genuinely feel worse off as a result of the change. As Geoff Gaines of KPMG has said 'it never ceases to amaze me the way in which change movers are surprised by the fact that not every individual shares their vision of the greater good'. The answer is to celebrate the differences as adding value and, having had an open debate, for the management to choose, announce the choice and say that everyone is now expected to work to it. The new strategy must be understood by everyone, even though not everyone will back it enthusiastically. The more power is held by the senior management, the more dissenters can be faced down. In a partnership organization it would be reckless to act radically in the face of the mutiny of a vital group of professionals.

Naturally, the best answer to the sceptics is to show that the changes can work effectively. In partnership change, in particular, the promoters of change need to put a tremendous and sustained effort into selling the merits of the proposed change through internal marketing. Should grumbles persist in a situation where the changes have been obviously fruitful, then some rearrangement of staff may become necessary (this is discussed in Chapter 10, Factors 11 and 13). The main point is that a dissenting minority should not be taken too seriously if, on careful analysis, their objections seem ill-founded. If they become destructive, they may have to go. Too many companies get sidetracked by their own factions.

FACTOR 5: HOW OPEN TO BE?

Tell people as much as practicable, taking some risks by being candid.

This turned out to be the most difficult issue on which to pronounce; the one where the answer was not obvious and where executives paused longest when asked the question. The basic dilemma is simple. If you, as chief executive, have a major strategic change in mind, with many foreseeable inferences, is it better to tell people everything—the ultimate destination, the route, the costs, the risks, the uncertainties and the opportunities—or should you trickle it out, stage by stage, telling people enough to take them on the first stages of a journey, but where you do not reveal the end goal?

At first sight, one's inclination is to tell all, and every executive wanted to be as open as possible. But they nearly all held back from revealing their total plans to all their employees. A brief summary of the conflicting inclinations helps to flesh out the dilemma.

The argument for telling all is, primarily, that it is ethical to be candid with people in the organization—after all, they are participants in the scheme of things and are going to be affected by events as they unfold. They will better be able to contribute if they know the ultimate destination, and their experience will be invaluable in steering the organization to the best advantage. It was also felt that 'you can't keep going back to people and asking them for more yet again'. The other element was that a really stretching goal will make people realize that a major change is in prospect and that some galvanizing transformation is needed. The firm may not reach its stated overall goal, but it should get further than if it sets a modest target and then finds that no one makes an effort for such a drab task, or they think that it is so easy that no effort on their part is required.

One counter argument is that, if you tell people too much they will give up, believing that the goal is unattainable. 'If I'd told them where I *really* wanted to go, they would never have believed me and they certainly wouldn't have agreed to set off.' 'Sometimes you'd be a mug to tell all. You'd just be causing greater misery. Demotivated people will act defensively.' Another objection to total candour is that neither the top management nor the chief executive know the ultimate destination or the route to it with reliable clarity. There are always uncertainties, but to reveal that you haven't come to terms with them will be disturbing to those below, who are comforted by having confident top managers who have answers. As Mike Bett, deputy chairman of British Telecom, pointed out:

> You can't say, 'I don't know where we're going, but come along with me.' 'Forget that,' they'll respond. Don't tell them the end is certain; you can't see that. But tell them as much as you can confidently. After all, if you are not confident, they'll ask who can be? And why should they be if you are not?'

But confidence helps to breed trust and if people feel that the management doesn't know where it is taking them, they may well decline to join the mystery excursion. People may sense that something needs changing but lose their faith that management knows how to deal with it.

Additionally, though lower down in priority, the executives' concern was the possibility that, through widening the circle of confidants, the firm's plans might reach its competitors. The overall dilemma was summed up by Lord Sheppard: 'Basically we share everything. They'll work it out if they're intelligent. If they aren't, they ought to go anyway. . . . There can be a gap between the strategic decision and the implementing of it. We have to keep quiet about companies and businesses that we might sell.'

Another chief executive put the issue starkly: 'I don't like having to lie to senior managers in my own firm.' Other views were almost as troubled: 'You can't reveal your full hand to the world at large—which includes your competition, with whom you may be tussling for control of certain assets, certain markets.' 'When we first developed our strategic vision, we couldn't publish it because people in half our businesses would have seen that they didn't fit. Even now, after selling most of those operations, there are queries about what we might do with some of the present businesses.'

Trying to judge the relative merits of these competing views, three factors stand out in the choice facing the top manager(s).

1. Your choice depends on the nature of the goal. If it is a positive and general aspiration then you can generalize the target and reveal all you can. 'We are going to knock the stuffing out of X, our major competitor' is, like 'Beat Benz', an uplifting way of stirring the animal spirits of the enterprising and raising their sights towards a new horizon. The route to that horizon may not be clear, but at least the prospect is enticing. Furthermore, it causes the organization to ask the questions, How are we going to get there? and What will we need to do? The overall goal makes you look at your competitors closely. A plethora of things immediately come to mind when faced with a dauntingly grand aspiration. Do we have the technology? If we aren't able to match them in the most demanding

markets at present, how can we ever beat them globally? Can we win globally if we aren't even in Japan yet? How much will we need to improve our products and our reputation in order to outstrip our competitors? The questions proliferate and force the organization to face up to its own deficiencies and illusions. The single goal may be exhilarating even though it is a great humbler when trying to turn aspirations into achievements. Sharing that exhilaration is generous as well as sensible. Such is the power of retrospection that many people in the organization will want to be able to claim at some later stage that they were deeply involved and responsible for the changing of the successful firm. As the saying has it 'Success has many fathers; failure is an orphan.'

If, on the other hand, the goal is to shrink the organization—that is, a cost-cutting or defensive move—then you may want to trickle it out to avoid demotivation, abandonment, fatalism, etc. and to see if, after the first stage or two, you still need to go further and if so, still in the same direction. This is particularly apt if you are not sure of the route or the organization's ability to complete the journey—especially if people's jobs are threatened. There can be more openness about the *process* of change. Limiting information is also relevant if you are clear that staff do not possess the required skills and you are not sure that they are up to acquiring them. But the main purpose of trickling out bad news is to sustain optimism and commitment to the organization's health rather than risk staff diverting their attention onto their personal survival strategies. You do not want the best people to leave, but it is often the most enterprising who do so. Nor do you want there to be so many prospective losers that they unite to thwart the strategy. Feeding information out in a controlled way can, provided that it keeps people adequately informed, give management more control over the behaviour of the organization and, if done sensitively, avoid imparting unnecessary stress to staff and customers.

2.   Can you see that far ahead reliably? In a pulsating world, long-term certainties are restricted to death and taxes. Discerning the shape of the world food industry in 15 years time is problematic. If your strategy is to become a major player in that industry, you may know current trends in food production and consumption, but the pattern of supply and demand can change quickly and you cannot know what existing industry assets may be snapped up or disgorged by competitors, nor what inter-govern-mental deals and GATT agreements will do to the shape of the industry. The overall goal can therefore be promulgated, but the exact route cannot, since you can only be explicit as far as you can be confident and you may simply have to tell people only one stage—even if you have a good idea about the second phase. 'You cannot say the end is certain because you cannot see that and you would be a fool to presume that you will not adjust your strategy, and even your goal, in the light of your experiences and any changes in competitive and market conditions.'

3.   The more general the aspiration, the more practicable it is to reveal the overall goal but not the detail, since you may not want to reveal the exact inferences but to leave some hope to all that they may be part of the successful team. To become the most efficient and prosperous retail bank in the country disguises the inference that some branches may have to close and some staff may lose their jobs. The more the organization is likely to change direction, the more sensitive is that news. As Mike Gifford of the Rank Organisation recalled, 'It was clear to me within a year (of taking over) that we should be a leisure and entertainment business. I absolutely wouldn't say that to anyone because I'd have left half the (diverse) Group with thoroughly demoti-vated businesses and the good people would have left. So our stated goals were only financial.'

Following his injection into Coats Viyella from Cadbury-Schweppes, Neville Bain, like other top managers, filtered information both by the sensitivity of the information being shared and the level in the organization at which to share it.

> You share the vision and what's involved in it at different levels. With the board and with your immediate reports, you tell the lot. If they don't understand the direction and the goal you lose a great deal and the management team suffers as well. I have to get that team in place, then I'm cheer-leading. Lower down in the organization people hear things on a need-to-know basis because there's a problem if you tell them the lot and then some bits just don't work. For instance, I had been very open about which businesses would be core and non-core for us, but then I wasn't able to sell some of the non-core businesses at a sensible price. I had the embarrassment of having to retain and fix them.

The key then is to cascade novel thoughts with some care, parading the ideas (which the top manager will already have worked out in skeletal form in his or her mind) via unstructured meetings with a small group of top managers, thus putting the ideas into their minds to get them used to it and to get feedback. The chief executive has to have a clear appreciation of the issues that are likely to be raised at this stage and a mental blueprint of the strategic change outline. The discussions will help that outline to evolve into finer detail. As the process continues (and the top manager must assume that gossip will cause an element of leakage, which may help to persuade others and also help the feedback process), he or she will increasingly want to involve all the key personnel who will support the strategy and guide the implementation: i.e. the skilled specialists who will be an intrinsic input to the initiation stage and others who will be involved or influential in the execution of the plan. Although the top managers cannot successfully delegate the overall leadership role for strategic change, the sheer volume of practical activity and the need to tailor solutions to local conditions means that many other personnel will need to become involved in the implementation process. They will need to be, and feel, involved in the ownership of the process in which they play a significant part.

Even in a high trust situation there will be limits to candour. How trusting will employees be if your predictions constantly turn out to be incorrect? Their confidence in management's capabilities would be eroded if errors are endemic. Having a single goal helps to resolve the dilemma because, except in gruesomely hard times, it will be upliftingly aspirational and general. Additionally, if more than a general goal is needed, but it isn't sensible to announce the core plan, then a statement of values, of what the firm stands for, can be helpful in setting the tone for strategy. Issues about personnel remain the most important and most contentious matter—jobs, roles, rewards, responsibilities, structure, prospects, security. In the early stages of an uncertain change, a high level of confidentiality will be needed and such issues cannot be approached with quite the same level of openness, despite the passionate wish by people to know where they do, and will, stand.

When the situation faced by the firm is threatening, there is a tactical trick (much used in the political world) that is used to affect attitudes. The leakage of an unapproved but authentic document which paints a dreadful picture of prospects is then followed by a denial from the company. When the eventual outcome is not quite so dreadful as the leak, then instead of saying 'Isn't this awful?' people are likely to conclude that it wasn't so bad after all. When British Rail was rumoured to be considering the closure of lots of rail lines, it was able to close a few without concerted resistance. When the BBC was facing job losses from reorganization in 1992, an internal task force prediction of 10 000 job losses was quickly disowned by the management. It will be interesting to see if the reaction is relief when the BBC job losses turn out to be only, say, 7000. That might, after the fright, sound positively soothing and welcome. It is a question of softening people up and getting them to see that their cup is half full rather than half empty. A consultant's draft report can be helpful here because, if the reaction to it is one of fury, the consultant can be disowned and sacked so that there is no lingering presence left to cast a day-to-day gloom over the organization. But the effect remains; the impact has occurred; expectations have been shifted. Like withdrawn evidence in a court case, the memory lingers on.

People will also set off down an uncertain track if they feel that they have no alternative.

> But once they have one, you have to paint a series of 2-3 year visions to keep them satisfied and motivated. The first one or two visions have to be reachable. People want to know where they stand and what they have to do and what is the first priority. If you don't tell them promptly, they'll work out their own version and those who don't like the look of it will begin to head it off. Once you publish the first chapter, people will begin to project the second chapter. As you get into the 3rd year, people have already begun to line up year 4. You may have to advance things and flex the plan to cope with that.
>
> (Geoff Gaines, KPMG)

Once again, the inferences are that it is prudent to have an outline plan for the first few stages and not just for stage one; and that some actionable, achievable first steps will help to build impetus and confidence.

Too much secrecy leads to feelings about 'not levelling with us' and of hidden agendas. Some decisions cannot be fudged and left until later. For example, if two units are to merge and the logic makes that obvious to one and all, it must be clear which of the unit managers is to run the merged unit and what is to happen to the other person. There is a limit to the amount of uncertainty and choice that people can absorb. Managers are used to absorbing much more quick-fire, discordant information than those below them. If the strategic logic indicates that a business is to be sold, the staff's motivation must be helped if the best are not to desert and the remainder to ease up and devote themselves to worry. Bribery may be an answer. When asked how he got such startling performances from the birds in his famous film 'The Birds', Alfred Hitchcock replied: 'We pay them very well.' One organization told the employees of one of its businesses that it intended to sell the operation and promptly put them on performance bonuses to encourage them not to lose heart and to stay and keep the business running well while it negotiated a sale—which included the maintenance of most of their jobs.

A better answer is to be open with employees while

ensuring that those who may become disadvantaged by the changes will be treated honourably. Then candour is less unnerving. It has been said approvingly of one commendably open and supportive chief executive, 'he is open to the point of indiscretion'. The overall conclusion is that you should reveal as much as you can reliably project, depending on whether the vista is appealing or intimidating, for as far ahead as you can, to people as far down the organization as you feel can be entrusted with the information.

FACTOR 6: COMMUNICATION

Effective communication is vital and almost impossible to over-do.

In changing situations, people in organizations often say that communications aren't working, even when they are. British Telecom's Research Centre, evolving as fast as it could into the commercial world from the public sector, found that its technical, specialist managers (not always the people most interested in matters of financial and commercial information) were claiming to be overburdened with popularized information—which they disparaged as 'the comics'—while simultaneously claiming to be 'told nothing'. Although feeling insulted by the simplifications of the considerable amount of written information that was reaching them, the irony was that a few basic questions revealed that they had scarcely a clue about the financial matters that they deigned as being beneath them. In short, they were being given information that they did not appreciate or comprehend.

In that case the specialists were unworldly about financial and trading matters, had received no training, had little innate interest in financial matters, had been offered no intellectual connection between the future of their jobs and their commercial circumstances and were suddenly being asked to become more financially and commercially alert. They were also being communicated with by written material when face-to-face presentations and discussions would have been far more convincing. It is a typical fault that, faced with the need for a rapid improvement in comprehension and commitment, managements veer away from provenly good communication mechanisms rather than gird themselves for a big, time-consuming communications push by executives, and think that videos and leaflets alone can fill the gap as they fail to engage the emotions and intellects of their employees.

This type of error creates ripples far beyond its immediate cost, for it is through the communication process that a management starts to predispose people to change. Those who have not normally been involved in strategy delibera- tions begin to recognize that there may be a need for a change of strategy, but without solid information they lack a sense of ownership or of control over the process, since a failure to communicate just results in rumour, a sense of isolation and a feeling of impotence. If there is a vacuum, rumour will fill it; and rumour is rarely charitable, though sometimes optimistic—which then leads to disappointment. The key communications challenge for managers is that, at a time when they are trying to promote an attractive general view of the future, rising concern causes their subordinates to require explicit and unambiguous detail, often in advance of the supporting decisions being made.

British managers in particular seem uneasy about in- truding into other people's work lives and prefer instead to maintain social distance. Nor do they always know what to say. One top manager admits that he tries not to visit a site where he knows that employees are to be fired because he then finds difficulty in sacking them. It is no wonder that major change is easier to accomplish in high-trust organiza- tions or brutal command companies.

Communications skills help to mould the group.[5] It seems that in building team spirit you cannot communicate too much—with one caveat. There has to be a logical, persuasive, believable, consistent message, which takes us back to the notion of a single goal embedded in a context of guiding principles. Communication within the firm has been aptly described as internal marketing. Since firms try not to neglect marketing outside, there is no good reason for neglecting the inside. The period of strategic change is a testing time. The organization's inhabitants have had their previous assump- tions disconfirmed and are in a vulnerable state until a new, more appropriate vision has been painted to give them heart for the work ahead.

The corollary of the need for a convincing message is that no management should fall into the trap of thinking that communication is helpful, regardless of the message; or that, out of it, will come amity, constructive alliances, understandings and agreements. In an unintended effect, it may confirm each person's worries, criticisms and alienation. As one appalled senior executive complained, 'I hadn't realized how negative our management was until we got together to try to change things.'

Communication is not an untrammelled good. It is always assumed that information is useful, but is it inevitably calming, empowering, liberating? Does it inevitably lead to better, easier, faster decisions? Excessive information may simply immobilize policy implementers with complexity beyond comprehension, options beyond choice and confusion beyond resolution. It is another fallacy of the educated but managerially inexperienced, that people can cope. Many citizens become overloaded, even distraught, when flooded with information. Two key tasks for a manager are, firstly, to identify the valid information and, secondly, to filter and structure it for the less skilled so that they do not become disabled by excessive, unintelligible information—which many managers then describe as 'telling them everything', which patently it is not. Managers cannot just throw down facts and abdicate their own interpretive role. They have a duty to explain matters lucidly, because employees need and deserve that help. Many (but by no means all) people have a high innate capacity for coping with difficult situations, provided that they are offered guidance and support. That guidance and interpretation is, after all, what teachers do. A supply of valid information is vital if people are to make informed judgements.

Managers cannot escape that duty. Despite any desire for self-responsibility and empowerment coming from employees, there are still persistent calls from below for leadership, instruction, specific and unambiguous signals. The idea that everyone wants to be empowered, to be partly responsible for the organization, is dubious. Who, and where, are all those below who are clamouring to be encumbered with all the confusing signals that batter top managements? Instead, you often find lower level employees who presume that management must (i.e. should) know what it is doing and that it is managers—not themselves—who are paid to decide who is to do what. When considering a problem in your own organization, and reflecting on higher paid superiors, can you honestly say that you have never thought: 'Well, that's their problem; let them decide; they wanted the job they've got and that's what they're paid for'?

But do communications have to be so problematic? After all, you hear the call for better communication in every organization. Have you ever known an organization in which the inhabitants declare themselves to be satisfied with internal communications? With all that angst, one might expect organizations to have responded to the challenge, and to know how to do it by now, with expertise, resources and proven mechanisms—even in periods of rapid change. It can be done. The successful merger of Beecham and Smith Kline Beckman has been a classic case of competent integration, aided by the chief executive involving his senior management in the development of the merged firm's strategy and by excellent internal communication. The lesson must be that communication in stressful change situations requires sustained and extensive interpretation and reinforcement. Competent, high-trust firms are in a position to communicate the same basic messages to all levels, from middle management to shopfloor, with nothing left out on the grounds that those below would not understand it. Those at the bottom might not grasp it all immediately and individually; but it is impressive how quickly the collective intelligence of the employee network starts to hum with analyses. Those below can seek guidance from the middle managers. The assumption, as in 'How open to be?' earlier, is that omissions of information have to be justified on grounds of commercial sense and not on a belief that those below won't care and cannot be helped to understand.

But there are still limits to the content of what is communicated. As was discussed above in 'How open to be?', the issue for top management is not whether to delegate that communication process to the lower levels of the organization but how far to share their own fluctuating uncertainties with their subordinates. It is all very well asserting that resourceful and intelligent people will act rationally in the service of the organization and its needs. That can be bunkum. The identity of interest between company and employee is rarely complete. Alarm can readily result from the surfacing of worrisome possibilities, and managements can say all they like about the speculative nature and improbability of some prospects and yet the perturbations in employees' minds will not be assuaged. Not all managements would be sanguine that privileged information would be treated with discretion, and they would be concerned that ideas thrown up for discussion could instead create dismay and reaction.

Consequently, there is an inhibition in many organizations about moving the discussions on possible strategic changes from top to bottom and back, since that would require a high-trust situation. The prospective losers from the touted changes would have to feel very secure not to entrench themselves or look for escape routes when faced with the likelihood of personal loss. Could people up and down the organization discuss the almost-unthinkable without crippling defensiveness? Discussing specific implementation options might reveal implications that top management will wish to conceal from other members of the organization until the options have been further developed, or dropped. Whether those who desire strategic change are seeking allies, mellowing opposition or behaving openly for principled reasons, the release of half-formed thoughts as grist for the organizational debating mill will be a matter of judgement and one that must be consciously addressed when building a model of implementation processes. Hence the dilemma for top management is how widely and freely to hold the strategic debate. The idea, ethically appealing as it is, that strategies can emerge with constructive efficacy from an open organizational debate, will depend markedly on the type of organization, the uplifting or depressing nature of the prospective change, the level of knowing responsibility held by employees and the organization's heritage of candour and trust.

Confident managers take the risk. 'Over-communicate on the action plan, even recognizing some negative trade-offs through unsettling people in parts of the business to be sold off and finding that you don't achieve all points on the action plan' (Neville Bain, Coats Viyella). As Waterman puts it, 'When the life of a unit is threatened ... the only way leaders can make it worse is by not being straight about the trouble (even pretending that things are all right in a hollow effort to protect morale).'[6]

Managerial trust gap

The communication problem is one of getting the strategic message meaningfully down a large and complicated organization. Not only does it have to reach every pocket of the organization with some inspirational appeal, but as it is cascaded down from the top, the top management begins to lose sight of the message, not to mention control of it. The message—even if it is a good one—then reaches the middle layers which, in an internal change, have most to fear (not as in a takeover change, where the middle layers may be the beneficiaries of the liberating flux). If, even worse, the staff have spent many years under the old regime, they are not going to find it easy to adapt to a new strategy. It is scarcely a wonder that middle management can resent and seek to undermine radical change in their working lives. This will happen less for the middle managers who are merely in that grade as they drive upward through a successful career. At the time of the change they still have prospects and ambitions on their way towards the top. The real problem comes for those on a plateau for whom middle management is their pinnacle of achievement. They cannot look forward with delight, or even equanimity, to the changes being set in train.

In the previously stable climate the middle managers knew how to interpret policies; in the new circumstances, with different rules, criteria, goals, vision, values, context, they can become lost, just at the time when their own subordinates are asking for more reliable, more authentic information and interpretation to help their own understanding of the new situation. In such a circumstance, there is high risk that communications will falter unless senior management makes strenuous efforts to augment its normal communication processes. Baxter Healthcare found that its merger needed a single goal to be communicated, which articulated the logic of why it had merged, what it was going to do and the principles on which it would operate, leaving little doubt or misunderstanding about its intent. It then explained its vision of how the organization could pursue performance and higher levels of excellence. Despite these endeavours, an enormous and corrosive information vacuum arose. Baxter Healthcare concluded that communication simply cannot be overdone.[7] As another, more disorderly, organization realized: 'We made the mistake of thinking that when you've told people something once, they must have heard it.'

In poorly organized companies, it is the dislocation of the middle management interpretive links that give the clue to communication failure, as the previous system loses capacity when the normal connections between top and bottom of the organization are weakened under the jolts of changing strategy. The middle layers include those who face career blockages, delayering, perhaps even redundancy, and who are not in a good state to deal with the messages for the future. Now they don't know quite what interpretation to put on the messages being received from above and, simultaneously, fear that they will not be able to cope in the new situation. 'When you're changing your own organization you are clearing out dead wood and its not easy to get the middle managers to help that much if they are the ones who will be going.'

The result is what Judy Lowe[8] has christened 'The Managerial Trust Gap' (Figure 7.1). Just as the manager is less sure of what the information means, and just when his or her own position is threatened and he or she is busy trying to judge and to act under the pressure from above, the manager is being asked for more specific information by anxious underlings who are trying to work out what they should now do and where they stand. The consequence is that the usual supply of authentic, unambiguous information drops owing to the manager's uncertainty, just as the anxious subordinates

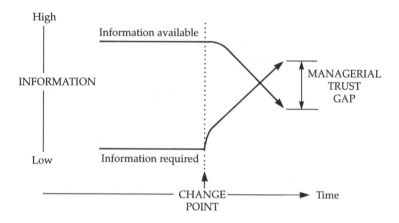

Figure 7.1   *Managerial trust gap*

demand more detail, more reassurance and more explicit information. While top management speeds up, the chivvied middle manager begins to display the white knuckles of the anxious learner driver wondering what to make of the incoming, overloading, signals. The subdued middle managers do not feel confident and, deprived of their normal quota of believable information, their subordinates' trust in them also goes down. If the projected changes are leaked, trailed, deduced or anticipated before any announcement, then the hunger for reassuring information will intensify before the actual announcement is made and a rapid response will be required. You have to move rapidly when cascading information down the organization, because the grapevine works so quickly.

Cascading information down from the top thus runs the risk that reassurance and comprehension may decline—not rise, because top management may be pouring extra information down through the communication channels without realizing that the signal to noise ratio has worsened dramatically. The top management's signal may actually be clear when transmitted, but is heard as noise by the recipients for lack of an interpretive framework that fits the new situation. 'The problem with cascading down the organization is that the person in the middle misinterprets stuff. The middle manager is also being put under more load when the organization is full of flux. People need more reassurance, more information, more comprehension, maps, guides and rules.'

No wonder senior managers then conclude that there is something to be said for bypassing people. Yet management cannot just bypass middle management in order to appeal directly to all staff. That can have superficial appeal in stressful situations, but it also has two chronic disadvantages. Firstly, bypassing demonstrates that the intermediate managers and supervisors do not count, are not well informed and cannot be allowed to brief and debate with subordinates—just when the subordinates are hungry for enlightenment from known and trusted figures. Secondly, faced with being bypassed, those managers and supervisors will become resentful and uncommitted and perturb their subordinates even more as it becomes clear that they don't know what is supposed to be going on either. Their sullen attitude can neutralize all the efforts of the top managers. Bypassing the middle management is only to be contemplated when it is the middle management's defensiveness that is already putting the strategic change at risk. This is why the excessive delayering of an organization at the time of making major changes so often has grim unintended effects as the changes are ill-interpreted by the depleted and jittery ranks of intermediate managers.[9]

A better solution than bypassing is to create dual channel communication which augments, rather than replaces, the normal cascading process. Cascading occurs when the intermediate levels of managers are briefed before they, in turn, become collaborators and brief those below. The managers are given supplementary information so that they can interpret for those below while feeling involved, valued and useful. The other channel is the direct link to and from top to bottom of the organization, in which top managers come to the units, make presentations and answer questions in general meetings that the intermediate managers also attend, having themselves been briefed by the top managers before the meetings.

Direct contact between top and bottom, in all but the most resolutely devolved organizations, is the most evocative way of showing that top management is involved and for top management to obtain feedback. Furthermore, that direct contact will likely be oral, face-to-face, and therefore be communication in a most potent form, because the body language, tone, interchanges and extemporizing all reveal more and make verbal contact highly influential. There are managers who deliberately eschew face-to-face contact for that very reason, but in stressful situations it is braver to face the music. 'It's no good using cascade briefing for these hard messages—the top man just has to get out there and do it himself.'[10]

Face-to-face communication also requires that the top managers listen. This is not always easy, for managers are used to giving information and instructions.

> You have to make listening legitimate so that it is respectable and produces no loss of authority. Lots of managers feel the need to tell people—and the people like that. They say 'Tell me that again. Give me the nuances; let me check it again' so that they can get another bearing on what they already know.
>
> (Geoff Gaines, KPMG)

Face-to-face meetings enable questions and answers to move the debate along quickly as a real transfer of views occurs, particularly in small groups. But that consumes more management time and managers have to be prepared to spend that time or to fully brief more subordinates. When change programmes meet problems, too often changes in the roles of key employees are not clearly defined; nor are key tasks defined in enough detail, and implementation problems are not relayed to top managers expeditiously, while the formulators of the strategic decisions are not active enough in the implementation phase.[11]

In a badly-run company the quality of dialogue is usually poor and this lowers its capacity for effective change when pressure mounts as a result of the poor performance. The better the two-way communication, the more sensitive the listeners, and the easier it will be for the firm's better informed, more trustful personnel to perceive and come to terms with radical possibilities. That will speed up decisions and their implementation. A good management creates opportunities to talk, listen, debate, develop ideas, identify and solve problems and to use the networks of contacts to progress the firm's strategies. Open debate also helps to get to the heart of what is to be achieved, rather than just fine-tuning the existing habits. Extensive lateral communication is also vital in transforming an organization's practices.

A competent management cannot evade the needs (a) to show that top management is involved, committed to the changes and listening to feedback and (b) to reassure, involve and support the intermediate layers of managers and supervisors so that they neither feel neglected nor look like ill-informed fools to their subordinates. There is no ducking the huge amount of effort that goes into a satisfactory communications programme.

REFERENCES

1. E. Margarit and A. Margarit (eds), *Isaiah Berlin; A Celebration*. University of Chicago Press, 1991.
2. Charles Hampden-Turner, *Charting the Corporate Mind: From Dilemma to Strategy*. Blackwell, 1990; also published as *Charting the Corporate Mind: Graphic Solutions to Business Conflict*, Free Press, New York, 1990.
3. Richard T. Pascale, *Managing on the Edge*, Viking, 1990, pp. 51–87.
4. M. de Boeuf, *The Greatest Management Principle in the World*. Berkley, New York, 1989.
5. D.L. Barton, and W.A. Kraus, Implementing new technology. *Harvard Business Review*, November–December 1985, pp. 102–10.
6. Robert H. Waterman, *The Renewal Factor: Building and Maintaining Your Company's Competitive Edge*. Bantam, 1988, p. 108.
7. Vernon R. Loucks, Strategy and organisational learning. Strategic Management Society Conference, San Francisco, October 1989.
8. Judy Lowe, Making change programmes work. Strategic Management Society Conference, London, October 1992.
9. Tony Eccles, Delayering myths and mezzanine management. *Long Range Planning*, **25** (4), September 1992.
10. Quoted in Kinsley Lord, *Making Change Happen*, published by Kinsley Lord, London, 1992.
11. Larry D. Alexander, Successfully implementing strategic decisions. *Long Range Planning*, **18** (3), June 1985, p. 95.

8 Leadership and capabilities

- Factor 7: The rule of proportionate responsibility
- Factor 8: The limitations of empowerment

FACTOR 7: THE RULE OF PROPORTIONATE RESPONSIBILITY

The more senior you are, the more responsibility you must take.

These dilemmas—how open to be; what management should and shouldn't communicate; how much unity is needed—all lead to the great divide in current management thinking about the way a management should behave. On the one hand, there is the view that involvement, participation, empowerment, team-working, cultural harmony and autonomy must be utilized, with the management acting as facilitators, guides, coaches, cheer-leaders and auditors of the efforts of employees and ever sensitive to the delicate psyches of staff. Management in this vision is all about process, culture, togetherness. It might be called 'Happy Families'.

The other vision, heavily influencing this text, is that managers have to be robust, responsible, ready to set an example and to fill any embryonic leadership vacuum. They cannot abdicate their role as controllers, leaders and risk appraisers and any attempt to offload significant responsibility onto employees is escapism. Empowerment is a case in point. Much lauded in political circles, a cynical definition of empowerment in the political domain is 'what you proclaim when you decide to dump the problem back onto the sufferers because you don't want to spend any money'. You then 'empower' the disadvantaged to solve their own enduring problems. It is a reminder of a scene in a political satire of the Thatcher era in which the actress playing the Prime Minister harangued the audience for their inadequacies, gradually pulled herself back under control, softened her voice, moved to the footlights and, to a roaring, immediate laugh of complete recognition, purred to the audience 'And remember. Whatever happens—it's your fault'.[1] In business organizations, the top management cannot run away from responsibility so brazenly. The chief executive may want the employees to be involved in product development, efficiency raising and to use all their capabilities. But the employees still don't run the company. The chief executive does.

People at the top generally do not arrive there solely by luck or by chance, nor even by hard work unconnected to talent. As Lord Weinstock has said: 'In theory empowerment is feasible. It's the least strain for the chief executive if everyone else is doing all the work. But it's patent rubbish. Do all the people who have got to the top arrive there by fate and accident?' This is the nub of the matter. Those at the top should have a broader and more strategic view, more experience, superior judgement, a developed sense of anticipation and better managing and coordinating capabilities. Otherwise the organization is saying that its management selection, appraisal and promotion systems are useless and that, rather than attempt any succession planning, it might as well buy a random number generator.

Managers are there, and often well paid, to take responsibility; to coordinate, judge, decide and guide. Supporters of power-sharing say 'you can't just tell people what to do'. But who claims that one *just* tells people what to do? It would be equally naive to proffer the opposite and say 'you should never tell people what to do'. The pretence that having a hierarchy of power must require an autocratic 'command and control' administration does no service to our thinking about the effective practice of management. Nor is hierarchy the same as bureaucracy. GEC has a clear hierarchy, but it makes decisions very quickly and informally when needed. Western firms are endlessly urged to flatten hierarchies to deal with turbulent environments, yet Japanese firms operate successfully in those turbulent environments despite having much steeper hierarchies.

The idea that a good manager merely orchestrates the endeavours of his or her personnel finds no more favour with Lord Weinstock:

> There are conductors and conductors. Some will stand in front of the orchestra waving the stick and beating time approximately. An undiscriminating public will give it a rapturous reception—depending on the publicity from the recording company. The great conductor will say what he wants and instruct and guide the instrumentalists. He'll stop again and again in rehearsal until he gets it right. Over the years they build up a relationship and how good the conductor is depends on the ambience, the stimuli, how good the players are, how he helps them to develop, how much commitment he shows and how much care he takes—as well as his talent.

The belief that an organization is a team of equals gives no credit to superior talent. In a 'one person, one vote' election system, the equal voters choose the administration. But the elected group then appoints managers and runs the administration; the voters don't. The religious belief that everyone has something to offer does not claim that the offers are of equal usefulness, even if a meagre contribution is of equal human merit when it is the best that an individual can manage. Everyone may have something to offer, but some are remarkably good at concealment.

The question is: Where, on a spectrum from domination to facilitation, should a management stand to run the organization to best effect? For example, it is said that the top cannot know enough to prioritize. Try telling a leading R&D-based company like Glaxo that it cannot (as it does) prioritize research from the top. Akio Morita, chairman of Sony, was equally clear:

> The innovation process does not begin by bubbling up from the research and development laboratory, or from brainstorming sessions with product planners. The innovation process begins

with a mandate which must be set at the highest levels of the corporation by identifying goals and priorities: and once identified, these must be communicated all the way down the line.

Mike Walsh, CEO of Tenneco, claimed that

> At the end of the day it (radical change) comes down to relentless leadership from the top, in which the CEO makes himself personally vulnerable at more points than you can keep track of.[2]

The key point to bear in mind is that teams can work well in hierarchies. The current fashion for opposing, even polarizing, teams and hierarchies is not at all helpful. Teams may jointly set goals, but who guides the team, draws attention to benchmarks of progress, maintains a sense of purpose and direction, orchestrates choice and evaluates the performance of team members? Evaluation by peers gives little weight to a good leader's better judgement, and peer group evaluations are not always constructive.

Teams are not as egalitarian as imagined; they develop pecking orders even in egalitarian organizations. Hierarchy is not destroyed, particularly when team members have roles outside the teams. As John Ricatelli, CEO of Wilson Sporting Goods, plaintively put it

> It's a dogma. Everyone now talks as though we all have to be in teams; that teams are productive beyond all other ways of working. If you destroy power structures, perhaps teams are necessary, but why destroy things if they work? Hard-driving individuals can achieve a lot, so is the belief in teams justified? We need to understand when teams do and don't work.

Involving everyone in the team may not help the decision process. Sharing decisions is not guaranteed to produce the optimal result if a radical change is needed rather than an adjustment within existing mind-sets. Hage claimed that the participation of a large number of individuals in the decision-making process is likely to dampen both the radicalism of the innovation and the speed with which changes are introduced.[3] Many others have drawn attention to the trade-off between participation and speed of decision. It takes time to get people at all levels to spot what the most alert and wide-visioned personnel have realized. The delays that arise with participation can only be justified if the longer decision time is offset by faster introduction of change by more knowledgeable or better motivated workers. If there is high trust in management and appropriate worker skills, then rapid agreement can be reached, but few organizations are in that laudable state, and the lower the level of employee skill or expertise, the less the demand for, or value of, participation in strategic decisions.[4] Hage considered that managerially driven organizations can introduce radical innovations speedily if the dominant coalition places emphasis on its goal and is positively oriented and committed towards change and innovation.[5]

Senior managers cannot easily escape from responsibility even if they have delegated authority and empowered their staffs. Ideas, unless they are actually subversive, are often escalated up the organization quite quickly because of the desire on the part of their initiators to gain the plaudits of those above for showing enterprise, originality, energy and commitment.

There is another reason for the escalation of proposals. The junior employees are also pushing the responsibility upwards as they seek backing for what they have suggested, both from the patronage of more powerful people in the organization and through using their seniors' access to resources in order to progress their ideas. A partnership between those below and the senior management is highly desirable because 'top management knows the direction; those below know the terrain'.[6] Of course, the junior personnel want credit for their inventiveness and to retain an element of ownership. But they—often politically experienced within the organization, and with the scars to prove it—know the old rule that responsibility for activities varies directly (though not necessarily linearly) with the seniority of the people who were involved: the rule of proportionate responsibility. Admittedly, this can lead to ludicrous situations such as the director general of the BBC being deemed to be its editor-in-chief and ultimately responsible for every single programme that is broadcast by the corporation. Cabinet Ministers are supposedly responsible for all happenings in their department. That they usually refuse to resign when some débâcle occurs is due partly to their brazening out the scandal, and partly because they can scarcely be held responsible for every single event—particularly when civil servants are past masters at the old game of 'he was informed, but not told' in which information is passed under the nose of the Minister, but in a camouflaged way so that he or she does not spot its significance. Nevertheless, senior people normally bear disproportionate responsibility for events that occur within their managerial territory.

Issues also have to be orchestrated in the political domain of the company. Resourceful personnel know only too well that a lot can depend on the power of those who raise the issues, their status, and how the issues get the attention of those powerful opinion formers and resource controllers and brokers. The top manager becomes inveigled into responsibility by those below. Patronage, power and responsibility go together. Child[7] and Pettigrew[8] have written extensively about the politics of organizational decision-taking, where the personal agendas of the top people influence the firm's actions; and about the market for attention in which top managers choose which initiatives to back and which to ignore as they select from the myriad requests for their backing and sponsorship. Much nonsense was written by lesser academics in the 1970s about boards of directors 'rubber-stamping' decisions at board meetings, because the observers saw only the board meetings, and so their observations failed to capture the subtle, extensive, informal negotiations that preceded them. Those pre-meeting manoeuvres occur in order to test the climate, to get the top people on board, to work through and trim, or neutralize, their objections. The board decision then becomes a final stamp of approval rather than a debating arena. Predecision negotiations make the managerial decision process quite subtle.

The jobs of managers may be complicated, but their responsibility is crystal clear. We should be sceptical about top managers who claim to delegate their authority to the point where they have become mere orchestrators. Senior management cannot just leave it to those below, no matter how willing, how skilled, how hard-working are the employees. The relevance of hierarchy will vary. A clear hierarchy of authority should be much better for saving the crew of a sinking ship, while innovative and creative work will progress better with minimal hierarchy. Even in empowered organizations, managers remain in charge. Both the team and its sponsoring manager need to 'own' the project, the task, the responsibility—whether it be for inventory, forecasting or information systems—in order to avoid an absence of ownership or a multiplicity of separate 'owners' tripping over each other. The team and its sponsor need sufficient slack time to perform the ownership role, as they think, develop, extend, refine, persuade, problem-solve and act to progress their work. In the case of radical strategic change, if managers do not take full responsibility, they cannot expect those below to carry them forward in the absence of managerial leadership. There is little choice but to lead from the front, and good managers willingly accept that focal role. All of the senior executives who were interviewed were utterly clear about their leadership responsibility, and the idea that good management happens by some delegated, natural process in the absence of leadership was not one of their assumptions or working rules.

FACTOR 8: THE LIMITATIONS OF EMPOWERMENT

Even enterprising employees need to be led.

The question to ask is how much responsibility the manager should, and could, disperse to those lower in the operation. Unless the omens are favourable, it may not be practicable to disperse much—certainly in the area of strategically sensitive matters—despite the overblown rhetoric of empowerment. 'Empowerment' has become a vogue word for the process of encouraging employees, including managers, to utilize their skills and experience more by giving them the power to use more judgement and discretion in their work. At its best, empowerment provides employees with enough authority, resources and latitude to be able to work effectively in the service of the organization.

But is empowerment in practice much more than delegation revisited, a new word for normal process improvement, a rematching of authority and responsibility in an era when customizing of products and services requires that discretion must be available at all levels, down to the customer-facing staff? Empowerment has not become fashionable through any moral imperative about enfolding employees in the schemes of the company; nor is it a response to higher values of democracy. Motives are instrumental rather than heroic, as managements respond calculatively to the needs of the business as they realize that their employees have immense, if incoherently organized and underused, insights and experiences. To inflate these factors into a grandiose crusade of power redistribution does little service to the merits of empowerment because, in practice, its limitations are often all too obvious.

Despite its appeal, delegation of power can be famously trivial. A major retail chain encourages its store teams to show initiative and responsibility. But they cannot alter prices, product specifications, decor, fittings, or initiate promotions at store levels and have virtually no say over the product range or the items that are stocked in the store. What initiative means is that, if they see hot weather approaching, they should order more sandals, sandwiches and soft drinks. All that they are empowered to do is to carry out the closely specified task with maximum responsiveness to given signals, with minimal discretion in their consequent actions. They simply have to keep things going, using minor discretions to pacify complaining customers and to tweak store operations ever more efficiently.

Similarly, the much vaunted 'Workout' programme at GE resulted in such supposedly noteworthy items as the moving of factory pipes so that product no longer spilt onto the floor and in persuading a manager to open closed windows to ventilate an over-hot workspace.[9] In neither case could the employees do those things without managerial authority. More interesting were suggestions to adopt a cheaper in-house design of protective shield, source paint from one not two suppliers to reduce inconsistency, and to connect cash registers to speed up the opening of new customer accounts. Again, the employees were not empowered to do anything but only to recommend. Decision and resource power remained firmly with management. The only alteration was that, with 'Workout', the responsibility for the burden of proof shifted, so that rather than the employees needing to prove their case, the decision onus lay on the manager, who could only kill the idea by explicit rejection. Yet it was still the manager's decision and the employees remained supplicants.

These examples remind us that much of empowerment is ordinary commonsense activity and simply resurrects recognizable past fashions in a new guise. The suggestion schemes that were favoured 30 years ago have been revived as a way of tapping workers' direct experience at the sharp end of the organization where products and services are made and delivered. Similarly, job enrichment, touted some 25 years ago as the route to capturing workers' latent skills in the service of the organization, and then sidelined as having insufficient productive effect, is once again recommended as another aspect of empowerment. Those who advocated worker participation 15 years ago as the route to harmony and productivity at work—only to see the appeal of *mutuality* (as power sharing was christened) crumble under the impact of free market economics and the unremitting hostility of Anglo-Saxon managements—can be permitted a wry smile. Now, as a branch of empowerment, it is deemed to be a prospective salvation for companies that are struggling to compete with fierce international competition.

These three elements (suggestion schemes, job enrichment and worker participation) have been repackaged to form a spectrum of empowerment for service companies by Bowen and Lawler in a three-part range consisting of 'suggestion involvement', 'job involvement' and 'high involvement'.[10]

Suggestion involvement

'Suggestion involvement' is akin to the suggestion scheme examples already quoted. Employees propose, but the management disposes. Ideas come from employees and management decides whether to adopt them. Empowerment in this mode is quite close to the Japanese technique of Kaizen: the continuous, everyday, small-step improvements in all aspects of a business, which encourages everyone to get involved in improving every day. An example would be the training of operators to carry out self-maintenance of equipment rather than wait for the attentions of specialists with elaborate maintenance routines. Employees' suggestions emanate from the context of their current jobs, though in terms of logical incrementalism the cumulative effect might have strategic connotations.[11] Kaizen's approach is one of problem-solving and management's job is to provide structure, systems, resources and control and planning functions for the people to add value.[12] The people do not do as they like, do not operate in a vacuum and suggestions have to be accepted by the firm before they can be actioned. Kaizen could be summarized as 'Policy down and micro-solutions up'.

Kaizen may be prevalent in advanced Japanese companies but there is a huge gap to be straddled by Western firms, as the following examples indicate. A few years ago, a group of senior executives of a medium-sized Western electronics company were being addressed by an industrial specialist lately on the staff of a Western Embassy in Tokyo. Did their firm have suggestion schemes, he asked, and if so, how many suggestions did they receive in a year? Yes, they replied; hundreds of ideas were proposed, some being implemented. How many suggestions did they think Hitachi got from 80 000 personnel, he asked? They guessed at between 5000 and 100 000. Last year, he told them, it was 4.15 million—an average of one suggestion per employee per week. There was a stunned silence. Then the executives recovered and began to fight back against the inference of this riveting news. 'Bet some of the ideas weren't any good,' they claimed. 'Bet some of them were the same.' 'Bet management had already thought of some of them.' 'Bet some of them were only put forward in order to look good' (as though that was an offence). He nodded each time and let them go on before eventually responding: 'Listen. You can slice up 4.15 million several times and it is still a very large number.' They agreed, gradually coming to terms with the implications, though little action ensued (that firm was later taken over after several more years of lacklustre performance). Similarly, Garratt wrote of another Japanese company which implements 5000 staff suggestions per day, or 1.25 million per year.[13] Toyota has been reported as receiving 2 million suggestions in 1992 from its 108 000 staff, 85 per cent of which were implemented.

The transfixing question that arises is not about the bald number of suggestions—daunting as that is—but the issue of process. How could a company actually deal with the effect of such a torrent of ideas? Who would consider and action them all? Clearly not the management, for it would have no time for anything else. The answers are that the suggestions could only be assessed and actioned at the level of first-line supervision, unless the employees were given the licence to implement their own suggestions without reference to even their supervisor. How else could you deal with 5000 to 16 000 ideas each working day?

This leads to the next question. How many Western companies are geared up with supervisors and employees capable and empowered to deal with such work at that intensity? Why would opening some closed vents in GE ever get to the level where a manager had to consider and adjudicate on such a minor problem? These examples reveal just how adrift Western companies can be from believing that suggestion involvement is all they need to have. Tom Peters has claimed that companies in which there is empowerment have dramatically higher rates of employee suggestions. But do they have anything more? In order to gain the advantages from employee involvement, there would have to be a fundamental shift in managerial power, communications, working practices and assumptions for companies to obtain and leverage the latent expertise embedded in employees' experiences and judgements—which is what GE has been seeking to do, but it faces a monumental task.

That such a shift would be fruitful is not in doubt. The Japanese companies that have relied on the triple thrusts of cost reduction, quality enhancement and product innovation have been greatly helped through harnessing the intelligence underpinning the vast numbers of suggestions and the worker commitment that lies behind them. Not only have many Japanese companies taken employees and their suggestions seriously; they have fostered a managerial climate in which Kaizen has flourished. They encourage shop-floor managers to solicit ideas by judging the managers on the number and quality of suggestions that are implemented. Some Western companies have embraced these notions in theory; in some cases, such as Xerox, they have sought to put them into practice; but the limited extent to which suggestion involvement has become second nature is worrying. Empowerment will not get far if suggestions are not sought and taken seriously.

Job involvement

The second category was that of 'job involvement' in which job responsibilities are enriched and team work is encouraged, all within the framework of the tasks that are to be performed. Employees have some autonomy over how the job is to be done, but not much freedom to choose what to do. Typically, that discretion is quite limited. It may encompass giving a complaining customer a benefit or deciding whether a customer request is reasonable to meet, but empowerment is often simply giving employees some autonomy over limited fluctuations in their work and improving their immediate working collaborations. In *Building the Empowered Organisation*,[14] all the examples quoted are of people, typically in multifunction teams, improving the performance of their existing operational tasks, not of redesigning what the task should be or of deciding anything strategic. Usually, what is being saved is time or manpower, with a resulting cost decrease. In less favourable experiences, workers below the level of team leader are more likely to reserve their positions, withhold their full commitment and retain traditional non-managerial perspectives. If there is a risk-averse culture, then people will be reluctant to take initiatives that could leave them open to castigation.

Yet, as with suggestion involvement, job involvement has great potential for enhancing productivity and quality through finding better ways of organizing and carrying out tasks. The managerial commitment needs to be of open communication, team-building, high-quality conflict resolution systems, openness to new ideas, candid debate, budgets for explorations and experiments and a general managerial willingness to relinquish some of the command and control impositions that shape a traditional administration.

High involvement

The third empowerment category was that of 'high involvement', which is akin to 'job involvement' but goes further in that employees participate in work-unit decisions. To do this effectively they need to have more open information, business and team skills. These high-involvement schemes, wrote Bowen and Lawler, are as yet uncertain in their feasibility or in their effect on the performance of the organization.

With a restricted focus on participation at work-unit level, this is still light-years away from having those employees become involved in the company's strategy. There is this odd idea among empowerment zealots that a workforce can only be motivated and committed if its members have perched on the chief executive's shoulders, so to speak, and become intimately involved and knowledgeable about the firm's strategy. It must be disappointing to those who peddle this line that many employees wish for nothing of the kind and would simply prefer to be told what the company's goals are, how it intends to pursue those goals, what that means for them and their jobs and what, in consequence, they will be required to do and how it will be measured and rewarded. In short, there are large numbers of employees who might be flattered to be taken into the firm's confidence but feel no more than a cosy glow of voyeurism, almost unrelated to their specific jobs.

The growth of professional practices and the influence of collegial gatherings, such as academic groups, has led observers who inhabit those domains to believe that the whole world already works like that. Or shortly will. Yet there are employees who cannot count; some cannot read, and a few cannot even organize their private lives with any marked degree of sophistication. These limitations may not be their fault, but they do not help the cause of empowerment.

In 1985, at a Motorola plant in Illinois that had an experienced and productive workforce, the employees were given a test which average 12-year-olds should pass. Questions included 'What percentage of 100 is 10?'. Sixty per cent of employees failed the test. [Aghast at the discovery, Motorola promptly launched a major drive to educate its personnel.] Similarly, the state telephone company in Illinois found that 11 out of 12 school leavers failed its entrance test, involving basic sentence construction and skills such that they could converse with a customer in explaining a bill, itemize charges or look up data in a basic data resources document.[15]

The US government's 1993 'Adult Literacy in America Report' found that as many as 44 million Americans could not calculate simple sums or find an intersection on a street map. A further 50 million could not use a calculator or understand a bus timetable, even though half had completed high school and at least 15 per cent were college graduates. The report concluded that nearly half of America's 191 million adults can scarcely function in a complex modern society.[16] The transition from a Taylorian task-specified world employing unskilled people to a world with complex jobs reserved for capable people will, if we do not train unskilled people better, steadily disempower them clean out of any hope of entering the workforce.

Yet, in the 1970s, it was thought that worker participation held the key to fruitful partnership between workers and managers, although many managements were sceptical, even hostile, to the idea of sharing power and tended to talk of involvement rather than participation in decision-taking. In Britain, unions implausibly sought power at the strategic level in firms, while rejecting the idea that they should then share responsibility for the decisions that they would jointly make.[17] If the 'power without responsibility' that they sought was, in Stanley Baldwin's cutting phrase 'the role of the harlot throughout the ages' (he was talking of popular newspapers at the time), it was not surprising that employers were less than ecstatic about worker participation. Much of the talk about worker participation abated as recession and rising unemployment clipped the bargaining power of workers and as the conflicts of interest for organized labour became more obvious. Yet, as economies have become more open, the last decade has seen major alterations in the attitudes of trade unions as the growth of international competitive pressures has curtailed their chances of controlling events in any one economy, and as rivalries and self-interest have prevented any effective cross-border alliances between unions. Their acceptance of competitive markets has led to radically revised assumptions about the nature of the world of work.

Given these changed attitudes and circumstances, a resurgence of managerial interest in high involvement is not surprising, though high involvement is usually couched as sharing work-unit decisions and does not involve joint corporate decision-making. But is there any sign that managements are willing to hand over much power to lower level employees? And if they did, would it help? The assumption underlying worker participation and high involvement is that the resulting decisions and activities will be of higher quality, and less likely to be contested, than if management specifies the rules that must be followed. The participative solution to a problem, be that modest or strategic, may be different but should be better—for three reasons: firstly, the lower level employee will be better able to gauge what should be done; secondly, that he or she will be better motivated than if merely carrying out procedures designated by management; thirdly, lower level employees are closer to the customer. This raises a number of questions.

The local perspective

Many organizational experts are convinced that with wider ownership of solutions, change becomes easier and solutions to problems more appropriate. But will the different solution be superior? It may be technically inferior, more parochial, though probably easier to achieve. One fundamental assumption about management hierarchies is that, the higher your position in the organization, the wider and wiser is your perspective. The lower level employee may be more familiar with the detail of the problem being faced, but more ignorant of the subtleties of the problem, more self-interested in the shape of the outcome, more short-sighted about its effects, and more unlikely to come to a considered view. A persistent complaint from corporate managements that hold discussions about performance with the employees of units is the blinkered perspective; and as one human resources director bemoaned: 'In three years of taking our corporate results road show round each of our units, we have never had a single observation or question about the Group. All the questions were about their own unit.'

A further problem with delegating power to lower levels is that a micro-decision made parochially by an empowered employee can have costly consequences if it impacts adversely on another part of the organization. No one who has run a factory will be unfamiliar with the costly nuisance of trying to produce a non-standard, unexpected, short-order product promised to a customer by a salesperson who was trying to be helpful. A car company that empowers factory production workers may not be grateful if the ensuing extra output cannot be sold, despite marketing's best efforts. Job-empowered workers will not necessarily spot the costs of the extra inventory and stock obsolescence that will result.

Yet without an irretrievable (in the short term) handing over of discretion and autonomy, empowerment will be just hollow; not necessarily a conscious hoax by senior managers upon those they seek to 'empower' below them, but a self-deception in which responsibility is down-loaded on to less senior personnel, while the real autonomy that would enable them to 'own' their empowered jobs is withheld. The power would remain with the person who authorized the empowerment. Employees can sense when they, and their managers, are disempowered. One particularly bitter labour dispute was noted for middle management's use of 'the magic phone'—that is, the phone calls made to senior management when the middle management had no discretion to agree a demand. In the end, the disgruntled employees simply refused to deal with them and insisted, successfully, on dealing direct with senior management. Soon after the dispute the middle managers joined a trade union and themselves united to negotiate with the company. They had become lost to management through being disempowered.

From studying Japanese management in Britain, Delbridge *et al.*[18] have claimed that total quality management (TQM) is meant to 'empower' workers to police their own performance but not set their own goals or target levels, and that this really means a management goal of 'total management control' because of 'increased surveillance and monitoring of workers' activities . . . heightened responsibility and accountability, the harnessing of peer pressure within "teams" . . . pushing back the frontiers of control . . . such that any gains made by workers are noticed and appropriated (by the firm)'. Tom Peters pointed out that flat organizations may have more control through rapid feedback, high deadline pressure and the criticisms of workers' colleagues about lax behaviour. These particular views may not be wholly persuasive, but they do illustrate the scepticism that excessive claims about empowerment can evoke.

The opposite of having power without responsibility is to be given responsibility without power—the role of the scapegoat throughout the ages. At its worst, this is just delegating blame. The dilemma for a management is where to set the limits of autonomy. As Hayek wrote, 'Freedom is a matter of choosing the right kind of constraints.' To solve this dilemma, Waterman recommended a combination of direction and empowerment so that guidelines and parameters are set by management.[19] In short, empowered workers have to be orchestrated by management. The orchestration might take the form of a phased release of power and discretion. For employees to be empowered, they have to 'earn' the right to the next level of self-responsibility; i.e. they have to show that they deserve and can be entrusted with it. Effective empowerment is thus delivered through a combination of power release and responsibility, with measurable performance criteria to gauge the effects. Empowered employees need managerial support rather than being offered fine phrases and then left to get on with it.

If facilitation and support were all that is needed from top management, and if the exercise of power and authority is so inappropriate, why haven't the shareholders sacked all the top managers of General Motors and replaced them with behavioural scientists? Would Ford be better run by a group of psychotherapists? One suspects not. And if top managers merely orchestrate the work of others, exercise no greater judgement and have no more responsibility for what happens, then why are they paid so much more than the average manager, let alone the average employee? Why aren't management jobs rotated round all employees if no more skill is needed to lead than to be led? The usual reason given to justify high managerial pay is that managers have high responsibility and high impact on performance.

An abdication of managerial responsibility is not practicable and, while empowerment should induce employees to own certain domains of problem-solving, it is not the same as handing over the organization to all its inhabitants. There would be a risk that people would believe that autonomy was complete, as expressed by workers' responses when being castigated for their behaviour in a worker cooperative: 'But we can do what we like; we're a cooperative.'[20] As another manager defined the general issue:

> Empowerment is not total freedom. It is freedom within a football pitch—the goal is still where it was and the rules are basically the same. Some people have felt that the pitch has been abandoned and that they are free agents with no rules and the terrain is up to themselves. Empowerment can become a way of life if you can unleash people's energies in a controlled way.

There are circumstances in which empowerment, like delegation, is difficult to arrange. A government department supplying statutory services will want its customer-facing staff to be consistent in the application of specified rules. Discretion in the provision of public services can be risky and lead to anomalies, rule drift and recrimination as initiatives become embedded as new practices. Charities, too, have a wide range of stakeholder constituencies, including government, general public, media, volunteers and donors, quite apart from the normal ones of staff, trustees and clients. Most actions by a charity will require at least tacit approval from these different groups, which means that strategic changes are more likely to be planned and negotiated than opportunistic. Such procedural requirements inhibit empowerment in practice.[21] Nor will a multiple-outlet firm, such as McDonald's, want product or service discrepancies between outlets.

If even the empowering of employees in a straightforward commercial firm does not remove many of management's traditional tasks of mediating both within the organization and with the outside world of customers and suppliers, then is the game worth the candle? Despite the overblown rhetoric of empowerment, the unequivocal answer is, yes. The need for involvement has intensified. The reasons for this are clear. It is a long time since Henry Ford said 'any colour you like as long as it's black'. Now, with 30 000 different specifications available for a BMW 3 series car and 12 000 000 (yes, 12 million) variants in a Japanese bicycle maker's range, the idea of customized products and services within a low-cost production system is well established. But how then do you organize to ensure flexible responses within the production system and how do you treat special requests that cross the boundary between what is proffered by the supplier and what is demanded by the general customer? Some latitude must be given both within the firm and to the customer-facing staff. With the growth of service economies, the number of staff who meet customers has risen, for service is often face-to-face or voice-to-voice. The socially unskilled or undertrained are then handicapped in the search for employment; previously they could be given tightly specified tasks and could hold down necessary manual jobs in factories, with no requirement to meet a customer.

Now organizations are more likely to need bright, personable, well-trained and knowledgeable staff, confident and able to use discretion in making speedy judgements often under pressure from demanding customers. It is just as well that we are trying to improve educational standards and information systems in order to create a more capable populace—which is particularly valuable in service businesses where junior staff not only meet customers but deliver the service. It is at the frontier of the service organization that knowledge and flexibility are required, with the lower level employee knowing enough to agree or decline to meet particular requests. Similarly, in factories, employees need to be able to interrelate in ways not required when closely specified tasks were performed in Taylorian style by narrowly focused specialist workers. Multi-skilling and teamworking requires interpersonal skills and the use of judgement in uncertain circumstances.

Drucker[22] is less persuaded of this need and makes the distinction between knowledge workers and 'employees who work in subordinate and menial occupations' who, he wrote, may see little change in their work from empowerment. It is the knowledge workers who may need enhanced autonomy to sustain their motivation, he claimed, because 'they cannot be supervised effectively. Unless they know more about their specialty than anybody else in the organization, they are basically useless.'[23]

There is a snag in Drucker's distinction. If Garratt is right, there may eventually be only four bands of people in organizations of the future: directors, managers, supervisors and customer-facing staff.[24] This last group must contain many of the people whose work Drucker sees as changing little as a result of empowerment. Yet it is precisely there that flexibility is required, certainly in service industries. The need to respond to immediate, face-to-face, customer demands for unanticipated service activities, requires knowledge, confidence, judgement, discretion and autonomy. The three 'menial' examples he gives are of supermarket sales clerk, hospital cleaner and delivery truck driver. But all of these serve customers face-to-face and need some discretion to do their jobs well. As one senior service industry manager stated: 'Empowerment is natural and necessary for customer-facing organizations.' These 'menial' jobs may have considerable potential; for instance, the delivery driver may become a goods merchandiser and salesperson at his or her delivery points. The question is how to achieve those potential gains.

Building capabilities

The task for organizations is formidable. Not only is there a competitive and customer-driven need to be more efficient and more responsive, but employees can be sceptical as well as reluctant to take on more responsibility. As one firm put it, 'there is a demand from below for empowerment before you give it, but then the demand evaporates when you do'; one would suggest that this may be because they have been given responsibility without much guidance or power. Yet employees hold priceless information as well as being in a key position in the effective delivery of outputs to customers. Empowerment provides a context to tap the value of their expertise and experience. Like an oil field, it is a matter of accessing it to raise the yield and the rate of extraction.

The conclusion would surely be that a gentle and protracted switch to an empowerment style would be sensible where management has the luxury, or foresight, to begin the process before a crisis arrives. The reason is that there is a hierarchy for empowerment. If the organization does not have suggestion involvement at shopfloor level, then how can it move to job involvement when still lacking the basic mechanisms of continuous improvement? Such a firm might be able to introduce job involvement at team-leader level and above because managers are more used to cross-functional liaisons, but its chance of doing so at operator level would surely be bleak. And without job involvement, could the organization move further to high involvement?

The qualms about empowerment's implications are not constrained to the shopfloor but also extend to middle management. Changing the (previously successful) habits learned over many years is not easy and 'the more you devolve, the more those in the middle need to know what those above them want. It's a big jump from top to bottom and there is fear at all levels.' It can be a tricky task for management to help people begin to feel embedded confidently in a new order. Working out new behaviours at levels unused to much autonomy can be painful and take a long time, so management must coax and guide the process.

If, at the same time, the organization has been delayered, there are fewer experienced intermediate managers to decode the signals and fit them into the organization's new framework.[25]

An organization can only afford to cull the layers of middle management if it has already devolved responsibility to those below that level and provided the support that makes empowerment and high involvement meaningful.[26] Otherwise, except in the case of bloated bureaucracies, a depletion of middle management's ranks will initially weaken rather than strengthen the firm.

It would seem that *high involvement* normally relates strongly to top management, *job involvement* to middle management, technical and professional staff and *suggestion involvement* to supervisors, technical and ordinary staff—with some job involvement also in work teams. A gauge of the extent of an empowerment power shift is whether it changes the organization's agenda or whether it changes the organization's decision processes and criteria. What happens when empowered employees want to do something with which the management fundamentally disagrees? A test of meaningful empowerment might be how much employees can decide *what* they do rather than just *how* they carry out (specified) tasks. Perhaps empowerment can only work when a powerful management is confident enough of its grip on the organization that it can devolve some power in order to hasten the implementation of its own overall policies. The best new thing about empowerment is the word *empowerment*, which is so positive that it has enabled managers to embrace old, well-known, more productive ways of managing that had previously languished. Tapping workers' talents for improving their own work still leaves management to cope with the dilemmas, boundary management issues, service level dilemmas, etc. Empowerment is a useful tool; it is not a panacea for managerial deficiencies.

Top managers frequently espouse the notion of empowerment. You can scarcely open an annual report or listen to a conference speech by a top corporate executive without being told that people are a huge, underutilized resource; and on go the platitudes, well meant but essentially vacuous unless translated into tangible practices. Some firms are getting there but many have scarcely started. A good test to put to a pontificating manager is to ask: How many suggestions does the firm get from its non-managerial employees? And from its customers and suppliers? How are they processed? Who decides which are to be actioned? How quickly? What are the rewards and prizes publicized and presented to the out-standingly meritorious generators of good ideas? While asking these questions, watch the body language of the executive. Too many respondents will display signs of embarrassment.

Fashions recur in organizations. Worker involvement in the 1970s; tough leaders in the 1980s; empowerment and teams in the early 1990s. The pendulum swings from a concern for the flowering of the individual to concentration on the performance of the collective. Each cycle attempts to find the best mixture and, as we learn more about organizations, each compromise gets that little bit better, a little closer to appropriateness for the situation. We should cherish the tensions as helping us to learn how better to manage. So what should a management *do* to maximize the leverage at its disposal?

REFERENCES

1. John Wells, Anyone for Denis? Whitehall Theatre, London, 1981.
2. Jacqueline M. Graves, Leaders of corporate change, *Fortune*, 14 December 1992, pp. 92–3.
3. Jerald Hage, *Theories of Organisations: Form, Process and Transformation*. Wiley, 1980, p. 193.
4. Hage, *op. cit.*, p. 99.
5. Hage, *op. cit.*, pp. 186 and 193.
6. Arnold S. Judson, *Making Strategy Happen*. Blackwell, 1990, p. 27.
7. John Child, *Organisation: A Guide to Problems and Practice*. Harper and Row, 1984.
8. Andrew M. Pettigrew, *The Politics of Organisational Decision-Making*, Tavistock, 1973.
9. *Fortune*, 12 August 1991, p. 19.
10. David E. Bowen and Edward E. Lawler III, The empowerment of service workers: what, why, how, and when. *Sloan Management Review*, Spring 1992, p. 31.

11. James Brian Quinn, Strategies for Change. Irwin, 1980.
12. *Industrial Management*, June 1992, p. 14.
13. Bob Garratt, *Creating a Learning Organisation*, Director Books, 1990, p. 72.
14. Kinsley Lord, *Building the Empowered Organisation*. Kinsley Lord, London, 1992.
15. The Money Programme. BBC, 17 January 1993.
16. *The Times*, 10 September 1993.
17. Tony Eccles, Industrial democracy and organisational change. *Personnel Review*, **6** (2), 1977.
18. Rick Delbridge, Peter Turnbull and Barry Wilkinson, Pushing back the frontiers. *New Technology, Work and Employment*, **7** (2), Summer 1992.
19. Robert H. Waterman, *The Renewal Factor: Building and Maintaining Your Company's Competitive Edge*. Bantam, 1988, p. xiii.
20. Tony Eccles, *Under New Management'*. Pan, 1981, p. 135.
21. Natasha Owen, Unpublished MBA Report, London Business School, June 1993.
22. Peter Drucker, The new society of organisations. *Harvard Business Review*, September–October 1992, p. 100.
23. Drucker, *op. cit.*, p. 101.
24. Bob Garratt, *op. cit.*, p. 63.
25. Tony Eccles, De-layering myths and mezzanine management. *Long Range Planning*, **25** (4), September 1992.
26. Edward E. Lawler III, *The Ultimate Advantage: Creating the High-Involvement Organization*. Jossey Bass, 1992.

9 Capabilities and structure

- Factor 9: Teams and leaders
- Factor 10: Structure and culture

Without the skills and confidence, neither the empowered nor their managers will be able to progress; indeed, if badly initiated, matters might worsen. Preparation is vital. Interpersonal and team operating skills, the understanding of data, specification of the ground rules and the conflict resolution mechanisms, improvements in communication and the spreading of information through the organization—will all need attention before empowerment has much of a chance.

It follows that, in order to gain the best effects from empowerment, three accompanying things are needed. Firstly, multifaceted teams are required to enhance coordination within and between functions and departments. Team work is habitually a feature of empowerment programmes that go beyond suggestion involvement to job involvement. Team-building is also a common feature of suggestion involvement, for example, in total quality management. Even with work-unit teams, the limited perspectives of lower level employees make it unlikely that a sizeable organization could make speedy, radical shifts in strategy or behaviour without overloading the empowerment structures and processes. Employees who face radical change tend to expect their managements to give an unequivocal lead and to define the policies that are to be introduced. Empowerment seems much more suited for the improvement of efficiency through incremental change in a relatively stable, non-radical circumstance.

Secondly, the top management needs to set up steering groups of senior and middle managers to guide the teams in order to give these managers a pride of ownership and a commitment to the teams' findings and proposals. This also reduces the chance that senior or middle management will disown or ignore the teams' findings or proposals. The top managers have the self-esteem of having orchestrated the changes; the senior and middle management can feel good about being involved and responsible. Thirdly, management needs to coordinate between teams and to specify the limits of acceptable action beyond which empowered employees cannot go without management clearance. The scope of a team's authority and responsibility must be agreed if frustration and dissent are not to occur, otherwise much energy will be wasted in establishing whether or not the centre's blessing was required for the action that is being contested.

The locus of power remains tilted towards management even when significant discretions are given to employees. It is worth remembering this when managements become captivated by the more exotic possibilities of empowerment—which absorbs within it an enticing but fallacious assumption. The fallacy is that in an organization there is a lump of power that is divided up and can only be redistributed. But power is not subject to Newtonian laws for its existence. Power can be created and destroyed. A key question is whether the act of empowering employees diminishes the capabilities of the organization or, alternatively, stimulates purposeful enterprise and vitality. The bulk of evidence is that it stimulates fruitful endeavour—provided that factions do not run self-interestedly amok. Much success can be engendered through helping employees, particularly front-line employees, to develop their own solutions to work-unit business problems, thus tapping the talents of the staff more effectively than do traditional styles of management. This is what happened at the highly successful joint venture between General Motors and Toyota in California, where workers have been given strong support in the form of training and consultation. Small worker teams analyse their own work in meticulous detail and, through controlling their detailed actions, raise their motivation, their cohesion and their productivity. The factory staff are there not to control, it is said, but to support the workers. But the teams are not encouraged to improvise the carefully worked out assembly procedures or to share the running of the plant.[1]

The suggestion here is that the six principal factors which determine whether the management should incline towards enfolding all their employees in a mutually agreed plan or towards powering ahead on its own are

- the organization's heritage of trust
- the relevant experience of strategic change available within the organization
- the urgency and scale of the change needed
- the type of organization and the markets it serves
- the skills and open attitudes of staff
- the power available to the chairman and/or chief executive and the mandate they hold for action.

Democracy is not always welcome

The choice of intervention style depends on the available time, skills, resources and power. Obviously there would be an inclination towards involving employees where trust is high, experience of relevant change is substantial, confidence and capabilities are good, the scale and urgency is such that there is time to have employees participate and the organization is in markets in which changes are normal. If, on the other hand, there is an urgent need for major change in an organization that has inadequate trust, little experience of change, and is in an industry that is unused to change, then a powerful chief executive will be needed to provide incisive and strong leadership in time to pull the organization into shape. In that situation, an injected leader would be expected to act decisively and his or her invocation of democratic processes would be seen by the new subordinates as demonstrating a lack of determination and vision. People need to be reassured that the leader is completely *au fait* with the situation— preferably to the point where he or she can quickly tell them if they still have jobs or not and what those jobs are.

The goal in both types of approach—involving or assertive—is to arouse followers via uplifting, transformational leadership so that talented employees accept the new strategy as a consequence of their knowing judgement.[2] But that goal cannot always be reached. This is where a great divide affects the way a management approaches strategic change. In the case of Takeover change and Injection change, dissatisfaction with existing performance lies behind the introduction of a new regime. The focus will be on creating winners, initial acts, galvanizing the climate and changing the structure. Owing to those pressures there probably will not be time to build a wholly voluntary consensus. The stakes are so high and time sufficiently short that negotiations and persuasion would flounder. Instead, steps have to be taken to ensure compliance, moderated by a desire to create the maximum impetus that won't be incessantly contested. Of course the chief executive will want the support of the employees, for there is little point in dominating if a resentful staff simply acquiesce sullenly. The executive will want to create winners, to demonstrate early successes and to sweep up staff into an enthusiastic and committed set of actions. But he or she cannot afford to cajole everyone, or to be patient for long about resistance caused by self-interest or incomprehension. Once satisfied that a sensible aversion to the planned changes is not being overlooked, he or she will have to countenance casualties.

In a stable circumstance, relatively unthreatened by outside forces, the management will focus on team-working, empowerment and 'stroking the culture'. This will be particularly evident in Partnership change where the power of the leader is limited and the professional employees have great autonomy. Where there is time to diffuse the issues, and where there are professionals who need to be persuaded, a weak power structure and distributed technical expertise, then a more involving approach won't be merely desirable, but inevitable. This may also be apt for Renovation change and Succession change when there is no vivid threat to existing stabilities. Meeting competitive demands through gradual improvement is an attractive, low-stress policy, though it would be a lucky, and happy, organization that managed to evolve at the needed rate via continuous, low-cost, low-stress transition. Where there is a competitive threat, a vigorous, leadership-driven change process will be the most effective way forward for Succession and Renovation change too. But whether the leaders push or cajole, the role of teams is vital.

FACTOR 9: TEAMS AND LEADERS

Good teams and good leaders support each other.

There are some general adages about teams in strategic change that appear to help in a wide variety of circumstances. This next is not a section on the detailed operation of teams. There are plenty of good books on how to build and run effective teams.[3,4] What follows is concerned with the rationale of developing and using teams as part of strategic change in the organization.

Building the top team

The first team to be tackled is the top team. This has already been discussed under 'Confusion on the board' in Chapter 4, which concluded that the top team must be, and must be seen to be, sufficiently united that backing for the strategic change will be sustained and is not likely to be undermined by disunity and squabbling, or by the top managers running for cover when the plan is put under stress—as it will be. The board's unity has to be matched by an obvious commitment to implement—perhaps being restructured itself in order to do so. As one executive put it: 'It wasn't until we made some changes in board membership that people realized the changes were for real'.[5]

Even at the top there will be awkward periods while people come to terms with the seriousness and scope of the changes that face them. Typically, an agenda is worked out by the chief executive for use at an extended, off-site discussion by the company's key personnel. That discussion should be discursive, not to encourage rambling debate but to give time for free expression of concerns and to let people absorb the new possibilities. It is not practical to force or bounce people into changing their mind-sets by proceeding with undue haste, particularly if their initial attitudes vary from complete support to wary cynicism. The amount of time and effort that will be required to get a strategy agreed will depend on numerous factors. These include such items as the degree of confidence that the other decision makers have in the chief executive, how much power is centralized, the risk of the strategy, its confidentiality, whether it is controversial, whether it will require significant internal or external realignments, the size of the organization, the number of decision makers who should be involved and the environment—political, economic and competitive.

Enfolding the participants: layered involvement

The top team will want to enfold as many factions in the business as is feasible into understanding, refining and backing the strategic plan. It is important to judge the level of agreement that would be necessary before residual objectors can be bypassed, faced down or removed from positions of influence. Because there will be a diverse set of groups and interests, this agreement must at least amount to a sufficient convergence among the functions, departments and sites in the organization to carry the day. Some of those groups may have little direct part to play in the development of the strategy, but be crucial to its being carried out effectively. They are part of the critical mass which, if not assembled, will never ignite.

If individual and group commitment is the key to successful implementation and employees' adaptability and willing involvement are needed, then as many as practicable have to be part of the decision process too. There will need to be a cascading sequence of layered involvement; first involving the board, then the board members' direct reports, then down thought the firm layer by layer. Much will depend on the information system and the top managers' willingness to actively seek and listen to feedback. Too many managers only want to hear good news and so they filter out bad news. They think that they are listening, but patently they are not. Not all objections to plans are the result of intransigence or wistfulness for old habits.

An important benefit from this involvement process is that it gives senior management (particularly those new to the organization) information about who are in favour of the changes, who seem good at their jobs, who understand the firm's competitive challenge and which departments and units are well managed and well motivated. A further benefit is that the cascading down of involvement in decision-making can enhance the practical strengths of top management's power by making it easier to implement the decisions effectively and expeditiously. In each case the cascading process is aided by forming teams to undertake elements of the planning and endorsement processes that the change will involve. Whether the teams orchestrate communications campaigns, or under- take investigations, or assemble resources, or draw up new guidelines and procedures—they can be designed to incorpo- rate people in the process and help to gain the commitment of others towards the strategic goal. Teams of people who have complementary skills should perform better if they can unite for a common purpose and hold themselves mutually respon- sible for the achievement of team goals. That requires that their team cohesion and their remit from their functions should transcend the competing claims of their normal functional loyalties.[6] The ideal condition is one where every function gains from the team cooperation and has something to lose if the team's work fails. The team can also become inspired by a clarion call from above.

Everybody builds up their own job. When you form a totally new division or you form a new team, you do it semi- consciously by persuading everybody, or allowing them to persuade themselves, that the job they're going to do is bigger than the one thay have got and that is why they went to do it. You may or may not need to pay more salary, but if you say 'I want you to do this and this and this', they get very excited. They build it up their own imagination.

(Sir Alastair Morton, co-chairman, Eurotunnel)

There will be at least three kinds of team below the board. The first will consist of teams at the existing units, be they sites, departments or businesses within the enterprise, each with its existing arrangements and each trying to improve to best effect in the new circumstances, using inputs from all factions in the unit. While each unit's management team works out its micro-strategy, the empowerment processes of suggestion involvement and, perhaps, job involvement can be fostered further down in the unit, thus enhancing two-way communication as well as encouraging progress on raising efficiency. The task for each unit team will be to shape the necessary changes, render them palatable and to strive to implement them with optimum effect. Because they are all in the same unit, provided that there are not too strong a set of competing matrix links in the organization, they all have the same objective. Familiar with each other and the existing situation of their unit, they are united—even if only in adversity.

The second kind of team will consist of new teams formed as part of the restructuring and reorientation being intro-duced to fit the strategic change. As with the first type, these new teams should be formed to look at how their area will function within the overall strategy and what the implica-tions would be for other areas. Teams will largely be composed of managers and specialists and have the brief to introduce new ways of working. Their early task will be to get a grip of the new situation and unite among themselves behind an agreed task.

Third will be teams which can be multifunctional, multi-disciplinary, cross-site, multilevel teams formed either tem-porarily, like task forces to tackle specific issues, or permanently because the changing firm requires new arrangements. People's lateral cooperation is vital if the organization is to be able to leverage strategy across units, functions and sites and to generate an integrated set of strategic changes. This is typically what happens when revising processes through 'business process re-engineering', or redesigning the work processes to make them more appropriate in an age of information systems.[7] Teams composed of people from different functions and departments will work better if the team members can 'deliver' their function or department and commit it to supporting the team's decisions. This requires team members to be respected in their own domains and they must constantly report back to their departmental colleagues and persuade them of the merits of the specifics of the strategic changes if the team is to be fully productive in its work. Teams also need sponsorship from heavyweight executives. Where re-engineering projects fail to deliver performance improvements, a lack of sustained and committed attention by senior managers is a material cause of that failure.[8]

With teams, there is always a potential for conflict. The very fact that the team needs to contain complementary skills in order to carry out its remit can breed alternative perspectives and engender conflict, though multifunctional teams are good for developing their members' general management skills. A further difficulty is that the fashion for personal performance incentives runs counter to the need for team cohesion and cross-functional cooperation.[9] Divisive incentive schemes may need to be suspended, bought out or worked round to diminish their adverse impact on the team cooperation that is now required. A key question in shaping the context of teamwork is: Does this help cooperation and progress towards the goal?

The more that management can set challenging, but achievable, targets based on existing abilities and can target tangible organizational benefits, the more likely that the middle managers will support the changes. One leader came unstuck through ignoring this adage: 'I made the classic mistake of confronting people with the weaknesses of their position and by inference themselves, instead of identifying and building on their strengths. Having realised this, I tried to make everyone feel that they could be winners, so that if the firm won, they would win too.'[10]

The general mission

To hold the organization and the teams together in the early stages it is helpful to have a relatively bland but unambiguous mission, such as 'we want to become the best middle-sized retail bank in France', so that all in the bank can agree the goal. More controversial consequences can then be introduced when a broad groundswell of support has been engendered and the teams have created some proposals that fit the thrust of the strategic plan. Drawing people into the general thrust of a strategy makes it difficult for them to object later if the specific proposals can be shown to be in line with the strategy—which they have already agreed. An aim should be to introduce any contentious initiatives in a form that makes objection difficult. Who could possibly disagree with aims of improving efficiency, enhancing customer service, raising quality, etc., except by showing that the specific plan wouldn't work and by proffering a better way?

This stepped sequence of change will help to concentrate energy and to lead people to the point of no return, where it is less constructive to turn back than to go forward. The leaders will want to create a vision of a logical future which illuminates the required steps and builds, to the maximum, on present capabilities and resources.

During implementation, as in the planning that preceded it, it is helpful to have extensive informal contact between departments and other groups in order to test ideas, to obtain feedback, to look for joint interests, to handle overlaps and gaps and to agree tentative timescales for benchmarks and target points. This should minimize the number of formal meetings and reduce the number of coordinating committees. However, there should still be quasi-ritualistic meetings in order to signal specific agreements and to review progress. This will not only have a positive effect on progress but commit those who would otherwise later say that they weren't consulted and had never agreed to the plan. Forcing people to put up or shut up is a necessary political precaution.

Building enthusiastic cohesion can be done by bringing teams together, having unifying events in which they present their implementation plans so that good ideas are transferred, mutual learning helped and each team's ideas are improved. Such events also allow those affected in other parts of the organization to add further support. This should be done early in the implementation process and again at intervals so that incompatibilities do not have the chance to become entrenched obstacles.

Avoiding over-control

One of the odd features of empowerment programmes that have accompanied the delayering of middle management is that the delayered organization is often subject to tighter central controls than were in force under the previous hierarchy. Partly this has been due to the growth of information management systems. It has also been due to management's unease about letting go of the reins.

> Paradoxically, an institution can foster individual hustle only when it adopts a centralised system to measure profitability and determine whether people are focussing on the right businesses, products, and customers. When managers can compare and monitor the money-making success of businesses and customers, they will happily delegate responsibility. Those who can't, become defensive and bureaucratic.[11]

Furthermore, the top management cannot supervise every single item.[12] Quite apart from the impossibility of one manager having a finger in every pie, if the leader is too autocratic and wants to orchestrate everything, that disempowers everyone else. If the centre too strongly controls the process, commitment from the remainder of the management will droop.[13] Managers need to resist the temptation to intervene, overmanage, overreact, and protect the team from responsibility. Instead they need to become better listeners, facilitators and coaches without abdicating their managerial responsibility.[14] The motto should be 'avoid meddling unless there is going to be a major mistake'.

The successful manager stays above the detail until needing to dive into it, constantly alert to signals from below.

> It's a matter of getting up above and staying up above. But it's in the top group or top person's head that this goes on, it's not in Committees and things. If you get dragged down into the day-

to-day, you lose your way (it is not a question of delegating because you have to be able to cope with the day-to-day or you won't understand why some things aren't working) but suddenly something triggers a lot of interest. That's the instinct of the entrepreneur or the manager, the antennae some call it. Sensing that there is a problem, observing that something isn't happening, starting to pay attention in however much detail it takes, right down to the clause in Paragraph 2, subsection 7, Part P.

(Sir Alastair Morton, co-chairman, Eurotunnel)

Hence, the management should set staged, overall specific targets and must resist the temptation to create endless lists of micro-targets. Leaving the teams some discretion means that managers won't have to keep check on endless elements one by one, and the staged targets help to give a sense of achievement as each target is reached and its achievement recognized and applauded by those above. Diffidence about delving into the detail dissolves a paradox for managers, for

if I want lower level employees to have more autonomy and responsibility in making decisions—how can I tell them how to implement? If they want to change my strategy, that's fine as long as it doesn't cost a lot in efficiency and it is a sensible alteration which helps the strategy to work. I would only resist if it went outside my chosen arena in terms of fundamental goals. I will lay down the framework and then let them find their best ways of implementing the strategy. But if I direct everything— why should they care whether it works or not?

The other merit of letting teams construct alternative change activities is that it subtly eliminates the option of not changing at all.

Keeping out of the detail also conserves top management's judgemental role for deciding on contentious matters. The more that senior management gets sucked into trivia, the less it will be able to arbitrate when deadlock occurs. Fussing around in the detail denudes a manager of that magisterial detachment that can be needed when arguments become strained. The manager should be enthusiastic, committed, provide guidance and support, but not get embroiled in the entrails of every debate. The general adage is that if you are going to give a team an agenda and let it work out the consequences for itself, then it needs to be a very good agenda. Again, that puts load back onto the senior managers to get the strategic remit properly worked out among themselves before launching it on those below.

FACTOR 10: STRUCTURE AND CULTURE

Use structure to change culture.

One failed endeavour in the writing of this book has been the attempt to avoid mentioning culture. It is an overworked word that has become a kind of sociological black box or dustbin into which is dumped almost any ill-defined element of the mistier aspects of organizations. It is not that culture lacks meaning when applied to commercial organizations, but as an aid to comprehension it muddies as much as it clarifies by the very breadth of its application to organizational life. It has also drifted in meaning from its earlier connotation of civilized refinement, and its antonym would no longer be barbarity but the absence of customs and conventions. Not one of the top managers who were interviewed mentioned it except in passing. Instead, they talked of restructuring and of changing behaviour.

The recent concentration on culture also reflects a fashion as well as a set of beliefs. The 1960s view was that structural changes in organizations should swiftly follow changes in strategy if performance was not to decline, which led to the belief that both strategy and structure should be changed together in order to avoid handicapping the organization in its drive for greater performance.[15] There was then a mercifully brief period in which whimsical observers claimed that structure was little more than an abstract construct and that what was important was the *process* of managing rather than any anchoring foundations of organizational structure. This was odd because it was often the same people who were concerned about contextual and situational factors, though strangely, structure was not usually deemed to be one of them. The consequence was what Chris Lorenz called 'the exaggerated view of some business academics that really good managers can make almost any structure work'.[16] Perhaps they can; but it isn't difficult to find evidence that a badly constructed organization will set manager against manager, department against department, business against business, company against customers. The amusing beer industry exercise in Peter Senge's book *The Fifth Discipline* shows that even intelligent people, each acting rationally within a destabilizing positive feedback system, will make a complete mess of the overall task when their information systems and job responsibilities are badly structured.[17]

Structure is not just about organization charts, as its dafter critics assert. It covers individual and departmental responsibilities at every level in the company, whether these be expressed as accountabilities, responsibilities, task descriptions, work flows, administrative processes, reward criteria, promotion habits, departmental boundaries and separations, coordination mechanisms, etc. Business process re-engineering is frequently a restructuring of the firm.[18]

The structure of a company is the way in which responsibilities are assigned, jobs are delineated, reporting relationships are determined and interactions shaped, both formally and informally. The organization's structure is a function of purpose; the way people and other assets are organized to carry out their tasks and the way those tasks are integrated into a coherent and efficient whole. It is an important element in the control and behaviour of the organization. As Sir Winston Churchill said, 'First we shape our structures and then they shape us.' It might be more accurate to define process as 'STRUCTURE IN ACTION'.

Structure is used to arrange and distribute power in the organization. Departments, and people, are rendered more or less powerful as a result of reconfiguring the company structure, altering tasks and roles, specifying relationships and processes, channelling communications and allocating stewardship over assets and resources. Structure is a device for predicting, shaping and controlling behaviour in organizations.

We reorganized so that the functional departments, which had been jeering and fighting with each other, just had to cooperate across the whole business because we made that the basis of reward. People only got promoted in their own function if the other functions concurred. The functional managers were furious because it took away their patronage and reduced their hold on their own people. They then tried to collude to not interfere in each other's patch, but they couldn't, given the pressures of the market-place—which was what had made cooperation sensible. That was why we did it. And it worked.

A firm's structure is, of course, an aspect of its culture, a manifestation of its assumptions about how the organization should and does work. Structure and culture are not independent of each other, but structure is a more tangible matter than some other aspects of culture. Changing the organization's structure has three merits. It has highly visible consequences which demonstrate change; it can make a substantial difference to behaviour as the self-interested adjust to the new arrangements and, in an organization with centralized power, it can be done without much delay. Comparable effects can be achieved from changing reporting systems and performance measures, but those changes are not so obvious to the wider audience of employees and the top management may want to shake up the organization to a greater degree. 'My management mentor said, change makes people think. So change something for everybody every two years, even if it's only moving their office; keep people used to change and to querying their own habits.'

Restructuring typically announces a change in the company's direction, its thrust, its priorities. IBM restructured its flagging personal computer operations in September 1992; the changing IBM culture simply could not have delivered better results without that rearrangement, along with the restructuring of the whole company into 13 business groups. 'What we've begun here is far more than a restructuring, we are changing the culture of IBM and changing it very quickly' said IBM's then chairman.[19] In July 1993 his successor shifted the power structure away from regional and country management towards the global product groups, insisting that these should have dedicated, not shared, resources in each country in which they operated. Outsiders might disagree that IBM has been doing enough to change appropriately but, given the difficulty of changing attitudes, it is evident that the restructuring forced the firm into a new position much more quickly than an attempt to change values or attitudes would have done. This again raises the question about the short-term immovability of a company's culture. The argument here is that you can shift the culture rapidly by acting on the structure, rewards and accountabilities if the situation is dire enough, if the top management has enough power and the will to use it, and if there is a decent cushion for those who have to change—or who have to go.

It should have been no surprise that Digital Equipment, faced with similar problems to IBM, needed to change at the end of 1992. Did it mount a culture change campaign? Did it seek to modify attitudes as the route to renewal? It did not. It reorganized into nine business units: five marketing groups (health; discrete manufacturing and defence; communications, education and entertainment; consumer and process manufacturing; financial, professional and public services) and four development and manufacturing groups (personal computers; components and peripherals; storage; multi-vendor customer services). The reorganization followed swiftly on the retirement of DEC's founder and the installation of a new president and CEO. A Succession change altered the rules of the game. New attitudes and a more market-oriented culture were expected to ensue. The change was not just symbolic (though that was important in showing that the old regime was over), but was deeply and incisively action-oriented. DEC could not afford to wait, hoping that people would eventually get the message of their own accord—thought doubtless DEC included many employees who could read the writing on the market wall. Taking people along with you voluntarily usually takes a lot longer. And it is a fortunate company that has that time and the foresight to initiate a new culture long before it is needed.

Procter and Gamble told its employees in December 1992 that it would be reviewing its operations world wide in order to make the group more efficient and competitive via a 'worldwide project to review work processes and structure . . . to ensure that the organizational structure is matched to the needs of the marketplace'. It did not attempt to alter the culture first; instead it set up a committee to analyse the group's structure and then draw up detailed recommendations. Apple Computers also restructured itself in the summer of 1993 in the wake of its falling profit margins. Merrill Lynch turned itself round in the late 1980s, largely by the use of changed reward criteria and reward structures.

Structure counts. It shows where resources are and who has access and control. A change of structure can boot an organization towards improvements. Being booted isn't comfortable, but it can work quite well and quickly if the underlying logic is sensible, by clearing obstructions and strengthening the forces that will help the strategic changes to work. As Geoff Gaines of KPMG has said:

> Changing the organizational structure doesn't drive strategy— but if you announce what the organization will look like at the end, there is no point in people going on as if the old structure will still be there. So people begin to act in that knowledge; they start to build new alliances, see new rivals and their attitudes and relationships evolve quickly as the smarter people make their new dispositions to get themselves into a strong position for what they can now see is likely.

Changes in markets lead to the need for some organizational evolution. Restructuring helps a company to shape, galvanize and control that evolution. Conversely, structural failures embed competitive disadvantages. One major international bank separated the careers of its domestic and international managers. When the globalizing of financial services required that the two divisions cooperate, not only did they resent that, but each had little understanding of or sympathy for the other. Only when the chairman restructured careers and organizational links to reward those who had experience in, and empathy for, both activities did the bank manage to mingle the separate careers. Some managers hated it and left; those who stayed made it a great success. The actual mingling took years; the changes in attitude and behaviour did not. Once the aspiring managers had realized that the changes were serious, cooperation ensued rapidly.

You may not be able to create growth directly by changing the structure, but the structure may not be conducive to growth and may simply inhibit improvements in performance.

Not only does a change in structure lead to changed behaviour, but it also affects the dynamics of the management. 'The young managers do change their views when the new structure is announced. It is an opportunity for them and it dislodges some of the frozen elements of the old structure. The middle managers with existing power positions find it more difficult' (Mike Heron of Unilever). How a company structures itself helps to reflect and determine how it sees its world. A company that believes that all its national markets are different will structure itself with independent, self-standing national units; a firm that believes that its customers are part of one undifferentiated global market is far more likely to have a global structure that allows little in the way of local quirks, except those needed to cope with local social and legislative features.

The problem arises when a company wants both the flexibility of local responsiveness and the economies of global integration and so needs a dualistic organization. Much has been written about such organizational dilemmas, building on Lawrence and Lorsch's classic study, which concentrated on the endless tension between the need for differentiation of the elements of an organization and the need for integration of those elements.[20] As these authors pointed out, the need for differentiation and integration varies, depending on whether the tasks are operational or strategic, and the choice can depend on functions, markets and technology. The choice may lead to the complexity of a matrix or multidimensional system, which means that the structure cannot be unambiguously precise. But that is no reason, or excuse, to pretend that structure is superfluous. When people are appointed to posts, they typically want to know about their place in the formal and informal structure as well as about the softer elements of organizational life which feature in its 'cultural web'.[21]

Structure is therefore important; it should be a deliberate choice of posture to divide up and coordinate tasks, given the organization's goals, capabilities and activities. Structure is a facilitating feature which enables, or restrains, people in the ways that they work together. It is also a signal of linkages, criteria, power and assumptions. To be sure, the people in key positions make a difference and breathe life into it but, as Sir Michael Angus said when co-chairman of Unilever, 'Structure is never as flexible as you think.' There are limits to the range of sensible choices that are appropriate for any given organization and, while structure does not wholly determine behaviour, it encourages certain forms of behaviour to flourish which, if the organization is well structured, will help it to pursue its goals more readily.

Miller and Friesen found that organizations pattern themselves into configurations of strategy and structure that best fit their particular domain or environmental niche—just as you would expect of any intelligent organization.[22] As Lord Sheppard commented:

> You have to keep an organization refreshed and relevant to the market place. Our global IDV drinks company has been fundamentally reshaped three times in ten years. It has been done smoothly, methodically, quickly and with good communication—the last time in the Autumn of 1991. The critical thing in any structure is to have flexibility and to evolve an organization to fit its markets.

Mike Bett of BT concurred:

> You need integrity in the sense that all the bits of the company fit together. So you say, we'd better put the power base where it should be. The structure becomes important. Get it wrong and there are problems. That's why the top group is important. You need to be able to rely on them behaving the same way so that the strategy is robust. It is important to avoid chaos and so it's vital to have the leaders thinking the same way.

Restructuring is also an important weapon in the picking of winners and in recapturing (or marginalizing) losers. In implementing a new strategy you need to structure the organization in a way that promotes the implementation decisions, so you need to involve people whose resistance or whose passivity will scupper the scheme; to reward those who implement and to provide encouragements for those who facilitate understanding and get the message across. Top managers' actions and perceived commitment and serious-ness about implementing strategy are important because they provide a clear signal to subordinate managers who can intensify or deplete their own commitment in the light of the signals received from above. An example would be the changing relative importance of engineering and marketing functions in the major US automobile manufacturers. One also restructures if the existing organizational and control systems have become inappropriate for the new tasks. A switch from a low-cost leadership strategy to a goal of high innovation will demand reconstruction of the firm's architec-ture.

This all puts a powerful question mark against the attitude change programmes that have affected organizations in the late 1980s. Organizational culture can be defined as a pattern of beliefs and expectations shared by members of an organization that produces rules for behaviour—norms—that shape the behaviour of individuals and groups in the organization.[23] More concisely, Sir Michael Angus has defined it as 'the way people behave when they are not really thinking about it'. Yet the evidence is that shifting attitudes takes much effort and time. If the organization is in a hurry, that may not be the most obvious place to start.

In the argument about the relative importance of culture, the chicken and egg concern has been whether you could alter behaviour and performance without first having a cultural change, or whether the culture changes when you make organizational alterations. As soon as you pose the dilemma, the answer becomes clear. How could you change the culture while the work goes on as before in an unchanged organization? Changing the culture in order to change the strategy is like an exercise in metaphysics and does not seem to be a sensible approach. In the absence of a driving force—a need to change, which cannot be ignored—why should the culture change? What, to the organization's inhabitants, would be the point of adopting different beliefs if there is no apparent goal apart from that of changing for change's sake? Why would the staff of British Telecom have become market and customer sensitive if they were not to be launched into a competitive market but were to continue as a public sector monopoly?

Lorsch has argued that strategic change always involves culture change.[24] It is undoubtedly true that the culture will change as the strategic shift unfolds, but changing the culture before the strategic drive is a time-consuming and suboptimal method. As others have pointed out, you cannot build new competences on an old, unchanged system.[25] Peter Drucker pointed out that culture is largely dictated by the organization's task, be it a transport company or a school, and there is little mileage in trying to change the organization's culture before altering the tasks of the people in it.[26] This emphasizes again the merits of structure and rewards as levers for affecting behaviour, followed by attitude and culture. Only when the existing culture is so inimical to any fruitful change in structure, reward and control systems and performance criteria should an organization embark on a culture change programme as its first initiative. That might be the case in a partnership organization where, if the people don't support and agree with the changes, nothing different can be done. Yet even there a subtle restructuring can lead to significant attitudes and behavioural shifts.

In the worlds of health and education, as well as in business, it is only when the rules, funding and competitive circumstances are about to change that people normally see and become involved in major cultural shifts. Changing shared values is arguably the most complex and least understood type of change, because most managements know so little about the shared values and how much they are shared. It seems axiomatic that changing the culture of an organization has to be an accompaniment to other changes. Changing a culture without an evident purpose and without some incentives seems to be an unlikely route for transformation.

In contrast, the idea that you cannot change behaviour and performance by altering structure is manifestly untrue. Change a reporting relationship and you change the power structure, the career structure, the information channels, the informal and network relationships and perhaps the performance criteria. Change the applauded, rewarded behaviour

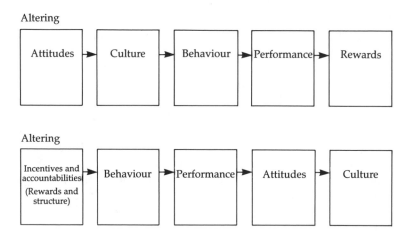

Figure 9.1 *Change sequence*

and people's behaviour and attitudes will adjust, often very quickly. Empirical evidence shows that changing organizational behaviour changes attitudes more than vice versa.[27] The behaviour component of culture (how people act in given circumstances) is much more amenable to alteration through incentives than the value component that underpins people's deeper attitudes.[28]

Instead, many 'culture change' advocates have believed that the effective change sequence is as shown in the upper line of Figure 9.1 because it involves people more and attempts to dissolve, rather than overcome, resistance. But resistance may be minimized only after much (expensive) time has elapsed and, even then, may only have been reduced at the cost of adopting a low common denominator of agreed action.[29] By contrast, the evidence of speedy but effective change is that the sequence is as in the lower line of Figure 9.1 and is not such an imposition as is commonly feared. If the new incentives, accountabilities, rewards and structure are sensible, people can soon become convinced of their pertinence.

As one chairman put it,

it does take a long time to change attitudes. People are conditioned by their experiences. Unless you can counter their historical experiences in the way you present things, they will find it difficult to change their attitudes. It's all about compensation. People understand that; they can relate to it. I was talking to one board about budgets and the need for improved performance. It was a very warm afternoon and with the effects of lunch, I could see that I was losing them. I realized that the only way to get them motivated would be to introduce an element of incentive. So I said, let's forget all that stuff about budgets, I'm going to introduce an incentive for all directors and managers based on profit achievement and return on assets so that as much as 25 per cent of remuneration will come from that. The atmosphere became electric. Everybody suddenly started to listen and the effects of lunch disappeared. The scheme had an amazing effect and the people there talk about performance now, knowing they are talking about their back pocket. You can change behaviour if you affect people in personal terms. This is why structure, remuneration and performance all go together. People want clear-cut management, which gives them confidence that they know what they have to do and what will happen if they achieve results. People relate to structure and reward systems.

It is easier for a manager to stop and start things than to change attitudes; and changing behaviour does not necessarily require a frontal attack.

Attitudinal and behaviour change is difficult to do; it's easier to change the structure. But you haven't made converts by changing the organization. They only behave when you are watching and monitoring, unless the rewards and sanctions fit with the new behaviour. What you really need to change is the way the place works. As long as the prime activity continues to be done the way it has been done, a lot of people will accept the new regimen—so if you can change the organization fundamentally without changing the work much initially, then you may be able to change the way staff think about the customer, or about quality, or about cost. The management's behaviour has to change to match the desired new culture. They have to give an example. You can't be crisp with three hour lunches.

(Geoff Gaines, KPMG)

In deciding how to go about it, the main ways to change behaviour are (a) to manage by example so that those below see what desired behaviour is and hence realize that management are both committed and involved and (b) by rewarding the new, desired behaviour—even giving rewards for well-intentioned but not wholly successful effort.[30]

The reward, measurement and control systems are vitally important. All such systems influence, and therefore distort, the behaviour of those involved. Indeed, they are there presumably to cause just such influence through focusing people's attention and affecting their actions. The trick is to ensure that the measurement, control and reward systems foster the desired behaviour rather than undermine it, as is too often the case when a management engages in a strategic change without fully considering the consequences of the systems for behaviour and performance. Job roles also have their effects, for

> individual behaviour is powerfully shaped by the organizational roles that people play. The most effective way to change behaviour, therefore, is to put people into a new organizational context, which imposes new roles, responsibilities, and relationships on them. This creates a situation that, in a sense, 'forces' new attitudes and behaviours on people.[31]

For example, if cross-functional teams are needed, but the vertical hierarchies remain strong for promotions, identity and reward, or if personal advance comes from influencing the functional chimney to which the person belongs, then there must be rewards too for cooperating across the functions. Sometimes an effect can be created by simple means. Procter and Gamble's solution to country managers having too much power was to give each of them a brand to manage as well—thus raising the status of brand management in the company and getting them to see the problems of the brand manager, so that they would think globally more often.

It is not actually desirable to ride roughshod over the old culture if it no longer fits; you should aim to be as supportive as practicable and to utilize its good features. Such harmony seems to be much more in tune with the Japanese company ethos. The Japanese process of obtaining consensus is called

Nemawashi (consultation before decision; i.e. before doing something, laying the groundwork for the objective). Nemawashi is its formal form (transmission of information and approval). Nemawashi is also a means of promoting information sharing within the company. In business, Nemawashi is the process of providing information to those concerned, and incorporating their ideas and opinions to build up a consensus beforehand. In Japanese companies most information is gathered through personal contacts. Therefore, multichannel information networks are important.

If you are in a traditional Japanese company with harmony, respect for age, loyalty both ways between firm and person—superior and subordinate—insignificance of the individual and of rank, then, because attitudes about the firm are more positive, implementation will be different than in a Western company having contractual relationships, labour mobility, individual decision-making and responsibility, with promotion based on personal performance. The Japanese lesson for Western companies is to communicate more with subordinates and build a more consensus-based style of leadership through values that become infused with common understanding. This is more important in a partnership organization where the prevailing management style has to be more 'persuading' than 'dictating' through the building of consensus with various alliances and coalitions within the group. Even so, involvement in Japanese firms has been more restricted to middle management than has been believed in the West and, in the recession of 1993, began to be blamed for slow decision-making, with some firms, such as Sanyo and Honda, regrouping to make senior managers more directly responsible for decisions.[32]

A further issue in the making of rapid changes is the relative state of different parts of the organization. Perceptions, capabilities and inclinations towards change will be at different states, and moving at different paces. Whether it is one section of the firm that is marching ahead; or one level in the firm that has become alert to the need for change, the overall current in the stream of movement will have eddies, backwaters and treacherous places.

I'm very wary of culture change programmes, particularly those with a mission statement, 6 thrusts and 17 behaviours—all listed in some brochure. Not every bit of an organization can move at the same pace. If you try it, you lose some hearts and minds. The key lies in establishing which bits are ready to move; encouraging them, honouring them, making them examples and providers of best practice to others.   (Geoff Gaines, KPMG)

So when radical strategic change is required, one should be sceptical about the efficacy of attitude change programmes. Structure (accountabilities and linkages if you prefer), reward and performance criteria and key appointments are far more potent and immediate weapons for the management to use to galvanize an organization. Structure at its best is a powerful device for making things happen.

REFERENCES

1. Paul S. Adler, Time-and-motion regained. *Harvard Business Review*, January–February 1993, pp. 97–108.
2. James MacGregor Burns, *Leadership*. Harper Collins, 1982.
3. R. Meredith Belbin, *Management Teams: Why They Succeed or Fail.* Heinemann, 1990.
4. Jon R. Katzenbach and Douglas K. Smith, *The Wisdom of Teams*. HBS Press, 1993.
5. Kinsley Lord, *Management Today*, January 1993, p. 25.
6. Review of *The Wisdom of Teams, Financial Times*, 14 December 1992.
7. Michael Hammer and James Champy, *Reengineering the Corporation.* Brealey, 1993.
8. Gene Hall, Jim Rosenthal and Judy Wade, How to make re-engineering really work. *Harvard Business Review*, November–December 1993, pp.119–31.
9. Paul Teevan, John Lockwood and Mike Walters, *Who is Managing the Managers?* Institute of Management, London, 1992.
10. John Clark, Unpublished MBA Report. London Business School, 1990.
11. Amar Bhide, Hustle as strategy. *Harvard Business Review*, September–October 1986, pp. 59–65.
12. Herbert Simon, *Administrative Behaviour: A Study of Decision-Making Processes in Administrative Organisation.* Macmillan, 1961, p. 227.
13. Michael Goold and Andrew Campbell, *Strategy and Styles.* Blackwell, 1987.
14. Howard Schwartz and Stanley M. Davis, Matching corporate culture and business strategy. *Organisational Dynamics*, **10** (81), pp. 30–48.

15. A. D. Chandler, *Strategy and Structure*. MIT Press, 1962.
16. *Financial Times*, 6 May 1992.
17. Peter M. Senge, *The Fifth Discipline*. Doubleday, 1990, ch. 3.
18. Hammer and Champy, *op. cit.*
19. *Financial Times*, 23 October 1992.
20. Paul Lawrence and Jay Lorsch, *Organisation and Environment*. Harvard, 1967. See also Gerry Johnson and Kevin Scholes, *Exploring Corporate Strategy*. Prentice-Hall, 1984; C. K. Prahalad and Yves Doz, *The Multinational Mission*. Free Press, 1987; Christopher Bartlett and Sumantra Ghoshal, *Managing Across Borders*. Hutchinson, 1989; Paul Evans and Yves Doz, The dualistic organisation, in *Human Resource Management in International Organisations* (eds. Evans, Doz and Laurent), Macmillan, 1989; Richard T. Pascale, *Managing on the Edge*. Viking, 1990.
21. Johnson and Scholes, *op. cit.*, p. 223; and Gerry Johnson, Managing strategic change: strategy, culture and action. *Long Range Planning*, **25** (1), 1992, pp. 28–36.
22. Danny Miller and Peter H. Friesen, Monumentum and revolution in organizational adaptation. *Academy of Management Journal*, **23** (4), 1980, pp. 591–614.
23. Schwartz and Davis, *op. cit.*, **10** (81).
24. Jay W. Lorsch, Managing culture; the invisible barrier to strategic change. *California Management Review*, Winter 1986, pp. 95–109.
25. Charles Baden-Fuller and John M. Stopford, *Rejuvenating the Mature Business*. Routledge, 1992.
26. Peter Drucker, *Post-Capitalist Society*. Heinemann, 1993; in conversation with Chris Lorenz, *Financial Times*, 11 June 1993.
27. John W. Hunt, *Managing People at Work*. McGraw-Hill, 1992, pp. 276.
28. John P. Kotter and James L. Hesketh, *Corporate Culture and Performance*. Free Press, 1992.
29. Tony Eccles, *Under New Management*. Pan, 1981.
30. Boris Yavitz and William H. Newman, *Strategy in Action*. Free Press, 1983.
31. Michael Beer, Russell A. Eisenstat and Bert Spector, Why change programs don't produce change. *Harvard Business Review*, November–December 1990, p. 159.
32. *The Economist*, 18 September 1993, p. 98.

10 Building on action and success

- Factor 11: Creating winners
- Factor 12: Fast change and initial acts
- Factor 13: Caring for casualties
- Factor 14: Minimizing unintended consequences

Having taken on board the need for teams *and* leaders; empowerment *and* leadership; structure and incentive alteration *rather than* direct culture change, what should management now initiate?

FACTOR 11: CREATING WINNERS

Personal success is a great motivator.

People like to win. Even at the graveside of a departed friend, all the survivors, (apart from the suicidal), have a slight feeling of gladness that they themselves are still alive, mixed with regret for the death. So it is in organizations. Sympathy for the redundant is tempered by relief that you still have a job and, maybe, a better, more secure job with bigger opportunities. If a de-manning scheme has been well devised, you may even have a sneaking feeling that most of those who are going were not contributing very much anyway. It is one of the reasons why, in a reorganization, people must be told quickly if they will still have a job, just as customers and suppliers must know how it will affect them. Because groups, departments and units that gain influence will become better motivated about changes than those that lose out, the more and the earlier that you can co-opt winners, the more impetus will grow behind the change and the weaker will be the forces of resistance.

This process is aided if the intellectual clarity of the planned change has a compelling logic.

> When the functional managers were appointed to the new executive committee, they had to stop feuding and instead had to cooperate to make the committee work effectively. They had to give up some of their insular attitudes and gradually this altered the perspectives of their own subordinates. As soon as it became clear that some young and middle managers were going to gain from this, progress began to be made as the key people were turned into winners rather than potential losers. This put pressure on the rest and almost everybody then bought in to the new scheme. The winners consolidated their position and most losers shut up and accepted what was on offer. We only lost a few reluctant and mediocre people. The process was significant and it sorted out the problem quite quickly, mainly because the changes were so obviously going to help. There were a few dodgy moments. But we never looked back.

For firms seeking a major strategic change, an essential first step is to undertake an analysis to predict who will gain and who will lose from the array of prospective alterations. The management must identify those groups that will be most affected by the new strategy and work out the impacts and how their consequences could be shaped beneficially. This is not to say that losers will not back the changes, but they will have to be persuaded of the overwhelming logic of the moves; be cushioned from the worst effects of their loss— both financially and emotionally—and be generally encouraged to look on the bright side without feeling too diminished by the changes.

The downside is that, if their resistance is likely to cause a serious problem for the implementation and if, on fair-minded reflection, theirs is not a cogent resistance, then the objectors must be rendered harmless before they can organize to undermine the changes. This may not require a confrontation, for bypassing them at this stage might encourage them to join in later, if by then they can see the changes as containing a positive opportunity for them.

Sometimes that is just not feasible. Not every loser can be turned into a winner. Nor is waiting always desirable. Patience must have its limits and objectors should be made aware of the perilous position they have adopted. The longer you leave a festering rump, the worse the problem is likely to get; the most you can hope for is that the objectors will drift out of the organization before their truculence infects others. The more likely outcome is that they will knuckle resentfully under, constantly diminishing progress through their sceptical querying of policy as they embrace the new strategy with suffocating indifference. They may have to be faced down quite quickly.

Hence the management needs quiet contingency plans that are not voiced too overtly, because that would give objectors a rallying point for prevarication and would signal a lack of managerial commitment to the chosen strategy or a lack of confidence that can only encourage dissenters to redouble their resistance. It would only be sensible to broadcast contingency plans if they were more draconian, thus making the chosen strategy relatively attractive for the waverers.

As one major corporation put it:

> Because we're a team company, we always hold a conference for the top managers, the senior implementers. They analyse and summarize for the board, which considers what's been said and then decides the policy. By that time the top managers own it, since they've become engaged in its development. If then people don't sign up to what's been agreed, we move them. We do it very nicely—but we move them.

The speedy selection of winners and losers is vital when one company takes over another—and it is much the same when a major reorganization requires decisive action to get the new structure into place and working. Obviously it helps greatly if the company is still profitable and can afford to lubricate the changes. When the losers are to be well paid off, their own inhibitions about cooperating in a downsizing operation will be soothed. Indeed they will, knowing the operating system well, often be more radical than the managers who may be fearful of brutal action in case it turns out to be crudely inappropriate. This is one reason why it is desirable to involve people in making adverse changes before you are forced to do so in poorer circumstances and why there is a trade-off between that and waiting until the crisis is obvious to all—by which time the lubricating funds may have depleted. The leaders cannot always afford to wait for the staff to realize the problem, but should reveal and explain matters as soon as possible.

> With our Lever Europe moves, national managements were worried because country management had to decline as European executive control was set up and numbers were to be reduced. We needed to get the winners and losers sorted. There was no point in hiding it. We made sure that our good national managers got good jobs somewhere else. You've then got to tell everybody the broad story and get them on board down to the shop floor.
>
> (Mike Heron, Unilever)

If you have to keep going back to make repeated adverse changes as events unfold, you need to provide a secure future for those who remain and give support to the leavers, otherwise mistrust will grow as people begin to fear the death of a thousand cuts. Top managers must release the bad news—if anything to exaggerate the awfulness of the situation—rather than carry out a gentler, but unstated decline, which will do little to build trust or quash rumour. Crisis can mobilize energy into fruitful forms, provided that staff are appropriately aroused. Plant makes the point that having too low security petrifies people, and having too high security renders them complacent and indifferent to external signals (see Figure 10.1).[1]

> If we are putting two companies together we go round, talking about the important issues and gauging who is good. Talking to people tells you who are the winners and losers. We quickly create an XYZ list. This puts the top people—including technical specialists who are vital; it's not just managers—into three categories. X you've got to keep, so you make sure they are in the know about the plans—which helps their motivation and signals their importance to them. Once the logic of the amalgamation is seen and this first group has signed up, you build the Y list of

people who you'd like to keep and the Z list who you would like, or will invite, to go.

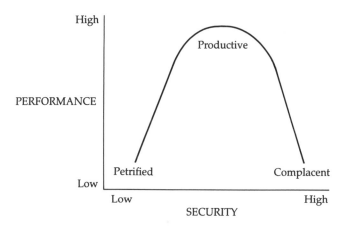

Figure 10.1   *Performance/security graph*

In one Injection change the chief executive recalled: 'We had immediately got rid of some people. After that in our first two years we didn't change anyone in the top management. Only later did we recruit from outside as well as promote from inside.'

'You should agree the organization structure very early and make the key appointments as quickly as possible. We pick the best available people from either "side" which means a heavy investment in getting to know people.' This fits with the principles followed in the merger which created Baxter Healthcare. In the 'One company principle', the integration of the two parts was forced by not continuing with the separate organizations. The senior managers were combined into the new teams, along with the 'principle of inclusion' in which all executives were put onto equal treatment in the two companies. It was always called a merger and not an acquisition, and there was equal representation on the task forces that were charged with bringing the two companies together.[2]

At the very least, the winners have to include key players from every section, function, department and unit—remembering that the personnel who are promoting the change may not be those who will be affected by it, nor will they necessarily implement it. Those people also need to be listened to and involved in the process. The more you can keep the single goal in mind and the less you prioritize between parts of the business, the less you set up rivalries and losers. You can adjust the performance targets of the losers to compensate.

Some staff turnover at the time of change enables a company to recruit better people, provided that it doesn't upset the 'X group', the irreplaceable staff. If they are highly mobile, they may need to be offered additional rewards in order to persuade them to stay. Getting rid of poor performers and notable dissidents sends a signal to the rest of the organization, just as talking to key people often reveals a lot of pent-up energy for change that had stalled because the previous management was inadequate. Sifting through the list of current proposals, or better, asking the remaining people what should be done, can yield a surprising volume of sensible initiatives that can be taken. There are usually several good ideas just waiting to be actioned, because prospective strategies lie dormant and organizations typically have several latent possibilities needing an event, an intervention, a fresh perspective. The process of consulting people generates and surfaces ideas. By the time you select the strategy, people claim that 'We've been saying that for years ourselves'. They own it and will back it, having moved on as they see what is coming. Inertia has been overcome and the impetus has grown. Obviously, the more change that can be well received throughout the organization, the better.

How much involvement and consultation is carried out will depend on the usual factors. How dire and urgent is the need to change? Do the initiators of the new strategy hold the trump cards that will force the changes through? How powerful and intransigent are the likely forces of resistance? How much will the changes violate the beliefs, values and interests of the participants?

What is fascinating is the extent to which radical change

liberates positive forces, even when all prior predictions would suggest that inertia and engrained habits would prevent any serious alteration of the existing situation. Those who have been antipathetic to the existing ways of working can be galvanized into rising up and overturning the previous regime's habits, aroused by the signal of change, the attraction of the new goal and the encouragement of the leader's new vision. The prospective winners from the changes will usually be happy to climb upon a promising looking bandwagon.

FACTOR 12: FAST CHANGE AND INITIAL ACTS

Early successes create productive momentum.

'If you don't do it in the first 100 days, you won't do it in 100 years' (Lord Sheppard, chairman, Grand Metropolitan plc). He continued:

> When we bought Pillsbury we broke the organizational link between Pillsbury and Burger King in the first week of our control. The old top management had all gone and we got to work and new top management was installed in weeks. Thirty to forty per cent of all the Head Office and Regional officers in both Pillsbury and Burger King left inside three months from the takeover. We explained what we were doing and why we were doing it and got a good reception from the staff.
>
> When we sold Intercontinental Hotels it was decided in the July, on the market in August and sold in December. The Heublein/Smirnoff acquisition began in the September and was completed in the January. We are very fast, so we're termed frenetic. But we can be fast because we have very short lines of communication; there is a two-way dialogue with almost daily exchanges that hone the process. Your dialogue must be with people who understand the vision and it helps when everybody has a good understanding of what the game is beforehand. Our management accepts change; it's taken for granted that you can't stay the same. We refuse to accept the fact that, because we are big, we must move slowly. You can make bold changes of strategy. I think it's much more difficult to implement it in 20 years than in 3 years—you'd have forgotten what it was.

As Lord Sheppard pinpointed, not only would you have forgotten, as a team you would no longer be there. Those who claim that a strategic reorientation takes many years seem to overlook the imperatives that drive a chief executive and his or her team.

> If it took ten years no chief executive would embark on a strategic change because it would be beyond his span of glory.

> A man in a hurry with only 5 years has to capture the existing anger, frustration and excitement and get people to go with it.

> If the top man is close to retirement when he's appointed, you know he'll either do nothing or run amok. It's a valuable and creditable leader who keeps his head and his sense of perspective under that strain. His great asset is that he can afford to be dispassionate, if only he can submerge his ego for the greater good.

Nor is the Grand Metropolitan example of speed an oddity. Neville Bain joined Coats Viyella as Group chief executive at the end of September 1990, having spent many years in Cadbury-Schweppes, latterly as deputy chairman and finance director. A speedy consultants' analysis helped to carry people along with the data as he took his Coats Viyella top team away to talk about the possibilities. He also talked with his board about the implications for Coats' seven key businesses and agreed the work plan. In mid-December 1990 a series of meetings was held to ensure uniform understanding from board level to two levels below. At the same time the decentralized structure was being put in place and some people were changed at top levels. Layers of management were removed and all key business areas started to report directly to him as Group chief executive from 1 January 1991—three months after his arrival.

> We then had to look at our stake in Tootal and, having found that an agreed coming together was not on, we bid for Tootal. While the contested takeover was in progress, the planning by Coats for integration of the two companies was at fever pitch because our management team was determined to start from day one with an action programme. Forty task forces were set up for

all aspects of integration. The bid succeeded on 20 May 1991. Two days later we held a worldwide joint conference of both Coats Viyella and Tootal top people to tell them of the early plans for integration and to appoint key Tootal people to the task forces. High priority was given to choosing the best people for jobs, so lots of our top team held discussions with the top Tootal people. [Bain himself saw 170 executives.] By early July 1991 the organizational structure with the top appointments was agreed; each of the main businesses had presented on their prospects and the forward plan for integration and disposals was agreed.

Seven weeks had elapsed.

As Amar Bhide wrote about financial services organizations: 'They move fast, and they get it right . . . what mostly counts is vigour and nimbleness . . . these high profits stem largely from superior execution or forceful opportunism, not structural competitive barriers.' And he quoted a banker, 'I don't view competition as an obstacle. Our most significant challenge is internal—making certain we manage our resources so that we are the best in the business.'[3]

Even an organization the size of British Telecom can reorientate itself quickly.

> In one year we completely restructured from having 30 geographical UK Districts each doing everything and run by general managers, to a customer-type based organization with three Divisions (Worldwide Business Communications, Domestic Personal Customers and Special Businesses Division for Yellow Pages, Cellnet, etc.) each doing its own marketing. Behind these three is a Network Division looking after the World Network and a Worldwide Products and Services Division. We've never ended a year with the same organization we started with; there's not always a complete reorganization, sometimes things are bolted together differently. The strategic change is not just structural; we've departed from having general managers to valuing people for their focused specialist skills—which changes their career routes. (Mike Bett, deputy chairman, British Telecom)

Tom Peters has commented on one 30 000 strong organization that went from nine layers to three in 90 days and also reported that when Percy Barnevik took over ASEA in 1980, he said to corporate staff, 'You've got 100 days to get a job in the decentralized companies or go.' ASEA's corporate staff went from 1700 to 200 in 100 days. When ASEA later merged with Brown Boveri to form ABB, again under Barnevik, the 4000 person staff bureaucracy went down to 100 in a year; the corporate centre going from 880 to 25 in that year.[4]

When Grand Metropolitan took over Burger King it found 13 layers of management above the franchisees of the restaurants, slowing down decisions and actions. Four layers were taken out within weeks—not an excessive delayering such as would have traumatized the management as well as being functionally counter-productive, but a tautening of responsiveness as the drive for greater effectiveness got under way.

Baxter Healthcare also came to believe in effective integration through 'the principle of immediate action', as compared to letting things settle down so that people get over the trauma, because it believed that rumours, distortions and productivity losses ensue.[5] The Rank Organisation agrees:

> If there is any error in acquiring, it is—don't touch it; leave it alone. If people don't listen, you shouldn't say 'It'll take time'. The longer you leave it, the worse it will be. This isn't a universal statement. You couldn't do that with a Japanese company; you would have to do it by consensus. But a Japanese company could have problems in another culture. Look at the problems Japanese consumer products companies are having in trying to deal with Hollywood moguls.

Rank also follows its own advice.

> In the case of the Mecca acquisition, we had worked out the organization before the offer to buy went unconditional. With one or two exceptions the whole management was in situ, all were in possession and with revised annual budgets at the start of the financial year ten weeks later, though it left some managers with a lot to do. There was shock at the way we did it because we'd got further in that time than Mecca had in two years with its acquisition of Pleasurama. But from the Group's view it was finished; it was all behind us within a month. There wasn't any other way to do it; we'd have had chaos.

Acquisitions feature strongly in these rapid movements.

With some strategic change goals the only way to make sensible progress is to acquire—whether it be a business, a top manager with skills not possessed in the organization, or through acquiring a good team—as one might do in financial services. Unilever, having decided to become a leading participant in the prestige perfumes market, realized that the only way to gain prestige brands in that industry quickly was to buy them.

In trying to transform an existing operation rather than absorbing an acquisition, it can be enough to install a new chief executive. 'We put in a good manager from another, barely related division with no experience in the industry. There was massive strategic and operational change in twelve months—and for the good. There are other ways, such as structural change or new technology.' Whether the fresh appointment results from Takeover, Injection or Succession changes, the new manager has to make an impact. 'When freshly appointed, you need to do something dramatic in your first 30 days or no one will believe that things are going to change.' This does not fit with the need to size up the situation first, work out the options, get people on side and organize to act effectively and to avoid clumsiness or the risk of derision. Therefore it can only be valid for major changes if the incoming manager has highly apposite experience, is very sure of the needed remedy or, if the organization he or she has joined is ripe for a timely push.

Yet doing something dramatic does not mean doing something that is too committingly important. A symbolic change can be a powerful signal.[6] Removing car park privileges, shutting the executive dining room, putting receptionists into the unoccupied marble hall, erecting a flagpole, mandating tourist class travel for all, introducing a prize—all these have knock-on effects through their visibility, without enslaving the organization to a new and possible defective strategy. New rituals percolate rapidly through an organization's consciousness into its inhabitants' behaviour.

Burning the boats was a highly symbolic act of war to show your own and your opponent's warriors that retreat was not an option. It can also happen in business organizations. When the dictatorial Cecil King was ousted from the

Mirror newspaper group by a board revolt, the symbolic purging was hilarious. He was a vivid character with a nice line in gallows humour. Once, when asked by a magazine survey on top managers' office furniture, what were his furnishings, he had replied: 'Very simple, very chaste really. Just a throne and a couple of prayer stools.' King had constructed a wood-panelled office with a working fireplace in the modern multistorey office block, which required a chimney to be driven up through the concrete floors to the roof. On his departure, in a ritual purification, the room was stripped back to the concrete walls, the fireplace and chimney dismantled and the room left bare and empty. The signal was that they wanted to start afresh without him.[7] They later got Robert Maxwell instead.

More pertinent is the firm where the management felt that employees would see, and appreciate, the efforts being put in to sell the expensive equipment they made. The one-class dining room had a long, large table for visitors (typically overseas and government buyers) and their hosts from the company. The lunch offerings were grand and the elegant table was decorated with fruit, flowers, fine china and wine glasses—all in the sight of those eating their normal works lunch. The visitors' meal, held frequently, was more lavish than most employees would have at the celebration on their wedding day. The centre table became known as 'The Golden Trough'. Its effect on motivation was not obvious, but calls for belt-tightening at the firm, let alone redundancies, were not well received.

Employees are good at semiotics—the study of signs and signals—and if, for instance, there is an austerity programme but the limousines stay and the gorgeous lunches are not curtailed, they become rightly cynical about the seriousness of the situation, or they conclude that there is one law for the management and another for them. Signals are important for announcing that 'things are now different round here' and 'I'm in charge'. They may also test whether you have opponents in the company and entice them to show their hand when there is only a low-cost issue at stake. You can then afford to rout them without much downside risk. Symbolic actions are highly visible at board level and a board-level restructuring is a powerful warning to other critics. Demoting or sidelining a resistant, but powerfully placed board member immediately signals a shift in the company's operating architecture.

Another frequently used signal comes from changing the information and control system. New criteria of performance, new data to be tracked and discussed; these convey a powerful message about the priorities of the new regime. Gabarro found extensive use of changes in information and control systems by newly appointed managers.[8] A sudden interest in cash management in an organization that has previously been indifferent, will signal a management priority and thoughtful managers will also start to take an interest in cash flow.

The influence of information

The organization's problem may simply be a lack of information. On arrival at Coats Viyella, Neville Bain asked key business groups to analyse their market prospects in detail. After some investigation, they returned, saying, 'We don't have enough information'. 'Dead right,' he responded. 'Go and get some.' He knew that unarguable facts would affect people's perceptions of the problems they faced and that by involving them in the search, they would more readily accept the inferences. Having then created a more widespread acceptance of the need for change, he could then initiate changes without provoking too much surprise or resistance. Disraeli had summed up the logic: 'As a general rule the most successful man in life is the man who has the best information.' Bain was confirming Waterman's view that information is the main strategic advantage and flexibility the main strategic weapon.[9] As Pettigrew found in the National Health Service, good data that are taken seriously and used to substantiate a case will improve the quality and conviction of a strategy because they show that the strategy is feasible.[10]

Such low-cost, uncontentious initiatives as information gathering will not need to be unwound if they turn out to be imperfect or off-target. That is why it is better, in inducing an early change, to set up, say, cross-functional task forces, than to appoint a deputy chief executive. The task force can be ended; its effects are reversible, whereas the new executive appointment is more permanent, more intrusive. The task force will eventually be disbanded, so it does not directly threaten anyone's job and it should have a major educative effect—as occurred in the BBC in 1991/92 with its formation of 15 task forces charged with generating new policies for the Corporation. And you can change perceptions quickly. Once people in the BBC had realized that the top management was serious about introducing a total costing system and an internal market called 'Producer Choice', speedy efforts were made to understand the implications—even by those most opposed to the changes. The key thing was the setting of an inviolable date for its introduction and a flat refusal to let it be put off by classical delaying tactics. The key factor in the BBC was that it became clear that those programme makers who made an early start would become winners through (a) being able to outmanoeuvre the late developers and (b) gaining managerial autonomy in the making of pro- grammes—their cherished activity. This latter element fits a valuable rule that assists attempts to change organizations— namely, the identification of a source of frustration that can be harnessed. Few programme makers could resist the chance of having more control over the making of their programmes.

Getting things to move quickly is greatly helped by early successes. As Pettigrew affirmed, organizations need 'islands of progress' to sustain energy and to develop positive self- esteem and momentum. That makes intermediate goals, milestones and markers important. With the amalgamation of 16 nationally run companies into the single business of Lever Europe

> it is the speed of innovation that gives Lever Europe its competitive edge . . . encompassing not only the development of a new product idea but also the speed and international scale on which it is launched . . . there were healthy doubts initially but once Lever Europe began operating, the consensus was that we had made the right decision . . . initially there was some concern

about the changes in structure, but the commitment from the board and the launch of successful new products convinced even the most sceptical that this was the only way forward.[11]

The same was true in Grand Metropolitan: 'The exciting piece of Pillsbury came when the people saw more R&D, new factories, getting rid of bad franchisees, dramatically better marketing.'

Rapid development of this kind presupposes that there is someone at the top with the vision, commitment, competence and control over resources (including people's careers) and whose resource and expert power affects the perceptions of colleagues and those on lower levels. There has to be leadership from those who are in charge. It is difficult to see how Lever Europe could have been formed through an upsurge from below when all 16 sets of participants were initially locked into their own parochial national enclaves.

Middle and young managers expect their top management to be wise, resourceful and to provide a coordinating lead. Isn't that what they are there for? Because of this belief, trust and hope that those at the top know what they are doing, and because of the often limited perspectives of those below, there is frequently no sense of urgency about strategy four or five levels down. Lots of staff, including managers, don't think in strategic terms. 'Those who think are stars', said one only mildly despondent top manager. Some of the trust, the belief that those at the top have a master plan, is actually quite flattering. It assumes that the top managers know what they are doing and are acting responsibly.

It also demonstrates that those lower down have not become alert to pressures on the organization, let alone enmeshed in working out how to deal with them. This is in contrast to Japanese firms which spend a lot of time and attention on intra-group communications and where few decisions can be made without consulting a wide range of interested groups. Anyone who might be affected in any way needs at least to be forewarned, if not asked to voice an opinion. This comes easier to Japanese managers who are judged as much by whether they can get the job done without disrupting corporate harmony as they are in delivering the goods. Persistent interaction makes it more likely that Japanese staff will be aware of pressing issues and they will have more interest in discussing solutions with their managers. Japanese firms have elevated competitive challenge and crisis to an art form. So what can a Western firm do, apart from resolving to gradually build up communications and involvement? It is no good saying 'embrace the Japanese way immediately' when that doesn't fit people's expectations, norms, values or assumptions about power and responsibility.

The key for Western companies is a set of three interrelated elements: a galvanizing event; a willingness by top management to give a lead and to indicate that commitment to fruitful change is mandatory for staff; support for those buffeted by the change. Kanter affirms that five factors are important in this process: a departure from tradition, be it an initiative or an accident that promotes new experiences or experiments; a crisis or galvanizing event; strategic decisions made by the firm, typically by its management or owners; individual prime movers, as with the pregnant executive discussed earlier; and what she termed 'action vehicles', such as a quality campaign or a customer service drive—something tangible to use to drive change forward.[12]

FACTOR 13: CARING FOR CASUALTIES

Caring for people is both morally and organizationally commendable.

An organization, like a society, is often judged by the way it treats the unfortunate. Whether they are unlucky, unworthy or simply surplus to requirements, the way an organization deals with its casualties is a component not only of its reputation, but of its ability to secure willing high performance from its personnel. Making old-time malingering seadogs walk the plank from a ship surrounded by ocean may have encouraged the others. But the rest of the crew had nowhere else to go. Short of mutiny, they had to perform or die. When, in a land-based organization, your best people can leave and get another job without difficulty or shame, the organization has to reconsider how it should behave towards its injured—if only as a matter of expediency rather than of honour.

A variation on the political adage 'Be nice to people on your way up; you may meet them again on your way down' would be for an organization to treat them nicely when it doesn't need them, in case one day it does. Gone are the days for most organizations when they could refuse to even consider taking back an ex-employee on the grounds that, in leaving, the person had shown that he or she had rejected the company community and should not expect to darken its door again. Not only do many organizations need all the talent they can get, but they need to retain the goodwill of their existing staff. A climate in which people have to calculate whether it is better to bail out before they might be pushed out is not normally conducive to high performance. That kind of climate is, instead, more likely to encourage employees to pursue short-term, calculative and end-game strategies.

Britain's Grand Metropolitan plc has a straightforward and commendable policy for the treatment of talent it doesn't cherish enough to want to keep: 'No compromise on high management standards' is coupled with 'Compassion in the execution'—and by 'execution' it does not mean the firing squad. This rapidly evolving multinational company is ruthless in the actual decisions it makes about the people it employs, but is then compassionate about the consequences of those decisions. Every effort is made to find a supportive way of handling the ensuing problems and to create an outcome that is approved both by those affected and by those inside who observe the process.

For Grand Metropolitan, caring for the casualties is not just a matter of compassion, worthy though that sentiment can be. It also has four effects. The first is to reinforce the self-esteem of those driving the changes. Knowing that you are treating the disadvantaged well is an uplifting reinforcement for your policy of change and removes some of the inhibitions that the senior people might hold that 'we can't really do that to him or her'. The second is to reduce the likely resistance to change because of the offsetting benefits that are available for the casualties. Indeed, as anyone who has made people redundant knows, such things as generous termination benefits can stimulate an enthusiasm for change to the extent that employees clamour for release—as British Telecom found in 1992 when thousands more than required applied for severance. The third advantage is that the survivors are given a signal that the costs of change will be cushioned and that future changes are not necessarily a threat, with all the motivating possibilities that the organization can accrue from its personnel having that comforting knowledge. The fourth effect is on those who are talented and well regarded but for whom no place can readily be found. Their departure is not a disgrace and, at other times, you might want them back. Indeed, organizations have been known to delayer imprudently and then to offer 'golden retrievers' to persuade key personnel to return.

Until recently, leading Japanese companies would have reduced casualties to low levels through programmes of redeployment, retraining, skill enhancement and the cooperation that stems from work security (not job security). The consequent loyalty, trust and commitment was believed to offset the additional costs through its effects on employees' behaviour. Some Western companies have begun to adopt similar schemes. Yet, in a turbulent world, it is a brave company that is prepared to turn its staff remuneration into a fixed cost, particularly as Japanese firms began to move away from such practices as the demographics in Japan swung in favour of employees. The *Financial Times* reported in February 1992 that, with twice as many jobs on offer as highly qualified young people at that time, skilled Japanese employees increasingly had employment options and 9 per cent left each year, with employees no longer being loyal because they were no longer powerless.[13] To counter this mobility, firms had started hiring mid-career employees and offering fast track jobs instead of relying on the harmony of promotion through seniority. Despite the Japanese labour shortage reversing into surplus by late 1992, companies continued to question the value of on-job training and their assumption that well-trained, well-treated personnel wouldn't leave. Japanese companies are beginning to adopt more Western, individualistic notions of careers, just as Europeans have taken on some of the American perspective that individuals are responsible for their own careers and as European and American companies have tried to adopt elements of Japanese high-security employment. Caring for the casualties has a moral as well as an expedient dimension.

FACTOR 14: MINIMIZING UNINTENDED CONSE-QUENCES

You cannot avoid all errors; but you can organize to anticipate some and to recover from others.

There are always unintended effects when a significant change occurs. As Tawney put it, you may be able to choose what kind of society to seek to have, but you cannot control the outcome of that choice. Governments are regularly embarrassed by the unexpected behaviour of the populace. The Education Act of 1844 led to improved conditions for children, but for short-term economic reasons it also led to the abandonment of large numbers of children who might have been retained by their parents if they could have continued to earn their keep. Leaving aside the problematic relationships between nation states and power blocs, the most vivid unintended domestic effect of this century is probably that of prohibition and the rise of the American mafia.

Unintended effects happen all the time. In the late 1980s it became the received wisdom in Europe that the way to combat violence within football grounds would be to equip each stadium with seating-only so that tightly packed standing crowds would be thinned out and calmed by being seated. This would also attract a better class of spectator. Shortly afterwards an affray occurred at a tense soccer match in Greece at an all-seat ground. And what weapons did the rival fans seize in order to throw and to hit each other? The seats.

At corporate level, it is a failure to predict outcomes that undermines the success of initiatives. One organization attempted to deal with deviant behaviour that involved false clocking on and off by blue-collar workers. After several months' work, a high-powered personnel and technical committee produced a secure device and installed the equipment. It took the workers just over half an hour to work out how to fool the system by using a folded cigarette packet and some cooking foil.

This is not to jeer at those responsible for such innovations, but to demonstrate the value of trying to predict outcomes of particular actions—which is just what planning attempts to do. It isn't possible to predict exact outcomes, but not all consequences need to be unforeseen. Nor are all unintended consequences adverse for the organization. There may be surprise at the specific occurrence, but not surprise that something like it does happen. Scenario-building can help improve the overall robustness and focus of a strategic change. When Pilkington invented the float glass technique, which transformed the world glass industry, it sought to obtain the best and most protective patents it could, using excellent patent lawyers. It also hired a second set of first-class patent lawyers to try to break the proposed patents, and then used the results of their endeavours to strengthen the firm's own patent applications. Pilkington also decided to license its new technology extensively and cheaply, thus avoiding the dislocation of the glass market that would have resulted from wounded competitors seeking to minimize their losses by cutting prices. It also almost eliminated other glassmakers' incentives to try to bypass the patents and the licensing charges. To sustain its competitiveness, Pilkington additionally wrote the licensing agreements in a way that gave it the benefit of any technical improvements that were made by its licensees.

One key to minimizing undesired effects thus concerns prediction through rehearsing the future (see Chapter 3, page 47)—which further undercuts the notion of letting strategy emerge—and seeking to anticipate deviations that might arise from the chosen plan.

It is tempting, because it is simple, to introduce one change at a time. In most complex organizational situations the temptation should be resisted. While full congruence of all factors is a perfectionist mirage, that is no excuse for the naivety of linear thinking in which each individual change plods after another, one by one. It is not that changing everything at once is sensible—though altering everything simultaneously in a coordinated fashion so that all elements move smoothly and harmoniously together would obviously be ideal, if only the organization could find that marvellous recipe. It almost certainly couldn't. In all but the most elegant of circumstances, a combination of unintended effects, urgency, lack of spare resources and the risk of dissipating energy through lack of focus, make multiple changes difficult to handle. More limited change initiatives become attractive. Afterwards, of course, critics will point to the unintended effects to show how you missed a trick with your limited changes. But would they, with their commitment to the splendour of fully congruent change, have ever got their act together to actually do anything in the first place?

What sensible strategy implementation programmes need is an anastrophic change (the opposite of a catastrophic change)—a coming together of elements to form a coherent, connected whole to the maximum practicable degree.[14] This fits with the notion of the firm as a cultural web wherein each part protects and reinforces any element that is attacked individually.[15] The important question here is: Does one have a choice in the number of interactive elements that can be changed simultaneously?

Choice may be a luxury. The organization in deep trouble may have to wage more campaigns than it would choose in calmer circumstances. Even then, it is not necessary to alter everything. There is a limit to the number of fronts that can be fought at the same time. Some constancy is comforting, and sanctuaries of stability are desirable.[16] As argued earlier, the culture may have to look after itself when urgency dictates the pace of change. Far more effective is an attack on a vulnerable leverage point, such as the reward system, or the performance criteria, or the information system, or the responsibility structure. The solution is to find a leverage point that is sufficiently strong and sufficiently influential that any change in that point results in productive change not only of itself, but in other factors that are affected by the force of its alteration.

A sensible firm will try to connect elements of initiatives to ensure that they fit together, and to ensure that the necessary resources are there to back up the plan and yet concentrate energies on a limited number of initiatives. The problem in BP in 1992 was that many different initiatives were being put into effect, and when the then chairman pulled people together to create a sense of achievement, morale plummeted even further when he indicated that he believed that they had achieved the goals of the earlier initiatives. They knew only too well they hadn't. His vista of further targets and goals made them realize that he didn't want to listen to the implementation problems of their existing initiatives. Their gloom hastened his departure.

The main thing is to avoid plain oversight in gauging how singular or how extensive the strategic change should be. Cost-cutting through delayering and reducing staff will look good on paper, but not if it is accompanied by an intensified drive for increased sales through new campaigns for which there are no longer the personnel. One well-known organization improved manufacturing cost efficiency by centralizing production only to find that the additional load on its unreformed distribution system swallowed up all the savings and more. Another large corporation delayered, only to panic when it saw the lack of coordination it had engendered. It then promptly destabilized its remaining middle managers by introducing another layer of management in order to recover from the effects of the original cuts. All of those problems were readily predictable. Any firm that is about to embark on a radical strategic change should ask about each of its operations:

- What will this change do (to this activity)?
- What will it be in the interests of the people involved to do (in the new circumstances)?
- How might this open us to competitor retaliation?
- Is there a vulnerable transition period (when the old is dismantled and the new not fully operational)?
- What contingency resources do we have that we would be willing to commit to the fray, or is success predicated on everything going to plan?

- Is there a more economical, least-action, more cost-effective way to achieve our goal?
- How confident are we that our staff are capable of making the strategic change work?

This last question is at the heart of the problem that bedevilled the BBC in 1993 as it introduced 'Producer Choice', its internal market system, into a large, bureaucratic organization, many of whose inhabitants were antipathetic to business values and unskilled in business techniques. The result was that progress towards financial efficiency was disorderly and deeply ruffling to its staff. Much of the initial disdain for Producer Choice was the inevitable accompaniment to shaking up that complacent organization.

The capacity to learn is a crucial element in making progress in organizations. Some analysts believe that the rate of knowledge accumulation is the sole source of competitive advantage, outside the good fortune of the advantage of natural resources or monopoly control of some aspect of the market system. Lacking that advantage, a successful firm can be copied, and assets can be acquired. Even the firm with matchless skills will only be able to stay ahead if it has the ability to organize better, and with better focus.

Nevertheless, given the rich texture of organizational life and the occasionally unexpected actions of competitors, government, suppliers and customers, the chance of anticipating all eventualities is not high, and the firm wouldn't know the probability of each possible deviation. It follows, therefore, that a recovery strategy is also needed. Sensitivity to unexpected effects is a matter of recovering from error by spotting their emergence, judging their likely effects and gauging the cost and possibility of curtailing or harnessing their consequences. This is where forces need to be marshalled, contingency resources deployed and error-recovery mechanisms put into action.

Initiative overload

Another objection to completely pervasive change programmes is that of overload. People are resilient; so, at times, are organizations. Yet how many hammer blows of change can an organization take at one time? It has already become apparent that, while firms which have delayered and reduced their workforce may have lowered their direct staff costs, their ability to flourish can be undermined by the sheer lack of personnel available to pursue initiatives and by the fatigue of those who remain. If you cut down or amalgamate marketing departments and then tell the survivors to intensify market planning, obtain and process market data, expand marketing initiatives, introduce a networked management information system, a new incentive scheme, capability training, cross-functional integrating teams, new product development and improved quality certification, there comes a point where nothing is done well or as intended. The several activities compete and the diverse crises that arise in their wake will disable the whole implementation process. Initiative overload is pernicious. One large engineering firm, hard-driven by its hard-bitten management, used to react to the anguished cry of 'we cannot do that on top of everything else' by replying 'there's always 2 a.m. on a Sunday morning'. That response eventually led to the fatigued executives being unable to prevent the firm's deterioration; it was taken over and its top managers were fired.

The aim must be to 'Avoid the death of a thousand initiatives' (Neville Bain, group chief executive, Coats Viyella).

The underlying objection to the perfectionist goal of making everything congruent is that the tensions, the contradictions, and the pluralities of choice cannot be wished away or reconciled. Constructive tensions are inevitable and can be valuable.[17] To the extent that tensions result in a high-quality debate that leads to the optimal compromise, that must be true. Compromise, by its nature, precludes optimization on competing alternative goals. The extent to which systems should be discretionary for responsiveness and mandatory for consistency will depend on the balance point of compromise that is chosen; just as will the balance between teamwork and individuality. But whatever the chosen balance, the need is to get on with it.

REFERENCES

1. Roger Plant, *Managing Change and Making it Stick*. Fontana, 1987, p. 147.
2. Vernon R. Loucks, Strategy and organisational learning. Strategic Management Society Conference, San Francisco, October 1989.
3. Amar Bhide, Hustle as strategy. *Harvard Business Review*, September–October 1986, pp. 59–65.
4. Strategic Management Society Conference, Toronto, October 1991.
5. Loucks, *op. cit.*
6. Karl E. Weick, *The Social Psychology of Organizing*. Addison-Wesley, 1969.
7. Graham Cleverley, *Managers and Magic*. Pelican, 1973, p. 12.
8. J. J. Gabarro, *The Dynamics of Taking Charge*. Harvard Press, 1987.
9. Robert H. Waterman, *The Renewal Factor: Building and Maintaining Your Company's Competitive Edge*. Bantam, 1988, p. 25.
10. Andrew Pettigrew, *Financial Times*, 8 November 1991.
11. Jon Peterson, chief executive, Lever Europe; Roy Brown, managing director, Lever UK, *Unilever Magazine*, **83**, 1992.
12. Rosabeth Moss Kanter, *The Change Masters*. Simon & Schuster, 1983, pp. 290–300.
13. *Financial Times*, February 1992.
14. *The Economist*, 4 January 1992, p. 68. (The word *anastrophic* was coined by Herrick Baltscheffsky, a Swedish chemist.)
15. Jerry Johnson, *Strategic Change and the Management Process*. Blackwell, 1987, pp. 223–4.
16. Andrew Pettigrew, Ewan Ferlie and Lorna McKee, *Shaping Strategic Change*, Sage, 1992, pp. 288–99.
17. Richard T. Pascale, *Managing on the Edge*. Viking, 1990, p. 53.

11 Maps for action

- A double distillation
- Shrinking the boxes: the time spectrum

How, then, do these 14 factors fit together? The first response is that there is no one universal way that fits all strategic change circumstances. Each change situation will have differences as well as similarities. Different priorities will need to be attached to each factor, depending on the firm's quirks, the substance, and the context of the particular change. Secondly, the 14 factors are not put forward as being the only way of categorizing facets of change. They come, however, from the distilled experiences of successful managers in companies that have been successful. Nevertheless, other factors could have been added.

There might have been a fifteenth factor about perpetual revolution, covering the ability to sustain continuous change. But this can be discussed quickly. Organizations typically seem to have bursts of change; bouts of rapid adjustment that take them to a new level of activity.[1] Only short periods of calm may be needed before the organization has recovered its breath and can tackle a new advance. Other work shows that some firms do not need that recovery period but can sustain continuous revolutionary change for a long time, as change follows change, provided that too many simultaneous initiatives do not overload the firm.[2]

What is clear is that any change needs to be supported and sustained if momentum is not to be lost. 'Our biggest implementation mistake was the gap between phases. Impetus dwindled' (Alan Penn, AEA Technology). So how should the management of an organization create and sustain that impetus? How, using the 14 factors as guides, should an organization change? What are the elements that underpin successful strategic change?

Successful change comes when the confluence of elements leads to a flowing tide of change. Indeed, we should recall the words of that well-known earlier observer of strategy implementation, William Shakespeare, who wrote

> There is a tide in the affairs of men
> Which, taken at the flood, leads on to fortune;
> *(Julius Caesar*, IV,iii)

The tide is created when those elements come together—with one significant difference. Compared to the oceans of the world, the elements that are involved in a successful change climate are far more in the control of those who are affected by them. Managers in particular can affect the tide of change. They have more power in their organizations than King Canute had on the beach.

Timing is also important and, unlike the tides, to some extent under managerial control too. The possession of a will to change is critical, for there will always be a reason not to do it: the time isn't right; we're not fully prepared; perhaps we should get more information; the threats to our future might go away; the changes would be disruptive and hurtful; these aren't the right changes. Early in his career, the author worked briefly for a frustrating manager who would pat his ever-bulging briefcase complacently and say, 'If I leave these problems for a while, half of them will go away.' And it was true. The problem was that the other half festered and got much worse. He was eventually replaced. He was not incapable; he just lacked the vital element of will.

A DOUBLE DISTILLATION

From the distilled managerial experiences that permeated the discussions about the 14 factors, a double distillation yields a set of eight elements, in the four categories, that are necessary in all types of change:

- Category 1 Purpose and initiative (Chapter 6)
- Category 2 Concordance and trust (Chapter 7)
- Category 3 Leadership, capabilities and structure (Chapters 8 and 9)
- Category 4 Building on action and success (Chapter 10)

Successful change demands that *all* these eight elements of Table 11.1 (which interweave with the 14 factors) be present in the organization which is being transformed.

These eight elements in Table 11.1 have been developed from work produced originally by Dean Berry[3] with three elements. These were later augmented by the CMI consultancy[4] to four elements and by John Hunt[5] to five elements and then by the author to eight elements.

Table 11.1 *Eight needed elements in successful change*

Categories	Needed elements	If missing, then	and reaction is
Purpose and initiative	1 Pressure for change	Low priority	Is there any need for change?
	+		
	2 A clear shared vision (of both goal and direction)	Fast start that collapses	Why are we doing this? Where are we going?
	+		
Concordance and trust	3 Effective liaison and trust	Suspicion and confusion	What are they up to? Do they know what they're doing?
	+		
Leadership, capabilities and structure	4 The will and power to act	Disorder and frustration	Nobody seems able to act. We can't do anything
	+		
	5 Capable people and sufficient resources	Helplessness	We can't do that with what we have
	+		
	6 Suitable rewards and accountabilities	Low commitment, feeble efforts	Why should we bother? The way we're organized, that won't work
	+		
Building on action and success	7 Actionable first steps	Haphazard efforts, false starts	Where should we begin? How can we start?
	+		
	8 Capacity to learn and adapt	Anxiety, early surrender	It's too risky; we'll never get there; it's beyond us

The four categories also map onto the 14 factors discussed in Chapters 7 to 10 (Table 11.2). So the key people in the organization need to ask themselves if they have considered the four categories, how confident they are that the eight needed elements are in place and, from that, whether they have convincing answers to the questions posed by the various factors.

Table 11.2   *Investigating the 14 factors*

Category	Factor	Question(s)
Purpose and initiative	1 The pregnant executive	Have we a champion? What dedicated group will drive this through?
	2 Single goal	What are we trying to achieve? Where are we trying to get to?
	3 Clarity of purpose	Why are we doing this? Is the logic clear?
Concordance and trust	4 The illusion of unity	Are we together on this? Have people bought in to the plan?
	5 How open to be?	Is there enough trust and shared agreement? How much dare we spell out?
	6 Communication	Do we talk and listen to each other fruitfully? Do people understand?
Leadership, capabilities and structure	7 Proportionate responsibility	Are we ready and willing to lead?
	8 The limitations of empowerment	How much do we help people to act responsibly?
	9 Teams and Leaders	Is it clear who is to be responsible for what?
	10 Structure and culture	Are we organized sensibly to pursue our goal?
Building on action and success	11 Creating winners	Do we reward commitment, success and meritorious failure?

12	Fast change, initial acts and early successes	How shall we show that it works?
		How shall we gain momentum and enthusiasm?
		How can we best make speedy progress?
13	Caring for casualties	How shall we treat the injured?
14	Managing unintended consequences	Can we adapt and learn?
		How shall we cope with contingencies?
		How resilient and flexible are we?

FACING AND TACKLING THE ISSUES

Where the key people do not feel confident about their answers, they need to reflect on the factors that perturb them and to fashion action plans to improve matters. There may be contention in the top management about which factors are awry in the firm and an analytical technique can be useful in focusing on the key issues and in teasing out the underlying causes of the perturbation. It can best be carried out by the managers at an off-site retreat, free of the daily stresses of the enterprise. It involves three judgements in each of two stages. The result should be a strengthening of the analysis of the challenges facing the firm, together with the development of plans for tackling them.

Stage 1: Using the 14 factors

The first stage utilizes the 14 factors as a basis for analysis; the second stage uses the insights of the first stage to tailor the key issues more directly to the specific circumstances of the strategic change that the organization faces. The first stage should not take longer than one hour to initiate and one hour to debate. Because it separates each individual's views, it also brings out the state of convergence or divergence between members of the management team. All this stage requires is that each individual be given a form such as Table 11.3—relating factors and capabilities—and be asked to complete it, alone.

Table 11.3 *Factors and capabilities*

Factor	Question(s)	Our current capability	Our ability to enhance that capability	The importance of the factor
1 The pregnant executive	Have we a champion? What dedicated group will drive this through?			
2 Single goal	What are we trying to achieve? Where are we trying to get to?			
3 Clarity of purpose	Why are we doing this? Is the logic clear?			
4 The illusion of unity	Are we together on this? Have people bought in to the plan?	4	4	10**
5 How open to be?	Is there enough trust and shared agreement? How much dare we spell out?			
6 Communication	Do we talk and listen to each other fruitfully? Do people understand?			
7 Proportionate responsibility	Are we ready and willing to lead?			
8 The limitations of empowerment	How much do we help people to act responsibly?			

9 Teams and leaders	Is it clear who is to be responsible for what?		
10 Structure and culture	Are we organized sensibly to pursue our goal?		
11 Creating winners	Do we reward commitment, success and meritorious failure?		
12 Fast change, initial acts and early successes	How shall we show that it works? How shall we gain momentum and enthusiasm? How can we best make speedy progress?		
13 Caring for casualties	How shall we treat the injured?	9	9
14 Managing unintended consequences	Can we adapt and learn? How shall we cope with contingencies? How resilient and flexible are we?		3

In the first of the right-hand columns, the individual should estimate, for each factor on a scale of 0 to 10, the present level of capability already available to the organization in the light of the specific strategic change that is required. A score of 10 would mean that the organization was already fully able to answer satisfactorily the questions posed by that factor; 0 would indicate that it had no satisfactory answer. In the next column, the individual should indicate how easy he or she thinks it will be to raise that factor's score towards 10. Zero would infer that it would be impossible to raise the score to 10; 10 would indicate that it would be readily practicable.

The final column rates the importance of that factor for the success of the mooted strategic change. Individuals should be told that the top rating for a factor of great importance is 10, that if they want to give extra weight to the importance of a particular factor, they can add one, two or three stars to emphasize its importance. A rating of 10^{***} would indicate an importance so strong as to be critical to the organization's very survival as a competitive force in its industry.

The resulting table will be an individual's map showing the factors that are important, the firm's ability to deal with them and how easy or difficult it would be to do better. Some factors will be of little importance and the firm will already have a high capability for dealing with them. For example, as shown in Table 11.3, if the company is growing and is wealthy or compassionate enough to have few casualties and to treat those generously, the first two columns of factor 13 (Caring for casualties) will score almost 10 and the final column about its importance will show a low number. There will be little need to consider factor 13 further.

If, on the other hand, disunity is rife, then factor 4 will have a low rating in the first column. If it also has a low rating for the organization's ability to improve in that area, the next column will be low also. If the individual deems this factor to be important for the projected change, then the final column of factor 4 will have a high rating, as shown in the table. This latter set of scores indicates that there is a worrying discrepancy between the importance of the issue and the company's ability to handle it well; the individual evidently believes that the organization has a real problem with that factor.

Once all those at the gathering have filled in their forms, the subsequent act of comparing individual's ratings will help to focus on the factors and capabilities that are commonly felt to pose a threat to the successful implementation of the strategic change. There may be strongly held views about the differences in valuation between individuals and so a vigorous debate should ensue about both the level and the range of judgements for each set of factor ratings.

Stage 2: Tailoring the debate

The debate will begin to consider the underlying causes of the problem factors. There will soon arise a need to move on to stage two of the analysis in order to evolve from the general 14 factor framework onto one that focuses directly on the specific circumstances facing the particular organization, because it is likely that some important issues will cover more than one factor. For example, the issue of information systems and information management could readily affect factors 5, 6, 8, 9 and 10. It is also likely that the relevance of the issue will affect different parts of the firm in varied ways—which may have led to some of the divergent views that surfaced in stage one. Furthermore, if divergence and argument have arisen from stage one, there needs to be a method of redefining the issue at stake in such a way that agreement can be reached to enable concerted action to ensue. Concentrating on the underlying issue of information management can help to take heat, though with luck not light, out of the debate.

The new set of issues that emerges in stage two will be unique to the situation in the organization, self-generated by the individuals present, and brought together using one of the techniques of structured brainstorming which help to bring out important matters in management gatherings. That will enable the participants to concentrate on the key problems of their own specific strategic change and, when done carefully, has the merit of valuing the contributions of all those present. That makes it more difficult for the opinionated to dismiss the concerns of other, more circumspect, managers, so that a higher quality debate should follow, leading to a high-quality action plan for the strategic change.

ENHANCING THE THRESHOLD

One would hope that this type of teamwork event would occur normally in an organization, not just when it became urgently necessary and not just at one level in the company. The merits of improved communication, practicable empowerment, fitting the structure to the tasks, and rewarding appropriately are all valuable whether the firm faces an urgent strategic change or not. They enhance the threshold of practicable change.

The whole notion of enhancing the threshold is not just to help the organization to hold its own, or to maintain current capability and relevance, where the forces of decay and the growth of obsolescence are just matched by the gains of experience and the refining of habits (Figure 11.1). The idea is to strengthen the organization through the growth of capabilities and the enhancement of the experience of changing, so that the forces of obsolescence are consistently outstripped by the confident ability to improve the firm's performance, year in and year out (Figure 11.2). Raising the sustainable capacity for acceptable change helps the organization to gear up so that, when a drama requires rapid change, the company can respond in a timely and effective fashion. It helps to get, and stay, ahead of the game.

This returns us to an earlier point. Being able to change more rapidly and more easily than your rivals offers a valuable competitive edge, for there are few competitive advantages that are not, in the end, whittled away by market changes or competitor actions. And competitors learn how to change more readily too. The perpetual modern litany that never has the pace of change been so fast—even if true—doesn't make change more difficult. Indeed, one can argue that it is easier, for four principal reasons:

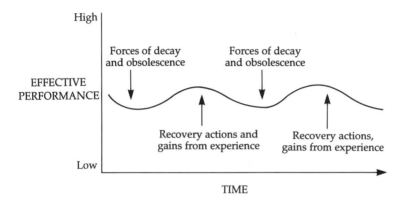

Figure 11.1   *Maintaining performance*

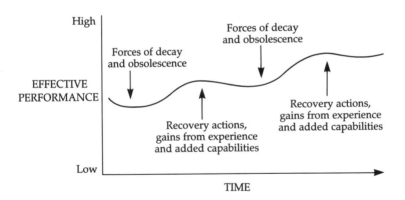

Figure 11.2   *Enhancing performance*

1.   Organizations have dismantled some of the more exotic, but difficult to manage, forms of organization—such as elaborate formal matrix systems—in favour of the clarity of responsibility of identified profit centres and the more careful linking of interdependent units.

2.   The advance in our understanding of organizational

forms and dynamics in this century has been substantial. We have learned, and continue to learn, how to change more effectively.

3.   Change is now easier because it is more familiar, more expected, seemingly normal, and so resistance to change has lessened. Benchmarking your competitors and transferring best practice are valuable stimuli for change.

4.   Because keeping up with, or ahead of, the competition is now more valuable, more resource is being put into it and, as privatization extends the realms of the market economy, more organizations are being moved from the protected to the competitive domain.

In addition to the top team facing and tackling the issues, implementation will likely utilize more than one of the many methods for creating significant change in an organization. These can include

- task forces
- action-learning projects
- special investigations
- competitor and market evaluations
- surveys of attitude, morale, climate or management styles
- intensified two-way communications
- use of change agents and change managers
- restructuring
- process re-engineering
- revised reward and measurement/control systems
- symbolic creations and destructions
- competitions and prizes
- setting innovation targets
- benchmarking best practices in and beyond the industry
- setting of stretching performance goals (provided that they are attainable and sustainable once achieved).

The aim, whatever the methods used, is to raise the firm's performance, including that of its ability to change again and to become steadily more resilient in the face of evolving challenges (Figure 11.3).

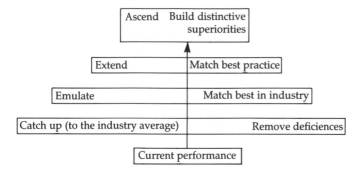

Figure 11.3   *Performance advance*

SHRINKING THE BOXES: THE TIME SPECTRUM

The advantage of being more able to adapt easily is matched by the competitive necessity to be more adept at changing, both in terms of effective capability and in readiness to act in a timely fashion. Without those qualities, the firm is restricted in its ability to engage in competent strategic innovation. The organizational ability to change speedily will depend on the firm's capacity for acting on three stages of the strategic process: (1) the time to conceive and decide the new strategy; (2) the time to plan, endorse and assemble the needed resources and capabilities; and (3) the time to implement—that is, to act on the conception, the plan and the endorsement. Given these three dimensions, the reduction in overall start-to-finish time for the strategic change can be called 'shrinking the boxes' (Figure 11.4). Shrinkage can also be achieved by greater overlap of the three stages—though excessive shrinkage and excess overlap are both counter-productive.

The length of time required for each of the three stages will differ. Self-satisfied and unthreatened partnership organizations might take years to endorse a major change. A small,

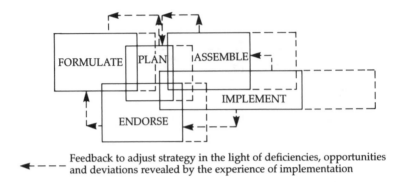

Feedback to adjust strategy in the light of deficiencies, opportunities and deviations revealed by the experience of implementation

Figure 11.4   *Faster strategic change: shrinking the boxes*

cohesive and well-informed firm might be able to obtain widespread endorsement and assemble the needed resources in a week.

Despite the desirability of reducing the length of time taken for each phase, of wanting to urge organizations to get on with it, one must not assume that the minimum time is the best. Timely strategic change is not the same as the fastest change, but is the ability to implement a change effectively and expeditiously. It requires a talent for combining carefulness with speed. Indeed, the firm's people may choose to moderate the pace of change—like a racing driver who slows down to conserve engine, tyres, brakes and fuel, but who is still trying to win. The more spare speed the driver has, and the further ahead the car is already, the more options are open to gain an unforced victory. So it is with organizations. The aim of a firm facing a major strategic change would be to avoid either excess length or excessive compression and to be in a position where it can choose the most appropriate pace of strategic change. Table 11.4 illustrates the spectrum of overall times taken in making such changes.

Table 11.4 *Spectrum of time taken*

Stage	Inadequate	Effective			Excessive
		Short	Optimal	Long	
1 Conceive and decide	Febrile	Confident	Reflective	Cautious	Feeble
2 Plan, endorse and assemble	Frenetic	Prepared	Resourceful and united	Careful	Sluggish
3 Implement	Hasty	Urgent	Incisive	Serene	Lethargic

Inadequate

The insufficient time shown at the 'inadequate' end of the spectrum would be inhabited by firms that engaged in ill-considered changes which they had scarcely organized and for which they were ill-equipped. Firms in this category would also include the most hyperactive, despotically run, unthinking, brutally indifferent to casualties, capricious organizations that one would care not to join. Speed of activity would be valued more than quality of action. It would be surprising if any of them had in place the eight needed elements for successful change (see Table 11.1).

Excessive

The longest set of stages at the 'excessive' end of the spectrum would contain companies that could barely arouse themselves from complacency to meet a challenge if it stood up and waved at them. Nor could they meet the test of the eight needed elements, because they would be the most lethargic, disunited, collectively unintelligent (whatever the individual intelligence of their inhabitants), unprepared, indecisive, disorganised, change resistant, badly informed types of organization. They would have the most unsupportive structure and decision systems and would have members who had inadequate, or inappropriate, skills as well as poor morale.

Effective

By contrast to these two extremes, the effective length of stage size and the most fruitful amount of stage overlap occur when particular conditions are present, and these will need tailoring to the particular situation and circumstances at that time and will depend on which of the types of change is in prospect, be it Takeover, Injection, Succession, Renovation, Partnership or Catalytic change. It is in the effective range of Table 11.4 that organizations can meet those eight tests and so can undertake strategic changes with some confidence of success.

Short

At the 'short' end of the effective range would be some Takeover and Injection changes, where the incoming managers are confident because of the relevance of their previous similar experiences (perhaps this is why they have been brought in). A rapid strategic change can also be accomplished if the people in the firm have open relationships, high mutual trust and enough relevant information, since speedy endorsement should be readily available. Alternatively, a highly participative firm that can speedily value and absorb the views of all employees with widespread agreement about the need for, and the choice of, strategic change, can move swiftly because the organization is united, with employees who are knowledgeable, capable, trusting and supportive and who are only waiting for the change to be triggered. Having adequate resources—including some contingency reserves to cope with the inevitable problems—will aid confidence as well as competence. The more the firm is prepared, the more it is poised for this kind of opportunity and the easier will be the planning, endorsement and assembly stage.

The speed of implementation itself will, in part, be driven from outside the firm by the urgency of the market challenge faced by the organization. Yet it will also be affected by the ability of the people in the firm to galvanize it into rapid action and, if they are thoroughly involved, they will then want and be able to take urgent action to move the firm into a better competitive position.

Long

A longer time frame would be relevant for uncertain situations, where premature or hasty action could be a mistake pending better information and analysis, or for a situation in which many people still need to be involved in the decisions— such as would be the case in a Partnership change. The 'long' end of the effective part of the spectrum will be inhabited by companies facing one of two circumstances: either they are in the luxurious position of introducing a stable transformation, having anticipated the need for change and having the time to do it gently, or they have internal circumstances that preclude quick action. In these pulsating times, the luxurious first condition is rare. It is the internal impediments that will typically retard the desirable pace of change.

A cautious and careful approach is necessary when there is an initial lack of trust and unity, little understanding of the need for change and no agreement between factions as to the actions that should be taken; a lack of required capabilities and relevant resources and, perhaps, a long lead time for acquiring them—all of which will handicap the promoters of change. The pace of change may need to be moderated when more initiatives are needed than people can cope with all at once; or where unprepared customers and suppliers need to be reassured and calming arrangements need to be negotiated and put in place.

Optimal

The optimal position would involve reflective, information-based, careful analysis; diligence in gathering data; judgement arising from measured debate; the generation of scenarios and possibilities; a mind-set inclined towards innovation and action; a culture that is united and change-oriented; an understanding of the twin needs for speed and care, via a planned and positioned strategy. There would be enough relevant resources; high skills, morale and commitment; united vision and strong collaboration; open communication with authentic information; knowing, intelligent employees; high trust and enthusiasm; self-belief. It would, in short, take proper account of the 14 factors discussed in Chapters 7 to 10. Their exact application will depend on the specific content of the strategic change being undertaken; its scale, scope, risk, urgency, familiarity, complexity, cost and value. The content will depend on the specific context in which it is to occur; the competitive and market circumstances, the resources and skills that are available and the organization's culture—particularly its inclination for innovation and its capability for handling change well.

FINALLY

We are moving towards the year 2000 with new emphases on management (a profession scarcely familiar at the beginning of the century), on the need to transform organizations so that they fulfil more of our needs, both material and spiritual. Advanced organizations have already shifted from narrower concerns about control, efficiency, data, procedures and managerial dominance towards the more fluid issues of networks, teams, influence, shared vision and voluntary commitment. The success formula of the future involves information, ideas, intelligence, interchanges of cooperation, the managing of permeable boundaries between what used to be separate activities—all the heartening panoply of the management style that fosters the talents of everyone in the organization.

Yet before we become too intoxicated by this vision of inspirational firms, it is worth remembering that managers do not habitually get to carry more responsibility by being average. They typically possess superior talents. Managerial skills in coping with fragmentation, handling vast amounts of puzzling information, synthesizing it, reconciling its conflicting tensions, dealing with variety, risk and responsibility, making judgements, then orchestrating the chosen actions are not universal human traits. Managers are capable above the norm. They are not merely the first among equals. They rarely get there by luck or by accident and, if some have, they seldom survive long in that post. Managers have usually risen to the top for good reason, having wider vision, greater relevant experience, being more alert, better at scanning information, more adept at using it fruitfully, more persuasive and more ingenious. They are, in short, talented.

So where does this all leave us? A summary would just reiterate the lessons of the 14 factors. We come back instead to the issues of will, of preparedness, of involvement of many people, of structuring the situation to optimize the likelihood of success, of teams *and* leaders, of empowerment *and* leadership, of arousing the organization through uplifting vision and exemplary behaviour. Of course it requires effort. There may be the odd setback. You cannot achieve radical change without resources and the commitment to use them. But strategic change doesn't have to take ages or be a grinding chore. Strategic change can be positive and exciting—one of the best, most fruitful, most productive activities a team can undertake. Despite the accent on the roles of management and leadership, the exercise of skills at work has high value for most employees, since work is a major source of life satisfaction. Of course, the good leader wants to create self-reliance rather than dependency on the part of those who are being led, and will endeavour to provide uplifting circumstances so that all the employee's talents can flourish fruitfully. Utilizing employees' energies, ingenuities and desires to achieve, is meritorious as well as sensible. Successful strategic change is an accomplishment of worth, and a source of pride. Yet it need not be too difficult, for as one top manager stated: 'Before we started, you would never have got me to say this. It is hard work, but one of the things you learn about change is that, once you've done it, it wasn't such a big deal.'

REFERENCES

1.   Danny Miller and Peter H. Friesen, Momentum and revolution in organisational adaptation. *Academy of Management Journal*, **23** (4), 1980, pp. 591–614.
2.   Leif Melin and Bo Hellgren, Patterns of strategic change processes— two typologies. Strategic Management Society Conference, Toronto, October 1991.
3.   Dean Berry, unpublished papers, 1988.
4.   CMI Consultancy, unpublished papers, 1990.
5.   John Hunt, *Managing People at Work*, 3rd edn, McGraw-Hill, 1992, p. 279.

Index